ROGET'S
Student
THESAURUS

Andrew Schiller

William A. Jenkins

HarperCollins*Publishers*

CONTENTS

First HarperCollins edition published 1991

Picture credits appear on page 447.
Library of Congress Catalog Card Number 90-5094

Library of Congress Cataloging-in-Publication Data

Schiller, Andrew, 1919-
   [In other words, a junior thesaurus]
   Roget's junior thesaurus / Andrew Schiller, William A. Jenkins—1st HarperCollins ed.
   p. cm.
   Reprint. Originally published: In other words, a junior thesaurus. Glenview, Ill.: Scott, Foresman, c1987.
   Includes index.
   Summary: An illustrated alphabetical list of words, their synonyms, antonyms, and the shades of meaning between them.
   ISBN 0-06-275005-4 (cloth)
   1. English language—Synonyms and antonyms—Dictionaries, Juvenile. [1. English language—Synonyms and antonyms.] I. Jenkins, William Atwell, 1922- . II. Title.
PE1591.S35   1991
423'.1—dc20   90-5094

ISBN 0-06-275005-4

91929394951 0987654321

INTRODUCTION

HOW TO USE THIS BOOK

WHAT IS A THESAURUS?

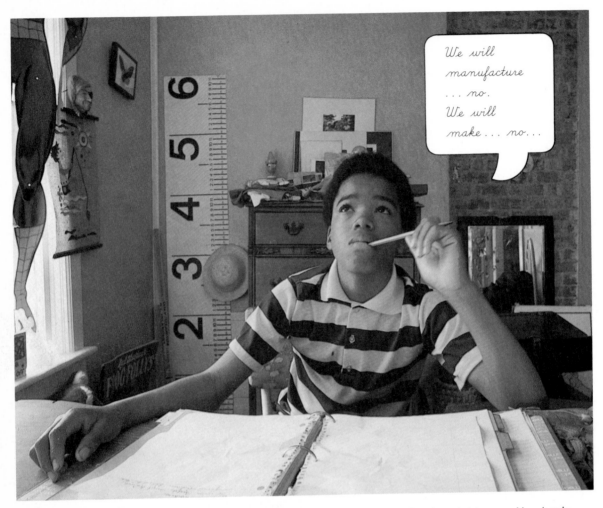

Imagine that you are writing a story about a clubhouse. You begin your story with this sentence.

• We will manufacture our clubhouse out of wood and nails.

When you read the sentence over you think, "Something is wrong. That sentence just doesn't sound right." So you read it again. This time you think, "I see the problem now. *Manufacture* is not the right word. *Manufacture* sounds like something you do with big machines, not with your hands." So you try another word in place of *manufacture.*

• We will *make* our clubhouse out of wood and nails.

"That's better," you think. "But *make* isn't the exact word I'm looking for. *Make* sounds too plain, too general. What do I do now?"

If you had a thesaurus you could pick the right word in a minute. A thesaurus contains lists of words to help you in your writing. These lists give you words to use in place of words that you are not happy with. For instance, on page 243 of this thesaurus there is a list of words you may use in place of *make.* Some of these words are: *build, start, create, shape.*

Which word will you choose? You will probably choose *build.*

• We will *build* our clubhouse out of wood and nails.

Now the sentence sounds just right.

Your thesaurus can help you with all kinds of writing tasks. Here is how Greg used his thesaurus to improve a movie review for English class.

Greg's assignment was to write a review of *The Frozen Mountain,* a movie he had just seen. Here is some of what Greg wrote.

The Frozen Mountain is a fine adventure movie about the lives of the pioneers. The photography is excellent, with many pleasant views of the Rocky Mountains. Kris Conant, a young actress, is the star of the movie. She plays the role of Jill Flowers, a pleasant woman with a pleasant smile.

Mr. Jackson, Greg's English teacher, read Greg's review. "Greg," he said, "you use the word *pleasant* to describe the views of the Rocky Mountains, the actress, and her smile. Try to find more precise words for *pleasant.* Use your thesaurus."

Greg looked up **pleasant** and rewrote his assignment. Notice how Greg changed his review.

The Frozen Mountain is a fine adventure movie about the lives of the pioneers. The photography is excellent, with many delightful views of the Rocky Mountains. Kris Conant, a young actress, is the star of the movie. She plays the role of Jill Flowers, a pleasant woman with a cheerful smile.

Which two synonyms did Greg use in place of *pleasant?* Compare the new review with the old one to find out.

How did Greg find the right words to describe exactly what he meant? The next four pages will show you how to use this thesaurus and how to find the exact words you need.

5

2 **3**

increase (v) *Increase* means become or make larger or greater or more. *Increase* is the opposite of decrease. A crowd *increases* as more people gather, or come together. In 1959, the number of States has *increased* to fifty. A driver can *increase* the speed of a car. Your strength and weight *increase* as you grow **4** older.

add *Add* means increase by joining or putting one thing to another. You *add* numbers in math. Theresa *added* more leaves to her leaf collection.

8 Theresa **added** one more leaf to her collection.

• attach *Attach* and *annex* are other good words to
• annex use for increase even though they are not real synonyms. *Attach* means join something to something else. The length of a freight train increases when a caboose is *attached.* A kite increases in weight if you *attach* a tail. *Annex* can mean increase by adding to something that is larger or more important. Hospitals *annex* buildings when more space is needed. A city may *annex* a suburb or surrounding land.

5

multiply *Multiply* means increase in number. Your fears might *multiply* in a scary situation.

extend *Extend* can mean make longer or increase in time. If you *extend* your visit with a friend, you stay longer than you had planned.

6 See also *enlarge.*

7 ANTONYMS: decrease (v), diminish, divide, subtract

1

213

6

1   This long section is called an **entry.** It contains the entry word and its synonyms, related words, and antonyms.

2   The entry begins with the **entry word** printed in heavy, black type. All entry words are printed in alphabetical order.

3   The **part-of-speech label** tells you how the word is being used. Some words, such as *increase,* can be used as a noun (n) or as a verb (v). Other words—for example, *fast*—can be used as an adjective (adj) or as an adverb (adv).

4   The **paragraph of explanation** tells what the word means and how it can be used in a sentence.

5   **Synonyms** and **related words** are listed in a column below the entry word. They are printed in lighter type. Related words are marked with dots to show that they are different from synonyms. Both synonyms and related words are close in meaning to the entry word. But related words have an extra-added meaning.

6   The **cross-reference,** which begins with the words *See also,* refers you to other words in the thesaurus. You can look up these words to help you in your search for the right word.

7   **Antonyms**—words that mean the opposite of the entry word—are listed in blue type at the end of the entry.

8   Many entry words have **illustrations** with **captions,** which help explain the meanings of entry words and synonyms.

THESAURUS EXERCISES

The exercises that follow will help you get to know your thesaurus. First, you will work with the parts of an entry. Then you will practice choosing synonyms and related words. Finally, you will practice choosing antonyms.

I. Reviewing the Parts

This exercise leads you through the parts of a thesaurus entry. When you finish, you will be ready to practice choosing synonyms and related words.

Directions Look up **delicious** on pages 114–115. Study the entry and answer the questions that follow. Look back at pages 6 and 7 if you need help.

1. What is the entry word on page 114?
2. What does it mean?
3. What are two synonyms for the entry word?
4. What are two related words?
5. What word is listed as a cross-reference?
6. What are two antonyms of the entry word?
7. Is there a part-of-speech label in the entry?

II. Choosing Synonyms and Related Words

Choosing the right synonym means picking the one that fits the context, or meaning, of a sentence. A synonym that works in one sentence might not work in another. For example, *add* and *extend* are both synonyms for *increase*. Read the meanings for *add* and *extend* on page 213. Then read the two sentences below.

> I *extended* two and two to get four.
> We *added* our vacation by a week.

Do the synonyms *added* and *extended* fit the meanings of the sentences? Why not? Try switching the two synonyms.

> I *added* two and two to get four.
> We *extended* our vacation by a week.

Now the two synonyms fit the meanings of the sentences!

Remember: You cannot simply use one synonym in place of the other. You must think carefully about each word's meaning. You must choose the synonym that fits in your sentence. Your thesaurus will help you do this.

Directions Look up **moist** on page 249. Read the meanings for its synonyms: *damp, humid, rainy, watery,* and *juicy* or *succulent.* Then decide which synonym best fits each sentence below.

1. Toby's hair was still   from his swim.
2. The soft, ripe pear was
3. During the   afternoon the roof leaked.
4. Her eyes were   because she had a cold.
5. The air was   after the heavy rain.

small   tiny

Some synonyms are stronger than others. *Small* and *tiny* are both synonyms for *little,* but an object that is *tiny* has less size than something that is *small. Small* describes a mini-bike better than *tiny. Tiny* describes a speck of dust better than *small.*

Directions Turn to the entry for **little** on page 236. Read the meanings of the synonyms. Then substitute one of the following synonyms for each use of **little** in the paragraph below: *small, trivial, brief, minute, tiny.*

There was a **(1.)** *little* incident during rehearsal. Roxie got a **(2.)** *little* cut on her finger. You could barely see the **(3.)** *little* jagged line. There was a **(4.)** *little* delay in the rehearsal. The nurse quickly treated the **(5.)** *little* injury.

Related words are not true synonyms of the entry word. Think of related words as words that have the meaning of the entry word and more. Use a related word instead of an entry word when you need to say more. For example, look at the related word *puny* in the entry for *little.* Read the meaning. Then decide whether *little* or *puny* best fits the context of the sentence below.

How can anyone who looks that (little, puny) lift those heavy weights?

Which word fits the context of the sentence better? *Puny* fits better because you need to use a word that says more than *little.* You need a word that says, "not only is the person little, but the person looks weak as well."

Remember: Always check the related word(s) in a thesaurus entry. Sometimes a related word is a better choice than the entry word or one of its synonyms.

III. Choosing Antonyms

Antonyms are words that mean the opposite of other words. Some antonym pairs are: *calm* and *excited; light* and *dark; shout* and *whisper.* You can use antonyms to contrast different things.

Directions Read each sentence below. Identify the two antonyms in each sentence.

1. We thought the story was true, but it was false.
2. Once the blue whales were plentiful, but now they are scarce.
3. The first day was bright, and the next one was dull.
4. His costume was unusual, but hers was ordinary.
5. Nan's job was easy, but Kate's was hard.

Sometimes you need to use an antonym in place of a *not* phrase. Here is an example.

- The weather was *not calm.*
- The weather was *stormy.*

The second sentence is more exact than the first. *Stormy* gives you a better picture of the weather than *not calm.* You can use your thesaurus to find exact words for *not* phrases.

Directions Turn to the entry for **real** on page 301. Find exact antonyms to replace the underlined *not* phrases in the paragraph below.

The witness gave testimony that was **(1.)** *not true.* She claimed that the will was **(2.)** *not authentic* and burst into tears. It was clear her grief was **(3.)** *not genuine.* Even her long eyelashes were **(4.)** *not the real thing.*

USING A THESAURUS WHEN YOU WRITE

The activities which follow will help you use your thesaurus to liven up your writing. You will learn how to select nouns, verbs, adjectives, and adverbs to use in letters, stories, and reports.

I. Career Day Project: Using Nouns

Mr. Trent's class was working on advertisements for a Career Day project. They were having trouble with the nouns in some of their advertisements. It looked as if they were going to have to use the word *instrument* in each one. Then they remembered to check a thesaurus. They found the words they needed in the entry for **instrument.**

Directions Look up **instrument.** Decide which word fits the context of each of the four advertisements that follow. Use the entry word or a related word to fill in each blank.

1. Special Spring Sale! See our line of tractors and other farm _____ at the Farmer's Friend!
2. No time to cook? Maybe you need a speedy microwave oven. At Cook's Corner you always find the latest in kitchen _____ .
3. Can't afford a new guitar? A new sax? A new drum? Come to the Music Makers! Specializing in used musical _____ for over 50 years.
4. Calling all carpenters! Electric saws and _____ kits on sale for limited time only at Woodworks.

Remember: When you cannot think of the right noun, look in a thesaurus.

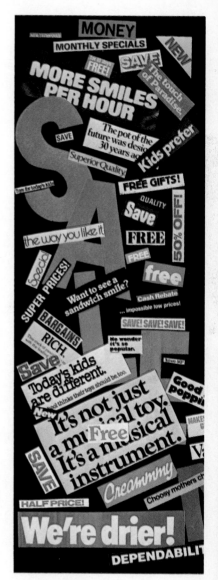

II. Mark's Letter: Using Verbs

   Read Mark's letter below. Mark used the thesaurus to find synonyms for the verb *run*, but he did not use the synonyms correctly. He used them without considering whether or not they fit his sentence meanings. Mark knew he needed to use the thesaurus again. This time he kept the meanings in mind as he used the synonyms.

Directions Read the entry for **run.** Find synonyms that fit the meanings in Mark's sentences. Then rewrite the letter. You may use *run* if you think it fits.

Remember: If your verb synonyms do not fit the meanings of your sentences, look at the thesaurus entry again. Read the meanings again to be sure that you understand them. Then use the synonyms that fit the contexts of the sentences.

---

                                    1 Roe Drive
                                    Houston, Texas 40002
                                    April 29, 19___

Dear Sam,
   Let me tell you about yesterday morning. Before breakfast I (1.) _fled_ around the block to get my daily exercise. Little did I know that I would be (2.) _galloping_ all day long. Later, on my way to school, I saw the bus was (3.) _sprinting_ ahead of schedule. I (4.) _escaped_ to the bus stop, but missed the bus anyway. By then the perspiration was (5.) _jogging_ down my face. I was ready to (6.) _abscond_ home and crawl back into bed. Yesterday morning was not a good morning.

                                    Your friend,
                                    Mark

III. Melanie's Report: Using Adjectives

Melanie wrote a report about Abraham Lincoln. Her social studies' teacher liked the report, but she thought it needed to be livelier. When Melanie read the paper again, she realized that she had used the adjective *great* in every sentence. It had spoiled her writing and made her report sound dull. She used the thesaurus to help her choose lively adjectives.

Directions Turn to the entry for **great**. Read the meanings for the synonyms and cross-references. Choose synonyms that fit the sentence meanings. Then rewrite Melanie's report. Note: You may have to add *most* to some synonyms.

Abraham Lincoln was truly a **(1.)** *great* president.
Some think he was the **(2.)** *greatest* president this country ever had. He held this **(3.)** *great* country together during the Civil War. The Gettysburg Address is still regarded as one of the **(4.)** *greatest* speeches ever given. Not every citizen saw Lincoln as a **(5.)** *great* hero. However, most people felt that he was a man of **(6.)** *great* honesty and vision. His nickname, Honest Abe, came about because of his **(7.)** *great* character. His death was a **(8.)** *great* tragedy for all.

Remember: Use your thesaurus to help you find livelier adjectives.

IV. Ted's Story: Using Adverbs

One day Mr. Trent gave his students an unusual writing assignment. They were to write a story about a visit to a haunted house. Mr. Trent reminded them to use the thesaurus when they wrote. He said, ''Pay close attention to your adverbs. Use your thesaurus to find adverbs that tell how people act, and when and where events take place. Not all words in your thesaurus are listed as adverbs, but you can make adverbs out of them. To turn words like *dreadful* and *dim* into adverbs, just add *-ly: dreadfully, dimly.''

When Ted finished his story, he wasn't happy with it. He had used the adverbs *suddenly* and *dreadfully* too many times. So he looked up **suddenly** and **dreadful** in his thesaurus, and found the adverbs he needed. Here are two paragraphs from Ted's story. Follow the directions to see how Ted rewrote them.

Directions Look up the entries for **suddenly** and **dreadful.** Make lists of adverbs from the entry words and synonyms. Remember to ad *-ly* to *dreadful* and its synonyms. Substitute adverbs from your lists for the italicized words in the paragraphs.

(1.) *Suddenly* I was filled with terror. A low moan had come (2.) *suddenly* from the next room. I knew (3.) *suddenly* that someone else was in the house. Just as I reached the open door, it slammed (4.) *suddenly* in my face. Then all that mattered was how (5.) *suddenly* I could get out of that house.

I was (1.) *dreadfully* frightened. As the misty figure moved in my direction, I stood and stared (2.) *dreadfully* at it. Could I hold in the fear that was growing so (3.) *dreadfully?*

Remember: Sometimes you must change the endings of words in your thesaurus to turn those words into adverbs.

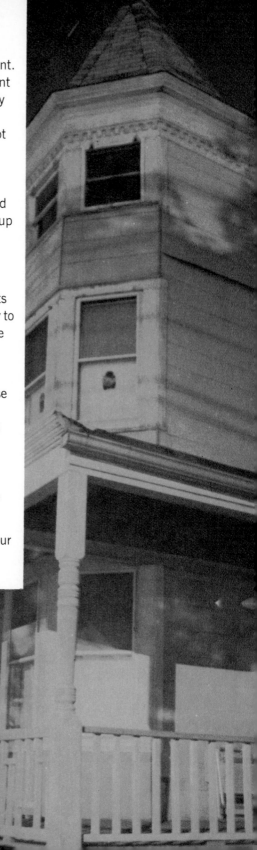

THE INDEX

This thesaurus has one more part: the index. It is located at the back of this book. The index tells you where each entry word, synonym, related word, and antonym can be found. When you need a new word to use in place of a word you are not happy with, turn to the index first. Look for the word you are not happy with. The index will direct you to a list of new, lively words to choose from.

Directions Study this part of page 434 in the index. Then answer the questions that follow.

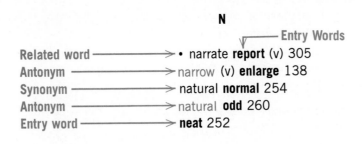

NOTE: Each page listed in this Index is the page on which the entry begins.
• Identifies related words.

1. What is a related word for **report?**
2. Under what entry word will you find *narrow?*
3. On what page will you find the entry for **normal?** for **neat?**
4. Is *natural* a synonym, a related word, or an antonym of **normal?**
5. On what page will you find *natural* listed as an antonym of **odd?**
6. How many entry words are listed?
7. How many antonyms are listed?
8. What part of speech is *narrow?*
9. How can you tell if a word is a related word?
10. What entry word is listed by itself?

OTHER USES FOR YOUR THESAURUS

As you know, your thesaurus is a source of synonyms, related words, and antonyms. It is also a source of idioms, and formal and informal words. Here is how your thesaurus can help you choose the right idioms and formal and informal words for your writing.

I. Idioms

Have you ever *put off* doing something? Has your dad or mom ever talked about how he or she *put in* a hard day's work? The phrases *put off* and *put in* are idioms. An idiom is a group of words with a surprising meaning. For example, you may think that *put in* means *to put one thing inside another.* But the idiom *put in* actually means *to spend time.* The English language has many idioms. In this thesaurus, idioms are discussed in the paragraphs of explanation.

Directions Turn to pages 23–24. Read the paragraph of explanation next to the entry word **act.** Then answer the following questions.

1. Which idiom means "follow through on something?"
2. Which idiom means "disobey or not act properly?"
3. Which idiom means "do something in place of someone else?"

II. Formal and Informal Words

Have you ever noticed how you talk differently to different people about the same things? Let's say you just took a camping trip. Now you are going to tell your teacher about the trip. Then you will tell a friend. Here are some of the words you will use.

like—enjoy	*purchased—bought*
adults—grown-ups	*finished—concluded*

Which of these words will you use when speaking to your teacher? You will probably use *adults, enjoy, purchased,* and *concluded.* Why? Because they are more formal words than *grown-ups, like, bought,* and *finished.* You use more formal words when speaking to adults, giving speeches, and writing business letters and reports. You use more informal words when speaking with friends and writing friendly letters.

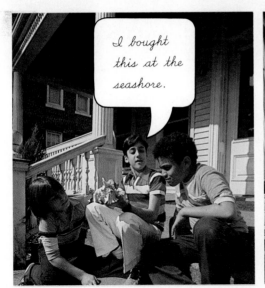

I bought this at the seashore.

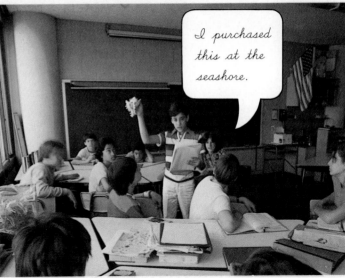

I purchased this at the seashore.

27 Lee Street
Chicago, Illinois 60623
May 12, 19___

Dear Uncle Ralph,

   Thank you very much for the wonderful book on aquariums. It is the perfect present! The day after my birthday, I purchased a tank, gravel, and other materials I needed. Once I connect the air pump, I'll have my "mini-ocean" ready.

   I hope you are well. Please write when you have time.

                         Yours truly,
                         Juan

27 Lee Street
Chicago, Illinois 60623
May 19, 19___

Dear Amy,

Guess what? I got the greatest book from my uncle. It's all about aquariums. What a terrific present! I went right out and bought a tank, some gravel, and other things. Once I hook up the air pump, I'll be all set to go.

So how are you? Write me soon.

Your friend,
Juan

Directions Use the index to look up each underlined word in the following letter. Rewrite the letter, using informal words.

Dear Freddie,

I **(1.)** commenced writing this letter as soon as Mom **(2.)** pronounced that I had not written to you in months! I just bought some **(3.)** contemporary football equipment. I'm **(4.)** endeavoring to make the park district's team. I **(5.)** desire to be a quarterback.

Do you still want to **(6.)** exchange your mystery books for my science fiction books? I also want to **(7.)** inquire about your dog, Sheb. How is his leg?

Best wishes,

Pedro

ON YOUR OWN

Now you have learned to use your thesaurus. You have also had practice in improving writing. What are you waiting for? It is time to improve your own writing. Keep your thesaurus. Use it the next time you write a letter, a report, or a story. Find the exact words to make your writing livelier, more interesting, and more effective.

ENTRIES

A COLLECTION OF ENTRY WORDS,
THEIR SYNONYMS, RELATED WORDS,
AND ANTONYMS

A

ability

Ability is being able to do something. You can be born with an *ability.* You can also develop an *ability* by learning to do something and then practicing it. For example, some people are born with an *ability* to carry a tune. Even if they never take singing lessons, they can sing. But no one is born with the *ability* to ski. Skiers must develop the *ability* to keep their balance and control their skis.

talent

Talent is some special ability that you are born with. A musician or a painter has *talent.*

skill

Skill and *dexterity* are abilities that you must develop. You develop the *skill* to do something by learning how it is done, and then by doing it over and over until you can do it easily and well. Typing is a *skill.* A good typist can type a letter easily and well.

Skiers must develop the **ability** to control their skis.

dexterity

Dexterity means skill in using your hands cleverly and gracefully—without fumbling or dropping things. For instance, a typist shows *skill* in typing accurately and fast. Carlos shows *dexterity* when he changes the typewriter ribbon.

ingenuity

Ingenuity is cleverness in inventing or designing things and in seeing new uses for everyday objects. It also means the ability to see, do, say, or use something in a different way. Amelia used a lot of *ingenuity* in designing a costume from an old curtain.

ANTONYM: inability

accomplishment

An *accomplishment* is something that has been accomplished, done, or completed. An *accomplishment* requires knowledge and, usually, hard work. When you have solved a hard math problem or learned to skate, you can be proud of your *accomplishment.*

achievement

An *achievement* is the accomplishment of something unusually dangerous or difficult. Because courage and effort are needed to achieve, an *achievement* is always admirable. The first space flight was a great *achievement.* The discovery of the polio vaccine was a great *achievement* in the fight against disease.

deed

A *deed* is anything that is done. You might call any kind or helpful or useful act that someone does a good *deed.* Some people try to do good *deeds* by helping others.

accomplishment continued on page 22 ▶

A

feat
exploit

A *feat* and an *exploit* are accomplishments. A *feat* requires more courage and strength than a deed. Climbing the mountain was a *feat* of skill and daring. An *exploit* is an accomplishment that requires even greater daring and heroism than a *feat.* Have you read any books about the *exploits* of Nellie Bly, the first woman news reporter?

ANTONYM: failure

account (n)

An *account* can be any description, explanation, or record of facts or real events. It is not a made-up story. It may be spoken or written. A charge *account* is a record of purchases. The eyewitness gave an *account* of the plane crash.

• article

An *article* is a written account of something that has happened or is going on. Newspaper and magazine *articles* keep the public up-to-date on current events.

• report

A *report* is a detailed account that is drawn up after some thing or situation has been carefully examined or investigated. The medical *report* showed that the patient would soon be released from the hospital. Mary's book *report* was so detailed that we don't have to read the book.

• version

A *version* is an account given from just one point of view. Your *version* of an incident

Mary's book **report** is so detailed that no one will have to read the book.

might be different from someone else's *version.* Each of the girls gave her own *version* of how the window had been broken.

• story

A *story* can also be one kind of account. A newspaper *story* is an account that tells what happened. It may also tell who, when, where, and why. A magazine article often tells a *story* but sometimes includes whatever the writer thinks about the *story.* A *story* made up to entertain someone or even to deceive that person is not an account—it is a different kind of *story.* Leon told us an interesting *story* of his adventures in Africa.

See also *history, story, tale.*

Leon told an interesting **story** of his adventures in Africa.

act (v)

Act means do something or cause something to happen. The firefighter *acted* quickly to put out the fire. Bubbles were produced when the acid *acted* upon the powder. *Act for* means do something in place of someone else. I will *act for* you while you are on vacation. *Act on* means follow through on something. The secretary *acted on* the boss's suggestion

act (v) continued on page 24 ▶

and typed the letter. *Act up* means disobey or not act properly. The dogs sometimes *act up* when they have to stay in a kennel.

behave

Behave means act in a certain way. Usually when you *behave* yourself, you are good and act the way you should. They *behaved* very nicely during the movie.

perform

Perform means act or do something. The plane *performed* perfectly on its test flight. *Perform* can also mean act or take part in a play or show. The dolphin *performed* some unusual tricks for the crowd.

function

Function can mean work properly or act as something else. The car *functioned* perfectly. Sometimes a football player *functions* as a coach.

See also *pretend, work* (v).

The dolphin **performed** some unusual tricks for the crowd.

action

Action means several things that are done or events that occur one right after the other. The fast *action* of a hockey game is hard to follow. A Western movie has lots of *action*.

act

An *act* is only one thing that has been done or accomplished. Throwing a ball is an *act,* but the *action* in a ball game is everything that happens during the game. An *action* is made up of a series of *acts.*

activity

Activity means action, often over a long period of time. The *activity* of the thief escaped the notice of the detective. I'm late for supper every night because of after-school *activities.*

Football players must get plenty of **exercise.**

process
operation
performance
work

Process, operation, performance, and *work* mean a series of acts or the way in which they are carried out. A *process* is the way in which you would do or make something. The *process* of cheesemaking has many different steps. The *operation* of a machine is the way it operates or acts or the way someone runs it. It takes time to learn the *operation* of a giant crane. A *performance* is the way a person or object acts or performs. The audience cheered the excellent *performance* of the rock group. The *performance* of the jet engine was perfect. The fast *work* of the crew kept the ship from sinking.

motion
movement

Motion and *movement* mean the action of changing place or position. Anything that is not at rest is in *motion.* The *motion* of the ship made me seasick. Some scientists study the *movement* of the planets. The *movement* of the curtain told me that someone was behind it.

exercise

Exercise means the action used to develop strength or skill. Football players must get plenty of *exercise* before a season begins.

behavior
conduct

Behavior and *conduct* mean action, either good or bad. The *behavior* of the crowd during the sale shocked the store manager. The *conduct* of the class improved during the school year.

See also *battle* (n).

ANTONYMS: rest (n), inactivity, stillness, idleness

A

active

Active is used in many ways. It means showing action, movement, or work. You are *active* when you play outdoor games, but you are inactive if you watch TV all day. Your brain is *active* when you are thinking about something, but it is idle when you're thinking about absolutely nothing. *Active* can suggest just slight action or movement, or it may mean that much energy and force are needed to accomplish something. A baby playing in its crib may be *active,* but certainly not as *active* as someone who is swimming.

lively
peppy
spirited

Lively, peppy, and *spirited* mean full of life and action. They can also mean full of, or showing, excitement. The *lively* kitten tipped over its bowl of milk. A basketball game can be *lively.* It is not slow or passive. A *peppy* person is usually full of fun. A good horse is *spirited.* There can be much excitement in a *spirited* discussion.

agile
spry

Agile and *spry* are words that describe quick actions and movements. An *agile* person moves quickly and easily. An acrobat has to be very *agile* in order to perform stunts. *Agile* can also describe a person who thinks quickly. It will take an *agile* mind to solve this puzzle. A *spry* person is one whose actions are unexpectedly lively. Quite often an old person who is unusually *agile* is called *spry.*

energetic

Energetic means full of energy. An *energetic* person likes to be active. Schoolchildren are *energetic* during recess.

An acrobat has to be very **agile** in order to perform stunts.

The painter applied color with **vigorous** strokes.

vigorous

You are *vigorous* if you are very active and energetic. Your physical health is so good that you do not easily become tired. Something that is done forcefully can also be called *vigorous.* The painter applied color with *vigorous* strokes.

strenuous

A *strenuous* activity requires energy and vigor. My father had a *strenuous* day at the office and was tired when he came home.

ANTONYMS: inactive, idle, slow (adj), passive

admire

Admire is one way to love and praise something or someone. You can *admire* someone's honesty. You can *admire* someone's skill in swimming. You *admire* a person if you look up to that person and respect something he or she has done. You may try to follow that person's example. You can *admire* your parents, a friend, or some of the famous people you know or have read about. Larry *admired* the courage of Harriet Tubman. You can also *admire* a beautiful object. There are many paintings to be *admired* at an art museum.

honor

If you *honor* someone, you show that you admire and appreciate that person and respect what he or she has done. On Mother's Day we *honor* mothers everywhere. We *honor* fathers on Father's Day.

respect

Respect means admire and show special care for someone. Children should *respect* their parents. When you show special care

admire continued on page 28 ▸

A

for the rights of others, you *respect* those rights.

regard

Regard means show respect and consideration. If you *regard* a friend's opinion, you listen to what your friend says and consider it important. If you disregard the rules of a game, you pay no attention to them at all.

ANTONYMS: dishonor (v), disregard

adore

Adore is one way to love someone or something very much. If you *adore* someone, you usually show your love and admiration through praise and through doing things for that person. You may say you *adore* your baby sister. But *adore* is a very strong word. People often use *adore* when they don't really mean it. You may say you *adore* chocolate pudding, but you really mean you like it so much you could have it at every meal.

worship

Worship means show great love or devotion. Many ancient peoples *worshiped* the sea or sun. Often people made statues of the gods they *worshiped.* These statues were called idols.

idolize

Idolize means worship an idol or someone you look up to as an idol. Often *idolize* means love something or someone foolishly. A sports fan might *idolize* a famous baseball player.

exalt

Exalt is the strongest word for adore. When you praise or honor someone above all others, you *exalt* that person.

adult (adj)   *Adult* describes someone or something that is fully developed. It can describe someone who no longer does things in a childish way. A frog is an *adult* tadpole. Voting is an *adult* privilege.

mature   *Mature* also describes someone or something that is fully developed. A baby is an immature person because it is not fully developed. A butterfly is a *mature* caterpillar. As a person becomes *mature,* he or she can take on responsibilities.

grown-up   *Grown-up* is an informal word used to describe an adult or mature person or thing. *Grown-up* behavior is not juvenile.

ripe   *Ripe* means fully grown or developed. It is usually used to describe fruits and vegetables that are fully grown and ready to be eaten. *Ripe* corn is ready to be harvested.

ANTONYMS: childish, immature, juvenile, green, unripe

A butterfly is a **mature** caterpillar.

A

advance (v)   *Advance* means move forward or cause something to move or be moved forward. Flood waters *advanced* toward the town but receded when the rain stopped. It can also mean put something forward like an idea or plan. Dentists in the community *advanced* a new plan for preventing tooth decay.

proceed   *Proceed* means advance or carry on an activity, perhaps after stopping. The train *proceeded* slowly out of the station and through the fog.

progress   *Progress* means advance steadily toward a definite end or goal. The construction of the building has *progressed* quickly.

A car **accelerates** when the driver steps on the gas pedal.

accelerate   *Accelerate* means advance by speeding up or cause something to move faster. A driver *accelerates* a car by stepping on the gas pedal and slows it by stepping on the brake. You might say you *accelerate* when you change from a walk to a run.

promote   *Promote* means advance upward, or to a higher position. Jake was *promoted* to editor of the school newspaper. A cause or idea is *promoted* when someone helps it along. Ambassadors of the United States *promote* good will abroad.

further   *Further* means advance something by giving help. The newspaper article *furthered* the candidate's campaign.

See also *grow, help* (v).

ANTONYMS: recede, slow (v), fall back, hinder, obstruct, stay (v), stop (v)

advise	*Advise* means give a person information or suggestions that may help him or her in some way. When Tom asked me if the test was hard, I replied, "I *advise* you to study every night for a week."
counsel	*Counsel* means advise. Someone who has knowledge or experience in something may *counsel* you by telling you what to do or say. Lawyers *counsel* their clients.
caution	*Caution* means tell someone to take time to think so that he or she can avoid being hurt or getting into trouble. If I had *cautioned* Susan about the broken alarm clock, she wouldn't have overslept.
warn	*Warn* means tell a person ahead of time about some danger or problem so that it can be avoided. The weather bureau *warns* people about a tornado.
admonish	*Admonish* means remind a person of something that ought to be done, or speak to that person about something he or she has done wrong. I was *admonished* to be careful of the flowers. Then I was *admonished* for not being careful of the flowers.

Kay will be **admonished** for not being careful of the flowers.

agree

Agree means have the same opinion or feeling about something as someone else. At first my idea differed from hers, but finally I *agreed.* If something is pleasing to you or healthful, it can be said to *agree* with you. The weather *agreed* with us.

consent
comply

Consent and *comply* mean agree to something that someone has asked or may want you to do. We asked if we could stay at Grandpa's, and Mom and Dad *consented.* When the supervisor told the workers to put down their tools, they *complied.* You *consent to* do something, but you *comply with.* Mom and Dad finally *consented to* let me go camping. The class *complied with* the committee's decision.

contract

Contract is a stronger word than agree. If you *contract* to do something, your words are usually put in writing. The builders *contracted* to begin the house next month.

admit

When you *admit* to something, you accept or agree that it is either true or false, good or bad. It was not hard to *admit* that the other team had better players.

approve

Approve can mean agree, but it also adds the meaning of having a good opinion about someone or something. Usually, *of* follows *approve.* Cindy hoped that the family would *approve of* her new wallpaper.

See also *promise* (v).

ANTONYMS: differ, disagree, disapprove, contradict, dispute (v), dissent (v), protest (v)

It was not hard to **admit** the other team had better players.

agreement	*Agreement* means an understanding or a promise reached between people or nations. It may or may not be written down. Alice and Marcos made an *agreement* to meet at eight o'clock. Not all the members were willing to sign the *agreement.*
• contract	A *contract* is a formal written agreement. The builders signed a *contract* promising to finish the house by the end ˙of September.
• treaty	A *treaty* is an agreement between states or countries. After the countries agreed to the boundaries, they signed a *treaty.*
• pact • compact	*Pact* and *compact* are other words for an agreement, usually between nations or groups of people. Peace was restored when the three countries signed the *pact.* The Pilgrims who came to America in 1620 signed a *compact.*

agreement continued on page 34 ▶

Peace was restored when the three countries signed the **pact.**

A

• bargain

A *bargain* is usually an agreement on the price of something. We made a *bargain* to pay more rent if the house were painted. *Bargain* can also mean something bought for less money than expected. Joan knew she had found a real *bargain* when she saw the old grandfather's clock in the junk store.

• understanding

An *understanding* can be an informal agreement. It would not be written. I reached an *understanding* with my friend in Tennessee that we would telephone each other once a month.

• approval

If you give your *approval*, you agree completely with someone or something. It is the opposite of disapproval. *Approval* also means praise. The audience showed its *approval* of the play by applauding. Peter tried to win his neighbor's *approval* by cleaning the garage and mowing the lawn.

See also *deal* (n), *pledge* (n).

ANTONYMS: disagreement, disapproval, contradiction, difference, dispute (n), dissension

alert (adj)

Alert means on the lookout for opportunities or danger.

watchful

Watchful has almost the same meaning as *alert,* but it is sometimes used with different words. You can be *alert to* traffic or you can be *watchful of* traffic. You can say someone is an *alert* driver or is *watchful* in a traffic jam. Airline pilots have to be *alert to* any dangers that might be encountered in a flight.

Airline pilots have to be **alert to** dangers.

awake   *Awake* is another word that can mean alert. Here is why. People who are asleep are not alert to what is going on around them, but those who are *awake* usually are. So you can say that people are *awake to* certain problems or *awake to* danger. Donna is a good lifeguard because she is always *awake to* the danger of someone's drowning.

vigilant   *Vigilant* means constantly watching for harm or danger. A forest ranger had better be *vigilant.*

ready   *Ready* means prepared for whatever might happen, good or bad. The goalie was *ready* to block the shot. After Yoshio had combed his hair, he was *ready* to have his picture taken.

quick   *Quick* means ready to act or to move fast. The fire department was *quick* to answer the alarm. A *quick* mind is the opposite of a sluggish mind.

ANTONYMS: asleep, sluggish, drowsy, dull, heedless, slow (adj)

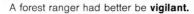

A forest ranger had better be **vigilant.**

A

allow

Allow is the opposite of prevent. *Allow* means let something happen or be done. The sitter *allows* the children to play outside until dark. Ball playing is not *allowed* in the park.

permit

If you *permit* someone to do something, you give that person permission. Something that is not *permitted* is forbidden. The principal *permitted* the students to use the gym at night. Some people allow something even if it isn't *permitted.* The manager allowed the dog to go into the store even though the store rules didn't *permit* it.

let

Let means allow. It is often used in giving suggestions and commands. *Let's* go to the park. *Let* go! It can also mean give permission. Tony wondered if his mother would *let* him go to the circus.

admit

Admit means let in or allow to enter. Amy was *admitted* to the hospital to have her tonsils removed. These tickets will *admit* us to the movie.

- endure
- tolerate

Endure and *tolerate* are good words to use even though they are not real synonyms of *allow. Endure* and *tolerate* can mean put up with something, especially for a long time. You *endure* something if you do not give in to it. The child *endured* the pain of a broken leg and didn't cry. We *tolerate* the nightly hooting of our neighbor's pet owl.

ANTONYMS: prevent, forbid, deny, prohibit

amuse

Amuse means pass time in a very pleasant way. If something *amuses* you, it holds your attention and may make you laugh or smile. It does not bore you. Something that *amuses* you can also make you feel happy and perhaps even excited. That book on the history of the circus *amused* Larry. You can also *amuse* someone else. I *amused* my brother until Dad came home.

entertain

Entertain means amuse and give pleasure. Movies and books can *entertain.* You *entertain,* too, when you have someone over to your house as a guest.

delight

Delight means amuse and give joy. The magician *delighted* the audience with his magic act. *Delight* can also mean be satisfied with something. Mother was *delighted* to see that the children had cleaned the house while she was at work.

interest

If something *interests* you, it holds your attention and makes you curious. The children were *interested* in dinosaurs.

cheer

Cheer means make someone who is sad feel happy. Visitors *cheer* patients who are in the hospital. *Cheer* can also mean shout encouragement. The crowd *cheered* the team on to victory.

divert

Divert means turn someone's attention from something that is worrying him or her to something amusing or pleasing. The comic books *diverted* the child's attention.

The magician **delighted** the audience with his magic act.

ANTONYMS: bore (v), annoy, disturb, tire (v)

amusement   *Amusement* is anything that holds your attention and delights you. It usually makes you laugh and feel happy. Reading a book, playing a game, going to a movie, and working on a hobby are all forms of *amusement.*

entertainment   *Entertainment* means amusement usually provided by someone or something. The animals at a zoo or circus provide lots of *entertainment* for children and grown-ups.

delight
pleasure   *Delight* and *pleasure* are feelings of happiness and enjoyment. You can show your *delight* or *pleasure* in something by laughing or smiling. You can show your displeasure by frowning. Max's *delight* in winning the raffle was apparent to all of us. It's a *pleasure* to talk to a good friend.

fun   *Fun* is anything that gives amusement or makes you laugh. Sophie thinks it's *fun* to twirl a baton.

recreation   *Recreation* is anything you find relaxing and fun. It is not work. Skating on a pond or rink is a good form of *recreation.*

Skating on a pond or rink is a good form of **recreation.**

cheer

If you give *cheer* to someone, you make that person feel happy. A letter from home always brings *cheer* to a college student. *Cheers* can also mean the shouting you hear at a football or baseball game.

diversion

A *diversion* can be an amusement or simply something that catches your attention and turns you away from what you may be doing. Movies and TV programs are good *diversions.* If you want a *diversion* from your work, you can take a walk. A good magician creates a *diversion* with one hand so the audience won't see what is really happening.

interest

If you have an *interest* in something, it holds your attention and you want to know more about it. But you may or may not be amused. You can have an *interest* in a very serious subject like the operation of a computer. Collecting model cars can be an *interest.*

ANTONYMS: displeasure, work (n), boredom, sadness

When Carrie and Arlene lost out on a chance to earn money, they felt **anger.**

anger

Anger is the strong feeling you have when something does not please you. You can feel *anger* toward yourself or someone else. You can feel *anger* at something that happens. Your *anger* would probably be directed toward yourself if you lost five dollars. If your little brother lost your five dollars, your *anger* would be directed at him. If you lost out on the chance to earn five dollars, you might also feel *anger.*

anger continued on page 40 ▶

A

irritation
Irritation is a feeling you have when you are annoyed or disturbed about something that keeps on happening. It was difficult to work with Kim because her constant whistling was an *irritation* to me.

vexation
Vexation means almost the same as irritation, but *vexation* implies a stronger feeling of anger. Grandfather says that when I am noisy, I am a *vexation*. When I am quiet, I am a pleasure.

exasperation
Exasperation is a sudden and temporary feeling of anger brought on by being repeatedly annoyed or irritated. *Exasperation* may be your feeling when you have just tried for the tenth time to phone your friend, and the line is still busy.

wrath
Wrath is a strong feeling of anger that often results in a desire to seek revenge. Roberta's *wrath* at not being invited to the slumber party caused her to make unkind remarks about her classmates.

rage
Rage is violent anger that may result in the loss of self-control. *Rage* usually suggests a boiling over of feelings. In his *rage* at striking out, Terry threw the bat to the ground.

fury
Fury is anger so violent that self-control and reason are forgotten. *Fury* is marked by such violent actions that the *fury* may seem like temporary insanity. In the movie we saw yesterday, a man's *fury* drove him to burn a barn.

ANTONYMS: pleasure, self-control, calm (n)

The mayor called a press conference to **announce** that she would retire in June.

announce

Announce means tell people something they don't know. Usually, *announce* means give out a public or an official statement. The mayor called a press conference to *announce* that she would retire in June. Due to the heavy snowfall, it was *announced* that there would be no school tomorrow.

broadcast

Broadcast originally meant to plant seeds by scattering them, or casting them, broadly. Now the word means make something widely known through radio, television, or a public-address system. At three o'clock we will *broadcast* the President's news conference over the public-address system. We sometimes also use the word when we mean tell something loudly or tell a lot of people over a broad area. His secret was *broadcast* all over the school by the end of the day.

herald

Herald means call attention to something important that is about to take place. Long ago a "herald" ran or rode ahead of the king's party announcing the king's approach to people along the way. The high-school band will *herald* the senator's visit. The birth of an heir to the throne was *heralded* all over the kingdom.

publish

Publish almost always means tell something in print. The magazine will *publish* the governor's speech. The names of all contest winners will be *published* in our next bulletin.

announce continued on page 42 ▶

announce continued from page 41

advertise

Advertise means call attention to something by telling people about it. Miriam *advertised* to the whole family that her birthday was coming soon. *Advertise* also means telling people about products and services so that they will want to buy them. There are many ways to *advertise*—on TV or radio, in newspapers and magazines, on billboards, or even in the sky. We can *advertise* our pet-sitting service by putting up posters in stores.

communicate

Communicate means talk with other people and listen to them. It also means share and exchange thoughts and ideas with others. The two girls used walkie-talkies to *communicate* with each other. Sometimes people *communicate* without talking. Indians in the Old West *communicated* by smoke signals.

ANTONYMS: conceal, hide (v), suppress, withhold

Annette and Elena used walkie-talkies to **communicate** with each other.

answer (v)

Answer means say, write, or do something as a result of what someone asks or wants or needs. You *answer* a question or a letter, a telephone or a doorbell. Usually you *answer* a question with words. But you might *answer* by shaking your head or shrugging your shoulders.

reply

Reply means answer. When you *reply* to what someone says, you tell that person something that is related to what he or she has said to you. When he told me to return my library books, I *replied* that I would

The mystery was **solved** when Max found the cat upstairs.

have to find them first. Sometimes you *reply* with action. Chuck *replied* to their angry question by calmly walking out of the room.

respond

Respond means react to something said or done, either with words or action. You *respond* to someone who is friendly by being friendly yourself.

retort

Retort means answer with a quick, sharp, and perhaps clever or funny reply. Should someone ask if you need a hand with your packages, you might *retort,* "No thanks, I've already got two."

solve

Solve is a good word to use when you mean explain something or find the solution to a problem. The mystery was *solved* when we found the cat upstairs.

ANTONYMS: ask, inquire, question (v), request (v)

answer (n)

An *answer* is something said or done as the result of a question or request. When you write a letter or ask a question, you expect an *answer.*

reply
response

A *reply* and a *response,* like an answer, tell you something you have asked or wondered about. If I ask you whether dogs lay eggs, I am sure your *reply* will be "No." A *response* is also an answer that tells how you feel about something. My *response* to Bob's suggestion that we go ice skating was, "I don't feel like skating today."

answer (n) continued on page 44 ▶

A

retort

A *retort* is a quick, sharp reply that is clever or funny or angry. When I told my little brother to be quiet, his loud *retort* was, "I am being quiet."

solution

A *solution* is an answer to a problem or puzzle. "The *solution* to your problem is to practice more," Paula's tuba teacher told her. I'll find the *solution* to this puzzle if it takes me all day.

defense

A *defense* can be an answer you give when someone suggests that you have made a mistake or have done something wrong. My only *defense* after breaking the window was that the wind carried the ball too far.

Ed will find the **solution** to this puzzle if it takes him all day.

ANTONYMS: question (n), query, inquiry, problem

appropriate (adj)

Appropriate means right and acceptable. Rules of behavior and good manners usually measure what is *appropriate* or inappropriate. There is an *appropriate* time to work and an *appropriate* time to play. It is *appropriate* to thank someone for a gift.

suitable
fit

Suitable and *fit* mean appropriate and ready. His clothing is *suitable* for warm weather. If a person is *fit* for a job, he or she is able to do it well. Some water must be treated before it is *fit* to drink.

becoming

If something is *becoming,* it is not only appropriate and suitable, but attractive. That new dress is very *becoming.*

qualified

Qualified is used to describe a person who meets certain requirements and standards.

44

COME TO OUR
BIG SAIL TODY TOODAY
TODAYE

Not everyone is **qualified** for skywriting.

A *qualified* pilot must have many hours of flight experience. Not everyone is *qualified* for skywriting.

proper
fitting

Proper and *fitting* mean appropriate and acceptable to a situation. A carpenter can work best when he or she uses the *proper* tools. Some people always know the *proper* thing to say. It is *fitting* to stand when you pledge allegiance to the flag. It is *fitting* to shake hands when you meet someone.

See also *correct* (adj).

ANTONYMS: inappropriate, unsuitable, improper, unfit

argue

Argue means give reasons for or against something. You might *argue* with people in order to convince them you are right and they are wrong. You *argue* in order to try to persuade them to accept your ideas.

disagree

You *disagree* with someone when you do not share the same opinion. You can *disagree* without having to argue. I *disagreed* with the umpire's decision but didn't say anything. The girls agreed to give their uncle a present but *disagreed* on the best gift to buy.

argue continued on page 46 ▸

A

The architects **discussed** floor plans.

discuss

Discuss can mean just talk something over. Persons who disagree may *discuss* their problem calmly and agree on a solution. The students *discussed* places to go on their class trip. The architects *discussed* the floor plans and decided to change them slightly to ensure the best use of space.

debate

When you *debate* with another person or group, you consider both sides of a question or problem. You defend your position and attack your opponent's point of view. There are rules to follow when you *debate* in public. You can also *debate* something with yourself. If you are lost, you might *debate* which street to take.

dispute

Dispute means argue angrily over something. It can also mean question what another person does or thinks. The contestants *disputed* the judge's decision, but they didn't withdraw from the contest.

quarrel

Quarrel means argue noisily. People usually shout when they *quarrel.* Most people don't enjoy being with someone who *quarrels* all the time.

See also *object* (v).

ANTONYMS: agree, consent (v)

arrangement

An *arrangement* is something made by putting things together in a certain way. Your teacher can change the *arrangement* of the desks in the classroom. A centerpiece on the table may be an *arrangement* of flowers. The *arrangement* of books on that shelf is alphabetical.

- order

Order can mean arrangement. The words in a dictionary are in alphabetical *order*. If everything has been straightened out and put in its place, it is in *order*. If your desk is in a state of disorder, you won't be able to find your papers and books easily.

- organization

An *organization* is the arrangement of parts to form a whole. A group of people working together to achieve a goal can also be called an *organization*. The United Nations is a world *organization* that is made up of representatives from many countries.

- system
- classification

A very detailed arrangement of things or ideas can be called a *system* or *classification*. The *system* by which books are grouped in a library helps you find them by title, author, or subject. In science you can study the *classification* of plants and animals.

- plan

A *plan* is the order or arrangement of steps in carrying out some activity. *Plans* to do something are first thought out and then may be written down. Having a fire drill without a *plan* would result in confusion. We haven't made *plans* for our vacation.

- preparation

Preparation can mean an arrangement made beforehand. Plans, ideas, or things are put in order or made ready for use. My parents made many *preparations* for my birthday dinner. The *preparations* for any space flight take many months.

See also *plan* (n).

ANTONYMS: disorder, confusion

A

attack (v) *Attack* means fight against or go against someone or something. Pirates used to *attack* ships and steal the cargo. A bear might *attack* a camper if it felt its cubs were in danger.

bombard *Bombard* means attack with cannon shells, bombs, or missiles. Francis Scott Key wrote "The Star-Spangled Banner" while Fort McHenry was being *bombarded.*

charge *Charge* means rush forward to attack. We *charged* our opponents' snow fort during the snowball fight. *"Charge!"* was the battle cry an officer would give to begin the attack.

ambush *Ambush* means attack suddenly from a hiding place. The outlaws *ambushed* the stagecoach.

storm *Storm* means violently attack an enemy's stronghold or fortress. A mob *stormed* and destroyed the Bastille, an old prison in Paris, on July 14, 1789.

invade *Invade* means attack, enter, and take possession of a place. When the troops *invaded* the village, they set up their headquarters in the town hall.

ANTONYMS: defend, protect, guard (v)

The outlaws **ambushed** the stagecoach.

48

attempt (v)   *Attempt* is the opposite of give up. It means make an effort to do something. The swimmer *attempted* to cross the English Channel. The pirates *attempted* to capture the ship and its cargo.

try   *Try* means attempt over and over to do something. It can also mean test or experiment with something. If at first you don't succeed, *try, try* again. I want to *try* a different recipe the next time. To "*try* one's hand at something" means attempt something new. *Try on* means see how something fits or looks on you.

undertake   *Undertake* means attempt something that you have promised to do. Our class *undertook* the job of raising money for charity projects.

endeavor   *Endeavor* is a stronger word than *attempt.* When you *endeavor* to accomplish or prove something, much effort is required. Amelia Earhart *endeavored* to fly around the world. Galileo *endeavored* to prove that the earth rotates around the sun.

strive   *Strive* is the strongest synonym for attempt. When you *strive* to do something, you have to try very hard. The firefighters *strove* to put out the fire before it spread. Sophia kept *striving* to be the best player on her basketball team.

ANTONYMS: give up, quit

49

B

basic

Basic describes the main part of something on which all other parts depend. The *basic* structure of a skyscraper is its steel framework. Without it, the whole building would collapse. An author develops a story from one *basic* idea.

fundamental

Fundamental can describe something like a foundation upon which other things can be built or added. One *fundamental* rule for drivers in the United States is to keep to the right side of the road. The Constitution is the *fundamental* law of the United States.

first
primary

First and *primary* mean before anything else. The *first* step in building a campfire is gathering wood, and the last step is lighting the fire. Learning to read is of *primary* importance. You develop reading skills in the *primary* grades. Red, blue, and yellow are *primary* colors. Other colors can be made from them.

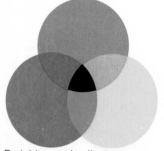

Red, blue, and yellow are **primary** colors.

necessary
essential

A part that is *necessary* or *essential* to something cannot be taken away from it. Tracks are *necessary* to a railway train. Wheels are *essential* to a car, but a clock is nonessential.

vital

Vital describes things that are basic to life or basic to staying alive. Food and water are *vital* to human beings. Breathing is a *vital* function of our bodies.

See also *important.*

ANTONYMS: last (adj), nonessential, trivial, unnecessary

battle (v)
Battle means fight against someone or something. People *battle* each other when they argue over something. Teams *battle* for victory. Doctors *battle* disease. The swimmer *battled* the swift current.

struggle
Struggle means work very hard or make a strenuous effort to do something. The hiker *struggled* up the steep mountain path. It took me hours to *struggle* through that assignment.

combat
Combat means struggle and fight against something. Forest rangers *combat* forest fires. You can *combat* a cold by staying in bed.

wrestle
Wrestle means battle or struggle against someone or something. You can *wrestle* with a person or with a problem. If you *wrestle* with a person, you may become bruised. If you *wrestle* with a problem, you may lose a lot of sleep.

grapple
Grapple is very much like *wrestle.* When you *grapple* with someone, you struggle with that person to get a better hold. When you *grapple* with a problem, you struggle with it to find an answer.

besiege
Besiege usually means surround and attempt to capture a fort or territory. The Vikings *besieged* the town until it ran out of food and ammunition. *Besiege* also means bother with requests. The jockey was *besieged* by fans seeking autographs.

The jockey was **besieged** by fans seeking autographs.

B

battle (n)

A *battle* is a meeting or a clash between enemies or people who have opposing goals. It can be between two armies, between two ships, or between two groups of aircraft. A *battle* might also be between two persons.

Battle can also be used for any kind of clash in which one person or idea struggles against another. There has always been the *battle* of man against nature. You might face a *battle* with your conscience.

action

Action can be part of a battle. Tanks went into *action* after the bombarding stopped.

combat

Combat means fighting in general. A *combat* may also mean a battle between two individuals. Soldiers must learn hand-to-hand *combat* as part of their training.

skirmish
brawl

A *skirmish* and a *brawl* are both rather small battles. Sometimes a *skirmish* is a short fight between a few troops during a battle or just before it. It doesn't last long. A *brawl* is any noisy fight or argument.

attack

An *attack* is a battle begun by one side usually taking the other side by surprise. Sentries guard an army camp against *attack.*

duel

Historically, a *duel* was a formal battle between two persons. Usually one person had insulted the other, and the one who felt offended challenged the other to a *duel.* *Duels* were fought with swords or pistols, and usually at dawn.

A **duel** was a formal battle between two persons.

A **contest** can be a game in which each side is struggling to win.

fight
conflict
contest

Fight, conflict, contest, are all general words for a situation in which people or animals struggle and strive to conquer, to win, or to be superior. A *fight* can be with words, with fists, teeth, claws, or with weapons. A *conflict* is any disagreement or feeling of disagreement. A *conflict* may be a world war, or it may be an argument over which TV show to turn on. A *conflict* can even be the struggle to decide between two good TV shows being shown at the same time. A *contest* can be a war or a battle, but it usually is a game in which each person or group is struggling to win over opponents.

See also *quarrel* (n).

beat (v)

Beat means strike someone or something over and over. My great-grandparents cleaned their rugs by *beating* them. That musician *beats* her drums loudly. *Beat* can also mean defeat or overcome. We *beat* the other team. I always *beat* my uncle at checkers.

beat (v) continued on page 54 ◗

B

Farmers in early times **thrashed** wheat by hand.

spank

Spank means beat with an open hand. Did anyone ever *spank* you when you were little?

pummel

Pummel can mean beat with fists. Lion cubs *pummel* each other with their paws when they play.

flog

Flog means beat with a rod or whip. In the days of sailing ships, sailors who disobeyed orders were very often *flogged*.

thump

Thump can mean beat, pound, or knock. When you're very nervous or afraid, your heart may *thump*.

thrash

Thrash means beat with a stick or whip. Farmers in early times *thrashed* wheat by hand to remove the grain. *Thrash* also means toss or throw yourself around. If you're having a nightmare, you might *thrash* wildly about in your bed.

trounce

If you *trounce* your opponents in a game or contest, you beat them by a large score.

See also *conquer, defeat* (v), *hit* (v).

beautiful

Beautiful is the opposite of ugly. Anything that you find very pleasing, attractive, or desirable can be called *beautiful*. Today *beautiful* is used to describe so many things that it may not mean much anymore.

pretty

Pretty describes those things that are pleasant and nice to look at but aren't grand enough or important enough to be called beautiful. A daisy is *pretty,* but you may not think it is the *prettiest* of all flowers. A face that isn't *pretty* might be called plain or homely.

handsome | A *handsome* person is good-looking. *Handsome* also describes those things that are very dignified, stately, and impressive. Buckingham Palace, the home of Queen Elizabeth II, is a *handsome* building.

fair | *Fair* can mean beautiful. The knights in the Middle Ages called young women, or maidens, *fair* instead of beautiful. We say the weather is *fair* when it is fresh and clear.

lovely | *Lovely* means very beautiful and delightful. It is a *lovely* day for a picnic. Horrid and hideous are very strong words to describe something that is not *lovely*.

graceful | *Graceful* means beautiful in form and movement. A good dancer has to be *graceful*. An elm tree looks *graceful* as it sways in the breeze.

beauteous | *Beauteous* means beautiful, but you would probably never hear it used today. People today speak of a beautiful evening instead of a *beauteous* evening.

gorgeous | *Gorgeous* means very beautiful and colorful. A *gorgeous* rainbow formed over the waterfall. The sun setting over a mountain range is a *gorgeous* sight.

exquisite | Something that is beautifully and delicately made or formed can be called *exquisite*. The spider web dotted with dew was *exquisite*.

ANTONYMS: ugly, homely, horrid, hideous, offensive

55

B

break (n)

A *break* can mean the act of breaking or coming apart. A *break* or fracture of a bone would have to be set by a doctor. A *break* in a water pipe could cause a flood. A tear, a rip, and a split are *breaks*.

A *break* can also be any kind of stop or a short rest in some activity. There can be a *break* in a storm. People who take a few minutes off from their work often call that period a coffee *break*. Radio and TV programs have station *breaks*. The program is stopped just long enough for the local station to identify itself.

interruption

An *interruption* is a breaking in on some activity. The most common *interruption* to your peaceful sleep is the ringing of an alarm clock. *Interruptions* during a phone call can be annoying.

pause

A *pause* is a brief break or stop. I waited for a *pause* in the conversation before asking my question. It can also mean a short rest or even a temporary cease-fire in war. There was a *pause* in the bombing.

intermission

An *intermission* is a planned break in a play or performance. You can get something to eat and drink during an *intermission* in a movie.

recess

A *recess* is either a short or long break from business or work. A judge can call a *recess* during a trial. Your lunchtime at school is a *recess*.

lull

A *lull* is a brief period of time when some activity is stopped. It lasts until the activity

They got something to eat during an **intermission.**

break (n) continued

starts up again. A *lull* in a storm is a brief period of calm, which does not last.

vacation

A *vacation* is a long break in someone's routine, everyday life. It is a break (and sometimes a welcome one!) in your school year.

breakable

Something that is easy to break is *breakable.* It can come apart, shatter, or be split into pieces. Glasses and dishes are *breakable.*

fragile

Anything that has to be handled carefully so it won't be broken is *fragile.* Postal clerks mark *fragile* on packages that could be damaged in the mail. Our new baby seems so *fragile* that I'm afraid to pick him up.

delicate

Delicate can mean extremely easy to break. Things that are *delicate* are usually lovely and very fine. The opposite of *delicate* is coarse. Thin crystal is *delicate* and must be treated with care. Some plane models are *delicate* to handle. An orchid is a *delicate* flower, but a dandelion is a tough flower.

brittle

Brittle objects are hard, but they snap or shatter if they are dropped or treated roughly. It is impossible to bend a *brittle* object. Glass is *brittle,* and so is ice.

crisp

Crisp means breakable when it describes certain foods. Crackers are *crisp* and crumble easily. Fresh lettuce is *crisp.* Toast, celery, and carrots are also *crisp.*

ANTONYMS: coarse, tough, unbreakable

B

build

Build means make something by putting materials or parts together. Carpenters *build* houses and office buildings. Birds *build* nests. Beavers *build* dams in rivers and streams. You can *build* a fire with kindling wood and dry logs. You can also *build* your hopes on something that you have counted on for a long time.

construct

Construct means build, but adds the meaning of making something according to a definite and often complicated plan. Architects, engineers, and carpenters are all needed to *construct* a skyscraper. You can *construct* a model rocket or a model ship according to directions.

manufacture
assemble

Manufacture means make or produce something using machines, usually in a factory. *Assemble* means bring or fit parts together. Each part of a car is first *manufactured,* and then all the parts are *assembled.*

fabricate

When you *fabricate* something, you make it out of many parts, according to a pattern. *Fabricate* can also mean make up a story to fool or deceive someone. She *fabricated* an excuse for being late.

develop

Develop can mean make a change, make some improvement, make available, or even grow. Exercise *develops* your muscles. A large oak tree *developed* from the young seedling. Construction plans for the shopping mall *developed* slowly.

ANTONYMS: demolish, destroy, tear down

Architects, engineers, and carpenters **construct** buildings.

C

calm (adj)

Calm means not excited or disturbed when you use it as an adjective. *Calm* people are relaxed. They don't get excited easily. How can I be *calm* when you are standing on my foot? *Calm* weather is not stormy. It is hard to stay *calm* when your team is winning.

quiet
still

Quiet and *still* can mean calm. A *quiet* person is not noisy or loud. A *quiet* street may have little or no traffic on it. *Still* adds the meaning of not moving. Sit *still.* A lake is *still* when there is no wind. An engine is *still* if it is not running.

cool

Cool people have a lot of self-control. They might be a little nervous, but no one would know it by their actions. They remain calm even in a dangerous situation. That pitcher has to keep *cool* if she wants to win the game.

peaceful
placid
tranquil
serene

Peaceful, placid, tranquil, and *serene* all describe something gentle and restful and calm. It is *peaceful* to sit by the fire after a long day of skiing. *Placid* waters are quiet and still. A *tranquil* person does not often get upset over anything. The Mona Lisa has a *serene* smile.

The Mona Lisa has a **serene** smile.

pacific

Pacific means peaceful and mild. When Magellan sailed into the South Seas on his way around the world, the waters were so calm and quiet that he called it *pacific.* Today we still call it the *Pacific* Ocean.

ANTONYMS: excited, stormy, noisy, loud, restless, nervous, disturbed

69

C

calm (v)

Calm means give comfort when it is used as a verb. It is the opposite of disturb or excite. You *calm* people who are afraid by talking kindly to them and making them feel less fearful. The jockey tried to *calm* the nervous horse. A person can be both *calmed* and excited by music.

quiet

Quiet means calm something or become still. The trainer tried to *quiet* the enraged lion. *Quiet* is often followed by *down*. Stir up would be the opposite of *quiet down*. The wind *quieted down* after the storm.

soothe

Soothe means calm or make less painful. You *soothe* someone's feelings when you make that person feel better. The police officer *soothed* the lost child. Cough drops can *soothe* a sore throat.

pacify

Pacify can mean calm someone's anger. We *pacified* the crying child by giving him a bottle of milk. The store manager tried to *pacify* the furious customer by giving back her money.

tranquilize

Tranquilize means calm or make someone feel less tense and nervous. A veterinarian uses medicine to *tranquilize* a frightened dog before setting its broken leg.

ANTONYMS: disturb, excite, stir up

The family **pacified** the crying child by giving him a bottle of milk.

Stillness can mean calm and the absence of motion.

calm (n)

Calm, when it is used as a noun, means a condition without excitement, disturbance, or much movement. A period of *calm* followed the storm. The doctor gave me a feeling of *calm* and well-being.

quiet

Quiet is freedom from noise and confusion. The *quiet* of the country was a welcome change after the bustle of the city.

stillness

Stillness means calm and the absence of motion. The *stillness* of the air warned of a coming storm.

peace
tranquillity
serenity

Peace, tranquillity, and *serenity* all mean a gentle and restful kind of calm. Being in the wilderness filled us with *peace* and *tranquillity.* There is *serenity* in the first warm spring day.

ANTONYMS: noise, confusion

carry

Carry means hold something while you move from one place to another. You *carry* such things as books, packages, suitcases, and bags of groceries. Trains, ships, and planes *carry* objects and people.

bring

You *bring* something if you carry it with you from another place to here. But if you carry it from here to another place, you take it. For example, you *bring* the bat here, but you take the bat home. Your mother may ask you to *bring* some groceries when you come home from school. If you are at school, your teacher may ask you to *bring* a note from home.

carry continued on page 72 ◗

carry continued from page 71

C

fetch

Fetch means go and get something and bring it back. Some dogs are trained to *fetch* rabbits.

bear

Bear can mean carry or hold something very heavy. Medieval kings traveled to neighboring kingdoms *bearing* many gifts. A bridge must *bear* the weight of many cars and trucks. You may also *bear* sorrow.

transport

Transport means carry persons or goods from one place to another, usually by some vehicle or machinery. A train *transports* people and freight. Milk is *transported* from dairies by refrigerated trucks.

See also *send.*

ANTONYMS: drop (v), take

A bridge must **bear** the weight of many cars and trucks.

catch (v)

Catch is a word that has many meanings. It really means to take hold of something that is in motion or in hiding. You *catch* a ball with your hands if you don't miss it. A cat *catches* mice. You might *catch* a cold if you are *caught* in a storm. You may *catch* a glimpse of someone, or a pretty picture

Mary **caught** a lot of fish on her vacation.

may *catch* your eye. Perhaps you *caught* a lot of fish on your vacation. You *catch on* to the meaning of something and *catch up* to someone who is ahead of you.

trap
net
snare

Trap, net, and *snare* mean catch an animal with something that will hold it once it is caught. The pioneers used to *trap* wild animals for food and furs. You can also be *trapped* in a room or building if there is no way to escape or get out. You *net* fish, birds, or insects when you catch them in a net. You *snare* small animals by putting a looped rope on the ground in such a way that it will pull tight and hold an animal that steps into it.

seize
snatch

Seize and *snatch* mean take hold of or take away something suddenly. Gail *seized* my arm to keep from falling, and then, after getting her balance, she let go of it. The dog *snatched* my candy bar and ran.

arrest

Arrest usually means catch a suspect and take that person to the police station. He or she may be released later. Something can also catch or *arrest* your attention if it makes you want to look at it or listen to it and causes you to forget what you are doing.

capture

Capture means catch or take hold of something by force. Wild animals are *captured* and then sent to zoos. We tried to *capture* the runaway horse.

ANTONYMS: miss (v), let go, release (v), free (v)

73

C

center (n) The *center* is a point inside a circle which is the same distance from any point on the outer edge of the circle. To draw a perfect circle you use a compass, placing the needle point on the paper and swinging the pencil point completely around it. The point where you put the needle is the *center* of the circle, no matter how large or small a circle you make. *Center* also suggests a point around which everything seems to turn, revolve, or rotate.
A shopping *center* draws shoppers from all around the area. The *center* of a hurricane is called the eye.

The point where you put the needle is the **center** of the circle.

middle The *middle* is not an exact point, but rather an area or space around the center. You could say Wednesday is the *middle* of the week. *Middle* also suggests what is between the beginning and the end—the *middle* of a story; the *middle* of the day.

heart We all know that the *heart* is the most important organ in our bodies. So *heart* means the innermost and most important part of something. Some people like to live in the *heart* of the city so they can walk to work. When you get to the *heart* of the matter, you get to the basic point.

hub The *hub* is the central part of a wheel. The spokes of a wheel go out from the *hub*. *Hub* can also mean center of activity. Railroad tracks go out from a center, which is called the railroad *hub*. Chicago is the railroad *hub* of the United States. New York harbor is a great shipping *hub*.

core   The *core* is also the central part of
        something. The *core* of an apple is in the
        center and contains the seeds. The *core* of
        a paragraph is the most important sentence
        of the paragraph. The *core* of an argument
        is the main idea you are arguing about.

nucleus *Nucleus* is from a Latin word meaning
        "kernel." Like a core, the kernel contains
        seeds. A *nucleus* is a center around which
        something gathers or collects. Downtown
        is the *nucleus* of a city. In science you
        would speak of the *nucleus* of a cell or the
        nucleus of an atom.

change (v) *Change* means make different or become
        different. You *change* your clothes. You can
        also *change* your mind about something.
        The weather can *change* from day to day.

alter   *Alter* and *modify* mean change only
modify slightly. A tailor *alters* a coat when he or
        she makes it shorter. An adjective *modifies*
        a noun, but it doesn't change the meaning
        completely. For instance, when you write
        "a little dog," the word "little" *modifies,* or
        describes, the word "dog." You *alter* or
        modify your ideas when you make them
        less strong or definite. My family *modified*
        its rule against pets when I brought home a
        kitten.

vary   *Vary* means change slightly so that
        something is not always the same. The
        temperature *varies* with the seasons. A
        pilot can *vary* the speed of an airplane.

change (v) continued on page 76 ▶

Transform means make a major change in appearance.

convert

Convert means change something for a different use. We *converted* the basement into a workshop. Petroleum is *converted* into gasoline.

shift
switch

Shift and *switch* mean change the place, position, or direction of something. A driver has to *shift* the gears in a car in order to back up. The wind *shifted* suddenly and caused the sailboat to capsize. The baggage car was *switched* to another track.

transfer

Transfer can mean change or move from one place to another. You may *transfer* a load of books from one arm to the other. You may trace a design on paper and then *transfer* it to cloth. Some students *transfer* from one school to another.

turn

Turn means change the position of something by moving. A wheel *turns.* You *turn* a key to unlock a door. You also *turn* the pages of a book. *Turn* can also mean change color. The leaves in autumn are beautiful as they *turn* red or yellow.

exchange

Exchange means substitute one thing for another. Marjorie *exchanged* the record for another one. We *exchanged* ideas on what we would grow in our garden.

transform

Transform means make a major change in the appearance or function or meaning of something. The Halloween costume *transformed* Jim into a ghost. Karen and Stan *transformed* an old box into an office.

ANTONYM: maintain

changeable *Changeable* means able or likely to change. The weather has been so *changeable* that I don't know whether to take sunglasses or an umbrella with me today. *Changeable* is often used to describe a person who jumps from one opinion or attitude to another. Jan is very *changeable*—one day she likes her new house and the next day she doesn't.

iridescent *Iridescent* describes something that shows changing colors. A fountain sometimes looks *iridescent* when it has the colors of the rainbow in it. A soap bubble can be described as *iridescent*.

reversible *Reversible* means able to move backward and forward or able to be turned around. A *reversible* coat has two sides that can be used as the outside.

fickle *Fickle* means often changeable without much reason. A *fickle* friend is not really a friend at all, because he or she may turn away from you at any time. He is so *fickle*—one day he's friendly and the next day he's not.

fluctuating *Fluctuating* means moving up and down. The mercury in a thermometer moves up and down during a day of *fluctuating* temperatures. Daily weather charts show *fluctuating* temperatures. Sometimes we say that a person has *fluctuating* moods. By that we mean he or she is up in the clouds one moment and down in the dumps the next.

Daily weather charts show **fluctuating** temperatures.

changeable continued on page 78 ▶

C

unreliable

Unreliable describes persons or things that seldom do what they are expected to do. An *unreliable* paper carrier won't bother to deliver papers in bad weather. An old car may be *unreliable*.

unsteady
unstable

Unsteady and *unstable* describe someone or something that is not solid or firm. *Unsteady* describes any kind of wavering because of a lack of support. Don't climb an *unsteady* ladder. *Unstable* often describes a person who is changeable or likely to break down under stress. An *unstable* person cannot handle problems as well as a stable person can.

ANTONYMS: true, reliable, stable, unchangeable

Fran and Billy **selected** a tie for Uncle John.

choose

Choose means make a decision to take, accept, or do something. You usually have a reason for *choosing* something. Whatever you do not *choose,* you reject or refuse. Tom *has been chosen* to represent our class at the student council meetings next year.

select

Select means choose from many things. You *select* presents to give your family and friends. We *selected* a tie for Uncle John. Your thesaurus will help you *select* the best synonym to say exactly what you mean.

pick
prefer

Pick and *prefer* mean choose a thing because you like it better than something else. Why did you *pick* the red sweater instead of the blue one? She said she *preferred* mustard to catsup on her hamburger.

elect   *Elect* means choose a person for an office or a position. United States citizens *elect* a President every four years. You may also *elect* to do something. When my family went fishing at dawn, I *elected* to stay in bed.

decide   When you *decide* on something, or *decide* to do something, you make up your mind by choosing from many possibilities. Have you *decided* which record album you want? Annette has *decided* to become a doctor.

    ANTONYMS: reject, refuse (v)

clear (adj)   *Clear* means bright or easily seen. It is the opposite of dim or dull. A *clear* day is not misty or hazy. You can see the sandy bottom of a *clear* stream. *Clear* can also mean easy to understand. It is the opposite of confused and obscure and vague. I had no trouble finding your house because your directions were *clear.*

plain   *Plain* means not only easily seen, heard, or understood, but also undecorated and simple. The point of the speech was *plain* to all. Some buildings are *plain;* others are ornate.

open   *Open* means plain and clear, with nothing to obstruct or hide or get in the way. It is pleasant to travel on an *open* road. Larry had an *open,* honest look.

transparent   You can see through something that is *transparent.* Window glass is *transparent.*

clear (adj) continued on page 80 ▶

clear (adj) continued from page 79

C

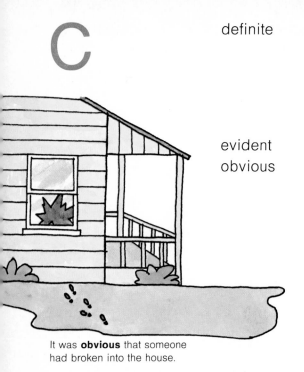

It was **obvious** that someone had broken into the house.

definite

Definite means clear and precise. It is the opposite of vague. A *definite* statement or answer leaves no room for doubt. I want a *definite* answer by tomorrow morning at the latest.

evident
obvious

Something that is *evident* or *obvious* is immediately clear and unmistakable. Her big smile made it *evident* that she had just learned she had no cavities. It was *obvious* that someone had broken into the house while we were away.

See also *visible*.

ANTONYMS: dim (adj), dull, confused, obscure (adj), vague, ornate, doubtful, indefinite

club (n)

A *club* is one kind of gathering. A *club* is a group of people organized either for entertainment or for working together toward a goal. Usually, members of a *club* pay dues and have regular meetings. Our *club* voted to donate some money to UNICEF.

• association

Association is another word for a group of people with the same interests. Often an *association* is made up of people in the same kind of business. My dentist is attending a convention of the American Dental *Association*.

• society

A *society* is an association of people who share an interest or belief and who work actively to support a particular cause. Our neighbor is a member of the *Society* for the Prevention of Cruelty to Animals.

80

- union

A *union* is an organization in which two or more people or groups join together, or unite, to form a larger group. A labor *union,* for example, is an association of workers who have joined together to assist each other and to deal with their employer. The United States is often called the *Union,* because the states are united to form a single nation.

- alliance

An *alliance* may be an association of several nations with the same goal. Nations in an *alliance* may agree to put together their resources for the good of all, or assist each other in case of attack.

- league

A *league* can be an association of ball clubs. There are major and minor *leagues* of both baseball and football teams. Nations may also agree to combine forces in a *league.* A *league* of nations is more tightly bound than an alliance, because the nations sign a formal contract or treaty.

- federation

A *federation* is the joining of several groups or states under one central organization. Some independent labor unions joined to form the American *Federation* of Labor.

clumsy

Clumsy is used to describe someone whose actions and movements are not graceful. The *clumsy* burglar knocked over the chair. *Clumsy* can also describe something that is poorly or roughly made or is difficult to handle. It was difficult to carry the *clumsy* packages to the post office.

clumsy continued on page 82 ▸

C

clumsy continued from page 81

awkward

Awkward can mean clumsy or embarrassing. Something is difficult to carry if it has an *awkward* shape. You would feel *awkward* if you called someone by the wrong name. Murray made an *awkward* jump for the basketball.

gawky
ungainly

You are *gawky* or *ungainly* if you often are clumsy because you don't seem to have control of your arms and legs. You are not able to move quickly and easily. Someone who is *gawky* might not play tennis well. The *ungainly* boy did not make the team.

Someone who is **gawky** might not play tennis well.

bungling

Bungling describes someone who often makes mistakes or something that is not done well. Her *bungling* efforts to pour the tea resulted in a broken cup.

ANTONYMS: graceful, dexterous, handy, skillful

come

Come is the opposite of go and leave. It means move to or toward. If you *come* here or *come* home or *come* inside, you move from another place to where you are now, or to where the speaker is.

Come is also used in other ways. Shirts *come* in many sizes. Spring *came* late this year. Have you *come* to a decision yet? My work is *coming* along nicely. My wish has just *come* true. This knot *came* untied. How did this situation *come* about? My bill *came* to three dollars.

A tornado is **approaching** from the southwest.

- approach

Approach means come near or closer to something. I started to *approach* the stray dog but changed my mind when it began to bark. A tornado is *approaching* from the southwest.

- arrive

Arrive means come to, or reach, a certain place. You should *arrive* at the movie before it starts. The train will *arrive* at eleven o'clock and depart at noon.

- appear

Appear means come into sight. It is the opposite of disappear and vanish. I saw a strange face *appear* at the window. A full moon *appeared* in the sky.

- happen

Happen means take place or come about—sometimes by chance. I just *happened* to see my cousin downtown. Accidents sometimes *happen*. It *happened* to rain. What *happened* to you?

- extend

Extend means stretch out or reach to a certain point. The table *extends* to a length of twelve feet. The teacher *extended* the deadline to Friday.

See also *grow*.

ANTONYMS: go, leave (v), depart, disappear, vanish, go away, quit, withdraw

A chair is **comfortable** when a person can relax and rest in it.

comfortable

Comfortable means giving or feeling comfort and pleasure. Something that is *comfortable* makes you feel good—not too hot or cold, not tired (maybe a little sleepy), just peaceful and happy. Clothes or shoes are *comfortable* if they fit well. Otherwise, they are uncomfortable. A chair is *comfortable* if you can relax and rest in it. You are *comfortable* with people who like you and who make you feel relaxed and happy.

satisfied
contented

Satisfied and *contented* describe someone whose wish or longing has been fulfilled. *Satisfied* means some need has been fully met. Eddy worked on his dune buggy until he was *satisfied* that it was as good as he could make it. One bowl of milk *satisfied* the kitten. *Contented* suggests a strong feeling of being *satisfied* with what you have or where you are or what you are doing. As long as the music played, the baby was *contented.*

easy

Easy can mean free from hardship, strain, worry, or discomfort. The host's *easy* manner made us feel comfortable.

cozy

Cozy describes a feeling of warmth, comfort, and friendliness that is very pleasant. It was *cozy* in front of the fireplace.

snug

Snug is another word that describes a feeling of warmth and comfort. *Snug* also suggests having just as much space as is needed, but no more. Su Lin felt *snug* in her sleeping bag.

84

cheerful

Cheerful means full of warm, pleasant feelings or giving these feelings to others. Everyone likes a *cheerful* person.

cheery

Cheery means bright and gay. The *cheery* card Lil sent helped me get well faster.

See also *convenient, happy.*

ANTONYMS: uncomfortable, uneasy, discontented, miserable, unsatisfied

command (v)

Command means tell a person to do something. Usually someone who *commands* other people has the right, or authority, to do so.

order

Order is like command but often means tell someone to go or come to a certain place. I *ordered* the dog to sit.

demand

Demand is a strong word for telling a person to do something. I *demand* we leave.

charge

Charge can mean tell someone to do a certain job. *Charge* isn't often used this way, though. Carlo is *charged* with tallying the results of the survey.

direct

Direct is a mild word that means tell or suggest to a person something he or she should do. *Direct* them to the buffet table.

instruct

Instruct means teach or tell someone the right way to do something. Our doctor *instructs* us to have a yearly physical.

See also *govern.*

ANTONYMS: comply, obey

The disappearance of the fish was of no **concern** to the cat.

concern (n)   *Concern* is the feeling you have when you really care about something or someone. When people have *concern* for you, they are interested in you; they care about you; they may even worry about you. The disappearance of the fish was of no *concern* to the cat.

interest   *Interest* is the feeling of being interested in a person or thing. When you have an *interest* in ice skating, you want to skate every chance you have and learn all you can about it. You can have many *interests.*

care   *Care* is concern plus a feeling of responsibility for something or someone. If you haven't a *care* in the world, you have nothing that you must do, think about, or worry about. Taking *care* of something means being responsible for getting it fixed, doing whatever it needs, or getting something done. The *care* of three gerbils, two mice, one snake, and two parrots is too much for me.

worry   *Worry* is concern mixed with fear about something that may or may not happen in the future. When the hurricane moved out to sea, my *worries* were over.

anxiety   *Anxiety* is a troubled and uneasy state of mind. Usually a person feels *anxiety* when he or she is fearful of something that may happen, or uncertain about what will happen. Gail's *anxiety* increased as she walked into the dentist's office.

ANTONYMS: indifference, unconcern

The athlete is in excellent physical **condition.**

condition

Condition means the way something is or the way a person feels at some time. A meteorologist reports weather *conditions.* The athlete is in excellent physical *condition.* A *condition* can also be something on which another thing depends. I'll go on one *condition*—that we leave early.

state

State is a good synonym for condition and is often used in its place. We sometimes speak of a country being in a *state* of war or a *state* of peace. Someone may describe conditions as a sad *state* of affairs.

circumstance

A *circumstance* is something that influences the way you feel, the way you act, or the way something is. The warm weather and good food were two *circumstances* that made Gil's barbecue a success.

situation

A *situation* can be thought of as a set or combination of circumstances. That scuba diver was in a dangerous *situation* when she got caught in some coral and the oxygen supply ran out. *Situation* can also mean the position or location of a thing. The *situation* of our house gives us a view of the whole valley.

status

Status can mean the condition or rank of a person in relation to other people. A major in the army has higher *status* than a captain. *Status* can also mean the situation at a given time. A teacher who has assigned a report to be handed in next

condition continued on page 88 ▶

C

week may wonder how much work you have done on it so far. He might say, "What is the *status* of your report today?"

confident

Confident means free from doubt. If you're *confident* something will happen, you firmly believe it will, and you don't worry about it. I'm *confident* the parade will still be held, but I'm doubtful about the weather.

sure

Sure is a good synonym for confident, but it is not as strong a word. When two people argue, each is *sure* that the other person is wrong. Are you *sure* you must go?

certain
positive

Certain and *positive* are strong words meaning confident. It is *certain* that the world is not flat. I am *positive* that five and five make ten.

self-reliant

A person who is *self-reliant* is confident of his or her own abilities. That person does not need help in accomplishing something. Bert is certainly *self-reliant;* he can do anything if he tries.

ANTONYMS: doubtful, uncertain, uneasy, unsure

confuse

Confuse means disturb or be disturbed. If something *confuses* you, it is hard for you to think or act clearly. Directions or questions might *confuse* you. You can be *confused* by a strange noise or an unusual sight. *Confuse* can also mean mistake one for another. I *confused* one telephone number with another and called a gas station instead of the pizza parlor.

CHIRP
CHIRP
CHIRP

Calvin was **confused** by a strange noise.

bewilder

Bewilder means confuse. Something that is very complicated, jumbled, or involved can *bewilder* you and keep you from thinking straight. The instructions for the card game have completely *bewildered* me.

dumfound

Dumfound means confuse and astonish. If something *dumfounds* you, it surprises you and may leave you speechless. Kinuko was *dumfounded* to find that she had really won the bicycle.

perplex
puzzle

If something *perplexes* or *puzzles* you, it is hard to understand or figure out. Trying to read the road map only *perplexed* her more. The instructions for assembling the model airplane *puzzled* me.

baffle

Baffle can mean confuse and amaze. The magician *baffled* the audience.

See also *disturb*.

ANTONYM: clarify

Twins create **confusion** for those who can't tell them apart.

confusion

Confusion is the state of disorder or not knowing what to do. A stalled car causes *confusion* on a highway. Twins create *confusion* for those who can't tell them apart.

bewilderment

Bewilderment is the confusion you feel when there are a number of different objects, ideas, or choices before you. Walking into a room full of laughing people might cause you *bewilderment*. Wayne's blank look showed his *bewilderment* at the auction.

confusion continued on page 90 ▶

C

confusion continued from page 89

perplexity

Perplexity is being confused, puzzled, and worried. I can't understand your *perplexity* over my simple question.

astonishment

Astonishment is what you feel when you are surprised, amazed, or shocked. The crowd looked with *astonishment* at the stunt driver's latest stunt.

ANTONYMS: calm (n), order (n)

conquer

Conquer means get the better of someone or something. Doctors *conquer* disease. Sir Edmund Hillary *conquered* Mt. Everest, the highest mountain in the world, when he reached its summit. *Conquer* and the synonyms listed here are often used by sportswriters and broadcasters to tell which team won a game. All of these words really mean win in warfare or battle with an enemy, but because they are such strong, colorful words, they are used in describing various situations.

overcome

Overcome means conquer an enemy. But you can also *overcome* a bad habit, a fear, or a fault. My little cousins soon *overcame* their fear of the dark.

overthrow

Overthrow means destroy and conquer. The rebels tried to *overthrow* their government and seize control for themselves.

rout

Rout means conquer and drive out an enemy. When you *rout* an army, you throw the troops into such confusion that they scatter and run away.

This ceremony was called a
triumph.

conquer continued

subdue

Subdue means defeat and bring an enemy or an opponent under control. The rodeo rider was able to rope and *subdue* the calf within half a minute. The wrestler *subdued* his opponent when he pinned him so that he couldn't move.

overpower
overwhelm

Overpower and *overwhelm* mean conquer something completely. But something can also *overpower* or *overwhelm* you if it is too much for you to endure. A severe headache may *overpower* you. Someone may be *overwhelmed* by sadness or despair.

See also *beat* (v), *defeat* (v).

ANTONYMS: submit, surrender (v)

conquest

A *conquest* is the winning of a struggle or a contest. A *conquest* is the opposite of a defeat. *Conquest* and its listed synonyms are also used in sports, even though they are strong words. The *conquest* of another country usually involves war. The enemy is defeated and forced to submit to the victor. Pizarro led the *conquest* of Peru. A *conquest* of nature sometimes means the successful end of some expedition or exploration. Sir Edmund Hillary achieved the *conquest* of Mt. Everest.

triumph

When the Roman armies came home from conquering new lands, they marched into the city and were received by the emperor. This ceremony was called a *triumph*. Today a *triumph* is an overwhelming and glorious conquest.

conquest continued on page 92 ▸

C

victory
A *victory* is the overcoming of an enemy, some obstacle, or a certain difficulty. A defeat is the opposite of a *victory*. Shouts of *victory* could be heard all over the battlefield at Gettysburg. The daring rescue at sea was a *victory* over death.

success
Anything that is attempted and turns out well can be called a *success*. Its opposite is a failure. Judy's experiment was a *success*.

achievement
An *achievement* is also the good result of doing something that is very difficult. Learning to communicate with others was a great *achievement* for Helen Keller.

ANTONYMS: defeat (n), failure

consider
Consider means think carefully about something. If you have an important decision to make, it is wise to *consider* every aspect of it before making up your mind. Before you buy something, you should *consider* its price. Had you really *considered* buying a flea circus? I am *considering* trying out for the track team.

weigh
Weigh means balance or compare the weight, value, or importance of two or more things. You use scales to *weigh* objects, but you use your mind to *weigh* opposite or conflicting ideas. A jury has to *weigh* all the evidence given in court before reaching a verdict.

ponder
Ponder means weigh or think deeply about something. Often you don't come to any decision. It is wise to *ponder* the lessons we learn from history.

Some people **contemplate** the stars for hours.

contemplate — You *contemplate* something when you consider it for a long time and keep your attention on it. Some scientists *contemplate* the stars for hours. Ben *contemplated* taking a trip to Europe.

study — *Study* means consider something carefully and in detail. You *study* science in order to learn and understand the subject. Mom *studied* the stock market before she invested her money.

reason — *Reason* can mean consider, examine, explain, or prove something. When you *reason* with someone, it may be to make that person change his or her mind. You *reason* something out if you think about it carefully, step by step.

ANTONYMS: disregard, ignore, neglect (v)

contain — *Contain* and its synonyms have many meanings. *Contain* means have or keep something within something else. The trunk *contains* old photographs. The book I'm reading *contains* stories by famous authors. *Contain* also means keep within limits. It was hard to *contain* our laughter because the joke was so funny. The pen was large enough to *contain* the hamsters.

hold — *Hold* means capable of containing. This gas tank contains only three gallons right now, but it *holds,* or is capable of containing, twenty gallons of gas. *Hold* also means contain or keep. "*Hold* your tongue" means keep quiet.

contain continued on page 94 ▶

93

Some families don't always **confine** their spending to things they really need.

An alarm clock is **handy** for getting up on time.

include

Something that is *included* in something else is part of it. The trip *includes* a riverboat ride, a tour of an old plantation, and lunch at a famous restaurant. The treasurer *included* all the expenses in the report. *Include* can also mean have in addition. The first-aid kit *included* splints along with medicines and bandages.

enclose

Enclose means surround or close in or hold in. A high fence *enclosed* the garden. The baby's arms *enclosed* the teddy bear.

confine

Confine means keep within limits. Our family doesn't always *confine* its spending to things we really need. It also means take away freedom of movement. I was *confined* to bed with a sore throat and a cold.

imprison

Imprison means confine or put in a prison. People are *imprisoned* when they commit crimes and are released after they have served their sentences.

ANTONYMS: release (v), exclude

convenient

Convenient describes something that can be done or used without much effort. Would it be *convenient* for you to stop at the drugstore on your way home?

easy

Easy means convenient because something is not hard or difficult to do. Using an electric sander is an *easy* way to sand.

handy

Handy describes anything that is convenient because it is close by when you need it. An alarm clock is *handy* when you have to get up at a certain time.

- comfortable

Comfortable describes someone or something that has or gives feelings of ease and restfulness. You can relax and rest on a *comfortable* couch, but you may become tense in an uncomfortable chair. You are also *comfortable* when you are with people you like.

suitable

You might use *suitable* when you want to talk about something that can be used in some situation even though it is not intended for that use. Two logs placed side by side made a *suitable* bridge across the stream.

ANTONYMS: hard, difficult, uncomfortable, inconvenient, unsuitable

conversation

A *conversation* is a talk in which two or more persons exchange opinions, ideas, or news. You have a *conversation* with someone about something.

chat

A *chat* is a very informal conversation, usually between friends. When you have a *chat* with another person, you talk about things that are interesting but not very important.

discussion

A *discussion* is usually a serious conversation. A question or problem is talked over, and some solution or conclusion is sought. A *discussion* can turn into an argument.

discourse

A *discourse* is a long, formal conversation. It can also be a long, carefully prepared

conversation continued on page 96 ▶

C

conversation continued from page 95

talk on a subject by one person. Sermons, lectures, and public addresses are *discourses.* The librarian gave a *discourse* on the use of the Dewey decimal system.

dialogue

A *dialogue* is a conversation between two or more people. A conversation written out for actors in a play is called *dialogue,* for example:

Jim: Where are you going?
Maria: Over to Judy's house.
Jim: May I come along?
Maria: Yes, if you'll help me carry
         these pamphlets.

Dialogue can also be spelled *dialog.*

parley

A *parley* is a conversation usually held with an enemy to settle a dispute or an argument. The cavalry officer walked out under a flag of truce and had a *parley* with the chief.

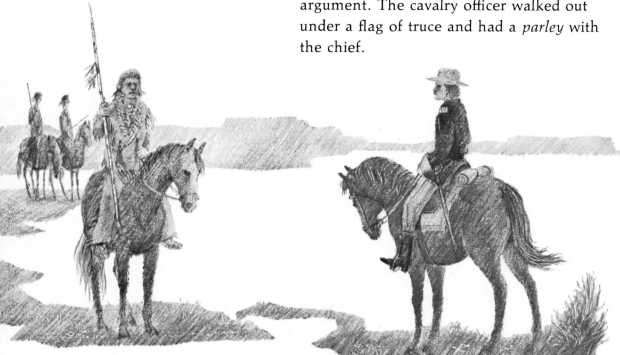

The cavalry officer had a **parley** with the chief.

copy (n)   A *copy* is something that is made to look like something else. People who study art might make *copies* of famous paintings. They would look at the originals and try to make their own paintings just like them. You can make a *copy* of a letter by writing it twice, or you can use carbon paper.

• duplicate   A *duplicate* is an exact copy or double of something. Did you have a *duplicate* of your key made?

• imitation   An *imitation* is a copy. It usually is made of cheaper material and is not as good as the original. An *imitation* of a diamond may be valuable, but it won't cost as much as a real diamond. An *imitation* is also the act of copying something. Can you do an *imitation* of Charlie Chaplin?

• likeness
• resemblance   Things that have a *likeness* or *resemblance* to each other are somewhat alike— especially in appearance. There is a great deal of *likeness* between most twins. You may bear a *resemblance* to your father or mother.

• image   An *image* is an exact likeness. You see your *image* when you look in a mirror. She is the *image* of her mother.

• picture   A *picture* is a painting, drawing, or photograph of something real or of something created by an artist.

• portrait   A *portrait* is a picture of a person. It especially shows the face of a person.

ANTONYM: original (n)

97

deal (n) continued from page 107

Aunt Joy and the car dealer struck a **bargain** on a car.

- exchange
- trade

An *exchange* or *trade* is a deal in which you give something and get something else in return. You may or may not be using money in this kind of deal. Stores make *exchanges* of clothing and other things with customers. The stock *exchange* is the place where stocks are bought, sold, and traded. Sometimes a baseball player moves to another team as part of a *trade* of players.

- bargain

A *bargain* is an agreement to buy, sell, or trade. It can also mean a real saving on something. Your aunt and the car dealer strike a *bargain* on a car when they finally make a deal. If your aunt doesn't have to pay as much as she expected, she gets a *bargain*.

See also *agreement*.

decide

Decide means make up your mind or come to a conclusion about something. Instead of staying home on a hot day, you may *decide* to go swimming. It was hard to *decide* which book to read. We tossed a penny to *decide* who would go first.

determine

Determine means decide definitely on something. The boys were *determined* to win the game, and they fought with all their might.

settle

Settle means make a final choice after you have cleared up all uncertainties and doubts. The committee finally *settled* on a day for the fair. You *settle* an argument

• misfor

• predic

• emer

• ani

• ol

• c

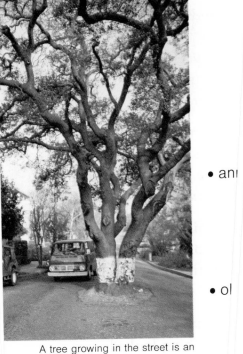
A tree growing in the street is an **obstacle** to traffic.

abbreviate

subtract
divide

Sumi **divides** a pie w
it into six pieces.

cut

S

A

111

when you decide who is right and who is wrong. When you *settle for* something, it may not be your first choice. I wanted a new bicycle, but I *settled for* my brother's old one.

Paco wanted a new bike, but **settled for** his brother's.

rule   *Rule* can mean decide what should or should not be done. The judge *ruled* that the lawyer was out of order. The referee *ruled* that the ball was out of bounds.

resolve   *Resolve* means decide on something once and for all. I have *resolved* to get up early every morning.

See also *choose.*

decision   A *decision* is what you decide. Every time you make up your mind, you make a *decision.* Choosing what clothes to wear is a *decision.*

settlement   A *settlement* is a decision made to settle a problem or an argument. People make a *settlement* when they come to an agreement or reach an understanding.

resolution   A *resolution* is a definite and final decision. It's what you resolve to do. Brenda made a New Year's *resolution* to make her bed every day.

ruling   A *ruling* is an official decision or statement made by someone in authority. We accepted the official's *ruling* that the other basketball team should get a free throw.

decision continued on page 110 ▶

judgment
verdict

decrease (v)

lessen

diminish
dwindle

reduce

shorten

hard

labori

comp

puz

A good detective can solve a
puzzling mystery.

dif

• h

• t

doubt (n)

A *doubt* is a feeling of not being sure or certain. You may have a feeling of *doubt* about someone who breaks a promise. You may suddenly have *doubts* about something you've always believed in—at some time in your life you might have had a feeling of *doubt* about the tooth fairy. When a person says "Without a *doubt*" or "There's no *doubt* about it," you know that person is sure that something is true. If you answer "I have my *doubts*," that person will know what you mean. A *doubt* can also be a feeling of not knowing what to do or what decision to make. Sometimes when you finally make a decision, you have a few *doubts* about it later.

misgiving

A *misgiving* is a doubt, especially about what will happen. You may have *misgivings* as you start to cross a creek by jumping from rock to rock.

distrust

Distrust is a feeling of doubt because you have no confidence in someone or something. The zoo keeper says he always approaches the lions with *distrust*.

skepticism

Skepticism is the feeling that you don't want to believe anything unless you have proof that it is true. Some people may show their *skepticism* when they ask you to prove something that you have just said.

suspicion

A *suspicion* is a doubt about something or someone. If you have a feeling of *suspicion* about someone, you feel that you can't trust or believe that person. As the snow began to fall, she realized that all her

• misfortune

Misfortune is the difficulty of having your luck turn bad. You could have the *misfortune* of slipping on a patch of ice and twisting an ankle.

• predicament

A *predicament* is a difficulty or situation from which there is no easy escape. When the villain in a silent movie leaves the girl tied to the railroad tracks and the train is coming, she is in a *predicament.*

• emergency

An *emergency* is a situation which occurs all of a sudden and which demands some kind of immediate action. To handle an *emergency,* a person must think and act fast. If you were cooking supper, for example, and spilled grease on the stove, you might have difficulty cleaning it up. If the grease caught fire, you'd have an *emergency.* You'd have to act fast.

• annoyance

An *annoyance* causes difficulty by getting in the way of your comfort and peace of mind, but it is not serious. Two people talking in a movie can cause *annoyance* to all the people around them.

• obstacle

An *obstacle* causes difficulty by standing in the way. You have to remove it or go around it. A tree growing in the middle of the street would be an *obstacle* to traffic.

• obstruction

An *obstruction* can be an obstacle or any other difficulty that holds something back or gets in the way or clogs an opening or passage. An *obstruction* in the water pipes caused a flood. Road workers cleared away all *obstructions* as they built the highway.

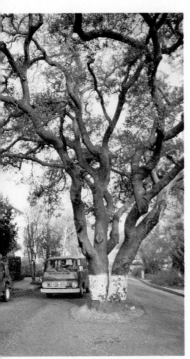

A tree growing in the street is an **obstacle** to traffic.

117

D

dim (adj)   *Dim* describes something that is difficult to see, hear, or understand. A *dim* room is poorly lighted. Voices on a telephone may be *dim* if there is a poor connection. We have only a *dim* idea of what we might be doing next year. If you "take a *dim* view" of something, you don't think much of it.

shadowy   *Shadowy* describes something that has shadows or gives out little light. It often means shady. It was *shadowy* in the forest.

indistinct   Something that is *indistinct* is difficult to recognize or understand because it is too dim or because it looks too much like something else. The voices in the distance were *indistinct,* not clear. The face in the photograph was *indistinct.*

obscure   *Obscure* means dim or hidden. The meaning of this poem is too *obscure* to understand. It might be difficult to find your way down an *obscure* trail.

vague   *Vague* describes something that is not clear or definite. The plans for the party are still *vague.* Eleanor's memories of her childhood are *vague.*

blurred   *Blurred* means with vague or indistinct outlines or edges. Everything looked *blurred* through the wet windshield. When I put on my glasses, the *blurred* type became sharp.

See also *dark.*

ANTONYMS: clear (adj), definite, sharp, bright, distinct, plain (adj)

Everything looked **blurred** through the wet windshield.

Some dogs are trained to **guide** the blind.

direct (v)   *Direct* means show or point out the way to someone. You would *direct* a person who is lost by giving directions. Can you *direct* me to the library? *Direct* also means manage or control. A police officer *directs* traffic. *Direct* can mean order or command. The air traffic controller *directed* the plane to circle the airport.

guide   *Guide* means direct someone to a place by actually going with that person. My cousin *guides* tourists through the exhibits at the museum. Sometimes you *guide* by leading someone or something in the right direction. Some dogs are trained to *guide* the blind. You can help small children write by *guiding* their fingers.

conduct   *Conduct* means direct or guide someone or something. An orchestra leader *conducts* the other musicians. The antique dealer *conducted* an auction at the old mansion. A social director *conducts* the activities on board a cruise ship.

lead   *Lead* can mean show the way by going ahead of someone or something. An usher *leads* people to their seats in a theater. The drum major *led* the parade. Marie *led* us out of the dark room when the lights went out during the storm.

steer   *Steer* means guide a ship or car in a certain direction. The sailor guided the ship by *steering* in the direction of the North Star. The driver *steered* the car around the block.

See also *command* (v).

119

D

disagreeable

Disagreeable means not to your liking. Anything that causes dislike, discomfort, or displeasure can be called *disagreeable.* You may talk about a *disagreeable* smell, *disagreeable* weather, or a *disagreeable* person. A *disagreeable* person may be unfriendly, annoying, or cross. *Disagreeable* people are hard to get along with.

unpleasant

Unpleasant is the opposite of pleasant or enjoyable. An *unpleasant* day might be boring, dull, or rainy. *Unpleasant* is the weakest word for disagreeable. Anything that makes you feel uncomfortable or uneasy may be described as *unpleasant.*

horrible
horrid

Horrible and *horrid* describe something that is very disagreeable and also frightening or shocking. *Horrible* is sometimes overused, so give it lots of rest. Getting lost in a large city can be a *horrible* experience. We saw a *horrid* accident.

offensive

Offensive is a strong word for disagreeable. When something is irritating or disgusting, it is *offensive.* Sometimes spoiled food has an *offensive* odor. You would draw away from an *offensive* sight. An *offensive* remark can hurt a person.

obnoxious
repulsive

Obnoxious and *repulsive* are the strongest words for disagreeable. You would try to avoid something that is *obnoxious* or *repulsive.* Rotten eggs have an *obnoxious* smell. This cough medicine tastes *repulsive.*

ANTONYMS: pleasant, attractive, acceptable, agreeable

This cough medicine tastes **repulsive.**

dishonest   *Dishonest* is the opposite of honest. *Dishonest* is used to describe some people and their actions. Someone who lies, steals, or cheats is *dishonest.*

untruthful   *Untruthful* and *deceitful* mean dishonest,
deceitful   false, and misleading. An *untruthful* account or story doesn't report the truth. Someone who is *deceitful* gives the wrong idea of things and makes people believe things are true when they are really false.

crooked   *Crooked* usually describes something, like a road or path, that has curves or bends. It is the opposite of straight. But *crooked* can also describe a person. A *crooked* person bends or twists the truth.

A **crooked** person bends or twists the truth.

untrustworthy   A person who is *untrustworthy* can't be counted on to do what is right and fair. That person isn't dependable or reliable.

dishonorable   *Dishonorable* means without honesty, honor, or respect. It is a very strong word. Some people have received *dishonorable* discharges from the military.

ANTONYMS: honest, straight, dependable, reliable, honorable, just, trustworthy, truthful, upright

D

disturb

Disturb means move something out of place or put something out of order. A breeze *disturbed* the quiet waters. The detective knew that someone had *disturbed* the papers on the desk. *Disturb* can also mean break in on something or someone or make a person feel uneasy and uncomfortable. Don't *disturb* me while I'm on the phone. The ghost stories we were telling last night *disturbed* me.

The detective knew that someone had **disturbed** the papers.

displace

Displace means move something out of place or put something in the place of another. After a flood, many people are *displaced* because their homes have been destroyed. Superhighways have *displaced* dirt roads between large cities.

disarrange
jumble

Disarrange and *jumble* also mean disturb by moving. You *disarrange* volumes of an encyclopedia when you change their order or arrangement on the shelf. You *jumble* clothes in a drawer when you mix or mess them up.

confuse

If something *confuses* you, it jumbles the order of your thoughts and makes it hard to think clearly. A complicated or puzzling problem may *confuse* you.

interrupt
interfere

Interrupt and *interfere* mean break into and disturb. You *interrupt* someone who is talking or thinking by breaking in with your own questions or remarks. You *interfere* when you take part in something that is none of your business or something that does not need your help or advice.

distract

It is hard to concentrate on what you are doing if something *distracts* you. Your attention is *distracted* by something that disturbs you. The bee buzzing around the ceiling *distracted* me while I was speaking.

The bee buzzing around the ceiling **distracted** Brenda.

rattle
fluster

Rattle and *fluster* mean disturb and confuse. If something *rattles* you, you may say or do the wrong thing. A lot of people crowding and pushing on a bus may *rattle* you. An embarrassing question can *fluster* you, and so can a lot of excitement.

upset
trouble

Upset and *trouble* can be used if something disturbs or worries you. A disappointment can *upset* you. You can *upset* your stomach if you eat too much. Bad news can *trouble* you. Eileen was *troubled* by nightmares and bad dreams.

D

dodge (v)   *Dodge* can mean move back and forth or from place to place or move suddenly in a new direction. In the game of *dodge* ball, players inside the circle must *dodge* balls that are thrown at them. *Dodge* can also mean keep away from something by being clever. The coach *dodged* reporters' questions by sneaking out the back door.

duck   You *duck* your head if you lower it quickly to keep from being hit with something. You probably know that *duck* can also mean push someone's head under water. Another meaning of *duck* is get out of or dodge something. We *ducked* out of the movie before Pat saw us.

avoid   *Avoid* and *evade* mean keep away from. But
evade   *avoid* usually means keep away from harm or danger or from something bad. If your older sister is on a diet, she *avoids* sweets. *Evade* usually means keep from doing or saying something by using a trick. You *evade* something if you don't face it directly. You may *evade* or dodge a question by asking another question or by changing the subject. You *avoid* dark caves; you wouldn't *evade* them.

When Miguel's older sister is on a diet, she **avoids** sweets.

doubt (v)   *Doubt* means feel uncertain about something. You *doubt* that you will stay downtown very long if you are uncertain about what you want to do. You could *doubt* that someone will keep a promise.

question   *Question* can mean feel a little bit uncertain. You *question* something when you wonder whether or not it is true or correct. You might *question* a friend's decision.

distrust   *Distrust* means doubt because you don't feel confident of or sure of something or someone. If someone lied to you, you might always *distrust* that person. The miser kept his money in a sock because he *distrusted* banks.

The miser kept his money in a sock because he **distrusted** banks.

suspect   *Suspect* means doubt or distrust something or someone. You can *suspect* someone of being guilty of wrongdoing even though you can't prove it. We *suspected* that birds were eating cherries from our tree.

ANTONYMS: believe, trust (v)

125

D

doubt (n)   A *doubt* is a feeling of not being sure or certain. You may have a feeling of *doubt* about someone who breaks a promise. You may suddenly have *doubts* about something you've always believed in—at some time in your life you might have had a feeling of *doubt* about the tooth fairy. When a person says "Without a *doubt*" or "There's no *doubt* about it," you know that person is sure that something is true. If you answer "I have my *doubts*," that person will know what you mean. A *doubt* can also be a feeling of not knowing what to do or what decision to make. Sometimes when you finally make a decision, you have a few *doubts* about it later.

misgiving   A *misgiving* is a doubt, especially about what will happen. You may have *misgivings* as you start to cross a creek by jumping from rock to rock.

distrust   *Distrust* is a feeling of doubt because you have no confidence in someone or something. The zoo keeper says he always approaches the lions with *distrust*.

skepticism   *Skepticism* is the feeling that you don't want to believe anything unless you have proof that it is true. Some people may show their *skepticism* when they ask you to prove something that you have just said.

suspicion   A *suspicion* is a doubt about something or someone. If you have a feeling of *suspicion* about someone, you feel that you can't trust or believe that person. As the snow began to fall, she realized that all her

Everyone in the room was placed under **suspicion.**

suspicions about a blizzard were true. Seeing a car race down the street at night without headlights on may arouse your *suspicion.* Everyone in the room at the time of the robbery was placed under *suspicion.*

ANTONYMS: confidence, belief, faith, trust (n)

dreadful   Something is *dreadful* if it fills you with dread or fear that something bad is about to happen. If you dread something, you are afraid and don't want to meet it face to face. A *dreadful* experience would be one that you could hardly bear to think of. A *dreadful* nightmare can make you shudder long after you wake up.

Most of the synonyms listed in this entry can be used wherever you mean *dreadful.* They are strong words, but many times people use them just to emphasize what they are describing. Something bad sounds even worse if you call it *dreadful.*

dreadful continued on page 128 ▶

A **frightful** scream in the dark would scare the wits out of anyone.

awful
: *Awful* describes something that is so powerful or dreadful it fills you with fear. A snowslide sweeping trees and rocks down a mountainside would be an *awful* sight.

terrible
: *Terrible* means causing fear or filling with terror. It describes something that threatens to hurt you—a *terrible* flood, a *terrible* storm, or a *terrible* headache.

frightful
: *Frightful* describes something that shocks or startles you. A *frightful* scream in the dark could scare the wits out of you. Seeing a *frightful* mask on a friend might shock you at first and then make you laugh.

appalling
: *Appalling* describes something so shocking or dreadful that it leaves you speechless. An *appalling* sight could frighten you so much that you might be frozen to the spot.

dull
: *Dull* means not bright or sharp. A *dull* day is cloudy. A *dull* person is not brilliant. A *dull* knife is not sharp enough to cut meat. *Dull* can also describe something that doesn't hold your interest. If a book is *dull,* you may never finish reading it. You might start to yawn if you have to listen to a *dull* story or a *dull* speech.

uninteresting
: *Uninteresting* can describe anything that doesn't hold your attention. Things that are common and ordinary are often *uninteresting.* You lose interest in them right away. But something that is odd, strange, or funny is likely to be interesting because it excites your curiosity.

128

tiresome
tedious

Something that is *tiresome* or *tedious* is dull because it is long and tiring. Cutting the grass can be *tiresome.* Riding in a car for a long time is *tedious.* Picking weeds out of a garden can be *tedious.*

monotonous

Monotonous means dull and not varied enough to be interesting. Doing the same thing over and over is *monotonous.* Practicing a piece for a piano recital can sometimes become *monotonous*—to you and to your family.

Practicing a piece for a piano recital can sometimes become **monotonous.**

boring

Boring means dull and monotonous. A TV show may be so *boring* that you turn it off.

insipid

Insipid means dull and uninteresting. A talk or speech is *insipid* if it doesn't interest you or hold your attention.

ANTONYMS: bright, sharp, brilliant, interesting, varied, exciting

E

eager

Eager means interested in something and looking forward to becoming involved in it. An *eager* person is seldom indifferent to anything. If you're "ready and willing" to start a race, then you've trained faithfully and are *eager* to get on with it.

impatient
anxious

Both *impatient* and *anxious* may mean eager, but *anxious* adds the meaning of worried or afraid. The children were *impatient* for the games to start (no fear, the games would start sooner or later). Barbie and Flo were *anxious* to leave on the fishing trip before all the campsites were taken (great fear, all of the campsites had been taken before).

keen

Keen means sharp—a *keen* edge on a knife is sharp and cuts fast and easily. A *keen* person is sharp and alert, greatly interested in and quick to respond to whatever has captured his or her enthusiasm. *Keen* tennis players keep an eye on the ball every minute and play as hard as they can.

avid

Avid is a stronger word than eager. It suggests greediness. An *avid* stamp collector never has enough stamps. An *avid* baseball fan would like to see a game every day of the year.

ANTONYMS: indifferent, bored, uninterested

An **avid** stamp collector never has enough stamps.

edge (n)   An *edge* is the line or place where something ends. It can be a boundary line. The driveway marks the *edge* of our property. At the beach you may stand at the water's *edge.*

outline   An *outline* is a line that marks the edge of something. It shows the shape of an object or area. A coloring book has *outlines* of objects. Children fill in the *outlines* with colored crayons.

border   A *border* can be an edge. It can also be the area that marks the boundary of something. The Mexican *border* is a southern boundary of the United States. We planted bushes along the *border* of our yard.

frame   A *frame* can be a border that holds and supports something. A window *frame* encloses glass panes. A picture *frame* holds a picture.

margin   A *margin* is a border with a definite measurement. The *margin* of a page is the area around the edge; it has no writing on it.

curb   A *curb* is the raised edge along a sidewalk or street. It is sometimes hard to ride a bicycle over a *curb.*

rim   A *rim* is the outer edge of something curved. The *rims* of some dinner plates are decorated. When the moon is covered by a cloud, you may be able to see just its *rim.*

edge (n) continued on page 132 ▶

When people come to the **brink** of a cliff, if they take one more step, they will drop off.

brink

A *brink* is the edge of something steep. When you come to the *brink* of a cliff, if you take one more step, you will drop off into thin air.

ANTONYM: center (n)

elastic

Elastic describes something that can be stretched or bent or pulled out of shape and then be returned to its original size without any damage. A rubber band is *elastic.*

expandable

You might say that a balloon is elastic. But you would be more accurate if you said a balloon is *expandable. Expandable* means able to be enlarged. You enlarge it when you blow air into it.

stretchable

To understand *stretchable,* think of yourself taking a big, long stretch after you have been sitting in one place for an hour or two. When you stretch, you become taller. *Stretchable* describes something that can be pulled or made larger in one direction—length or width.

resilient

Resilient is a good word to use when you mean that something easily slips back into shape when pressure on it has been removed. A tree is *resilient* if it can remain standing through a hurricane. Something *resilient* will bend but won't break. It is not brittle. A *resilient* person is one who can undergo trouble without losing his or her good nature.

springy

Springy means both elastic and resilient. Something that is *springy* can easily withstand pressure and just as easily return to its original shape. A trampoline is *springy.* Jumping on it will make you bounce.

A trampoline is **springy.**

flexible

Flexible describes something that bends or turns without breaking. A *flexible* pipe can be bent in any direction to go around objects or corners. A *flexible* shoe bends and gives as you walk. A *flexible* person can change plans or ideas quickly if it becomes necessary.

ANTONYMS: brittle, inflexible, rigid, stiff

133

E

enclosed

Enclosed means closed in or held in some way. An *enclosed* porch is not an open porch but one that has walls and perhaps windows. *Enclosed* also means placed in an envelope. Father always looks at the advertisements that stores *enclose* with their monthly bills.

surrounded

If something is *surrounded,* it is enclosed or cut off on all sides. If your dog runs out of the yard, your friends might help you catch her by forming a circle around her. *Surrounded,* she couldn't get away!

blockaded

Blockaded means enclosed and cut off from everything. Ships couldn't get into the *blockaded* harbor.

fenced

Fenced is enclosed with a fence, railing, or wall. A *fenced* yard is safer for little children than an open one.

limited
restricted

Limited and *restricted* mean kept within limits or bounds. A *limited* time is usually given for a sale at a store. If you get home late from a friend's house, you may be *restricted* to your own house every evening for a week.

ANTONYMS: open (adj), unlimited, unrestricted

end (v)

End means stop doing something or come to the last part of something. It is the opposite of begin and start. This story begins and *ends* happily. When an argument starts, I always try to *end* it at once.

cease

Cease means stop or come to an end. The applause *ceased* as the curtain came down.

halt

Halt means end suddenly for a certain period of time. You *halt* if you stop when you are marching. But you might start up again. The hikers *halted* at the river.

finish
complete

Finish and *complete* mean end naturally what you started to do. You *finish* something when you have done everything that is necessary to end it. An author *finishes* a novel when he or she has written all of it. You usually *complete* a task that has been assigned to you. Have you *completed* your homework yet? I can't *complete* it until I *finish* reading the poem.

Something **terminates** when it stops and doesn't start again.

terminate

Something *terminates* when it stops and doesn't start again. You can *terminate* something that may or may not have been completed. The parade began at 169th Street and *terminated* at 180th Street. José *terminated* his subscription to the paper.

conclude

Conclude means finish something or come to a stop. It is the opposite of commence. She *concluded* her speech just as time ran out. A play commences when the curtain is raised and *concludes* when the curtain is lowered after the last act.

close

Close can mean end something by limiting the time. The swimming pool opens the first day of summer and *closes* after Labor Day.

ANTONYMS: begin, start (v), commence, open (v), originate

E

end (n)   The *end* is the last point to which something can go. Our house is at the *end* of this street. It can also mean the last part of something. *End* is the opposite of beginning. We were very tired by the *end* of our bicycle trip.

finish   The *finish* is the end of something that has been started or begun. *Finish* is usually used for the end of a race or fight. I was late for the start of the race, but I was there at the *finish.* In western movies, the sheriff and the outlaws usually fight to the *finish.*

conclusion   A *conclusion* is an end. George brought the meeting to a *conclusion.* Our teacher told us that at the *conclusion* of this book we will have a test. The detective came to the *conclusion* that the butler committed the crime.

termination   *Termination* means the end of something that has stopped but may not have been completed. A snowstorm caused the *termination* of the search.

close   A *close* is an end or a limit of time. At the *close* of day, the street lights come on.

See also *edge* (n), *limit* (n), *object* (n), *result* (n).

ANTONYMS: beginning (n), start (n), origin

endurance   *Endurance* means the power or ability to withstand hardships or difficulties. The swimmer showed great *endurance* when she swam across the English Channel.

stamina

Stamina is a good synonym for endurance. It means the strength to do something strenuous without giving up. Someone with a lot of *stamina* does not tire easily. The athletes who take part in the Olympic games need to have *stamina*.

backbone

Backbone means endurance plus strength of character. Gordon had the *backbone* to stand up for what was right even though his friends laughed at him.

fortitude

Fortitude is a very strong word. It means lasting endurance and bravery in the face of danger. Someone who possesses *fortitude* is patient, uncomplaining, and courageous. The pioneers of the American West had the *fortitude* to overcome many hardships and dangers.

See also *bravery*.

ANTONYM: weakness

The pioneers of the American West had the **fortitude** to overcome many hardships and dangers.

137

They used bits of paper to make a **fake** snowstorm for a play.

fake (adj)   *Fake* means not real. Some *fake* furs look almost real. You can use bits of paper to make a *fake* snowstorm for a play.

imitation   *Imitation* means fake. Plastic material is used to make *imitation* leather.

counterfeit   *Counterfeit* money is very carefully (and dishonestly) made to look exactly like real money. A *counterfeit* painting may be an excellent copy of a famous painting, but it isn't as valuable as the original.

false   *False* is not true. A person may make a *false* statement either by mistake or on purpose to deceive you.

unreal   *Unreal* means not real or genuine. You may have a dream that seems real, but whatever happens in a dream is *unreal.*

untrue   If something is *untrue,* it is false or incorrect. You may hear a rumor about something and then find out it's *untrue.*

ANTONYMS: real, true, genuine

150

fall (v)

Fall means come down from a higher position or come down suddenly. It is the opposite of rise. Snow *falls.* Leaves *fall.* You may *fall* if you stumble on a rock. *Fall* can also mean become less or lower. Her voice rises when she's angry and *falls* when she's calm. A river *falls* after a flood. You also say that you *fall* asleep or that night *falls.*

descend

Descend means fall or come down slowly and gradually. An airplane *descends* for a landing. It ascends when it takes off and rises in the sky. The road *descends* into the valley.

drop

Drop means fall or let something fall suddenly or unexpectedly. Petals *drop* from flowers. Dom *dropped* the mirror when he heard the loud noise behind him.

swoop

Swoop means drop swiftly in order to seize something. The gull *swooped* down, caught a fish, and flew away.

sink

Sink means fall or become lower gradually. A boat that fills with water will *sink* to the bottom of a lake. In a silent movie we saw, a carpenter was hit with a board and *sank* to the ground. The sun *sinks* in the west.

fail

Fail can mean fall short of what is expected. You will get in trouble if you *fail* to pay your income tax. If you *fail* to get to the airport on time, you will miss your plane.

ANTONYMS: rise (v), ascend

A carpenter in a silent movie was hit and **sank** to the ground.

F

famous

Famous means widely known or honored. One act can make you *famous,* or a whole life well spent may make you *famous.* The pitcher who helps a team win a World Series is *famous* for a while. After a few months or years, that same pitcher may be forgotten and be living an obscure life. A *famous* doctor may have saved many lives.

famed

Famed is another word for famous. A *famed* restaurant is one that is well known for some special food served there. Certain parts of our country are *famed* for their mountains or weather or seashore.

noted

Noted means famous because of some accomplishment. We learned that Holland was *noted* for growing tulips.

notorious

Notorious means famous because of something bad or at least something not very good. A certain shop may be *notorious* for charging high prices. *Notorious* is almost always used when outlaws are described. Jesse James was *notorious* for robbing banks and trains.

renowned

Renowned means famous and highly honored. A *renowned* pianist may be asked to play for the President.

distinguished
eminent

Distinguished and *eminent* mean noted for excellence and having a reputation above others. Who is the most *distinguished* person in the Senate? Some *eminent* doctors met to discuss the latest developments in medicine.

ANTONYMS: obscure (adj), unknown

fast (adj)   *Fast* is the opposite of slow. As an adjective, *fast* means moving, happening, or acting with speed. A hot rod is a *fast* car. Hockey is a *fast* game.

rapid   *Rapid* means fast in movement. A *rapid* river has a strong current. A sluggish person does not walk at a *rapid* pace.

speedy
swift   *Speedy* and *swift* mean fast moving or happening very fast. A *speedy* person hurries along and is not poky. In ancient Greece, *swift* runners delivered messages between cities. Rabbits are *swift* animals.

quick   *Quick* means fast in doing something. Mom had a *quick* breakfast before leaving for the office. *Quick* can also mean alert or fast in learning something. You may be *quick* in foreign languages. Or you may be *quick* to notice something new or different.

fleet   *Fleet* can be used to describe an animal or a person who is very fast and swift. Deer are *fleet*. The *fleet* dancers hardly touched the ground.

The **fleet** dancers hardly touched the ground.

instant
immediate
instantaneous   *Instant, immediate,* and *instantaneous* can all describe something that is made or done without delay or at once. You can cook *instant* rice in a very short time. I gave an *immediate* reply to the invitation. When I stepped on the snake, its reaction was *instantaneous.*

See also *sudden.*

ANTONYMS: slow (adj), sluggish, poky

153

F

fast (adv)   *Fast* tells how quickly someone moves or acts or how quickly something happens or is done. I ran up the stairs *fast* and came down slowly. The accident happened so *fast* I couldn't tell whose fault it was. If your watch is ahead of time, it runs *fast;* if it is behind time, it runs slow. Synonyms for the adverb *fast* have the same meanings as the synonyms for the adjective *fast.*

rapidly   The river flowed *rapidly,* not sluggishly.

speedily   Gretchen skated *speedily* to the end of the block and was back in a flash.

swiftly   The rabbit darted *swiftly* into the hole.

quickly   I *quickly* reeled in my fishing line.

fleetly   The antelope ran *fleetly* across the prairie.

instantly   Come home *instantly.*

immediately   I answered his letter *immediately.*

instantaneously   The tree caught fire *instantaneously* when it was struck by lightning.

See also *suddenly.*

ANTONYMS: slowly, slow (adv), sluggishly

The antelope ran **fleetly** across the prairie.

fasten

Fasten is used in many ways. It means attach two or more things together or make something stay in place. You can use a clip to *fasten* papers together. Locks *fasten* doors and windows. *Fasten* can also mean fix or hold your attention on something. The little children *fastened* their eyes on the toy trains.

secure

Secure means make something safe by fastening it firmly. Ropes are used to *secure* a boat to a wharf.

tie

Tie means fasten with string, cord, rope, or ribbon. I have to wrap and *tie* this package before I can mail it.

Romero has to wrap and **tie** this package before he can mail it.

bind

Bind means tie or fasten tightly. You *bind* a cut when you wrap a bandage around it. The cowhands *bound* the steer's legs with rope and then branded the steer. We also say that a book *has been bound* when the cover is put on.

fasten continued on page 156 ▶

F

Galley slaves were **chained** to their oars and forced to row the ancient warships across the sea.

chain	*Chain* means fasten with a chain, or series of metal links. In history we read how galley slaves were *chained* to their oars and forced to row the ancient warships across the sea.
tether	*Tether* can mean fasten something. You might *tether* a dog to a post so it can move around but can't wander away from your yard.
hitch	You *hitch* a horse to a post when you wrap the reins around the post or slip them through a ring. A stalled car is *hitched* to a tow truck with chains and hooks.

ANTONYMS: free (v), loosen, separate (v), sever, unbind, untie

fear (n)   *Fear* is familiar to most people. It is an unpleasant and upsetting feeling people have when they are threatened with danger. When Arnie heard a strange noise at the door, his *fear* carried him right up the stairs and into a closet. Sometimes we use *fear* to mean only a mild concern or worry about something. I have a *fear* that rain will spoil our day at the carnival.

fright   *Fright* is sudden fear. The sound of a siren always gives me a terrible *fright*.

alarm   *Alarm* also means sudden fear. You feel *alarm* when you suddenly become aware of danger nearby. *Alarm* showed on the driver's face when the bus skidded on a patch of ice.

dread   *Dread* is intense fear of something that may happen. It suggests fear of facing whatever is coming. The thought of returning to the empty house at night filled her with *dread.*

panic   *Panic* is sudden and extreme fright, which results in unreasonable and frantic activity. It was the driver's *panic* that caused him to step on the gas instead of the brake after the car went over the curb. *Panic* is often used to mean the fear felt by a group, not just one person. A shout of "Fire!" in a crowded theater can cause a *panic.*

terror   *Terror* is extreme and intense fright. The approaching flood spread *terror* throughout the town.

ANTONYMS: calmness, fearlessness

157

F

fierce

Fierce can be used to describe people or animals or things. It means wild or threatening or cruel. The *fierce* dog sent the letter carrier running. Walt became *fierce* when I broke his favorite toy. A *fierce* rainstorm caused the failure of our electricity.

ferocious

Ferocious means extremely fierce and wild. The most *ferocious* tiger is a hungry one. *Ferocious* usually describes actions like those of wild animals. Wendy grabbed a shovel and began a *ferocious* attack on the snowdrift.

violent

Violent means uncontrolled and destructive. Hurricanes and tornadoes are *violent.* People are sometimes *violent* when they become very angry or upset. The umpire's decision caused a *violent* reaction among the baseball fans.

raging

Raging also means violent. The *raging* fire destroyed everything in its path. "The dog chewed my new book and ruined it," roared my *raging* sister.

savage

Savage means wild or uncontrolled. The elephant herd made a *savage* attack on the village.

See also *wild.*

ANTONYMS: gentle, harmless, mild, tame (adj)

fight (v)

Fight is an everyday word. Chances are that it is even more an everyday action. You probably *fight* the idea of getting out of bed when your alarm goes off.

The **raging** fire destroyed everything in its path.

At breakfast if you drink your milk too fast, you may have to *fight* for breath. It's easier to *fight* for the last pancake than it is to *defend* the things you say in an argument with your sister. She may *attack* your excuse for forgetting to wake her. The two of you may *argue* over whose turn it is to feed the dog.

You might be trying to *fight* your way through a difficult assignment in school. During the long afternoon some people have to *combat* drowsiness or *fight* to stay awake. After school you may help your basketball team *fight* for the championship. Your team may be *battling* for first place or may be *struggling* up from the bottom.

On a rainy day you could *fight* an icy wind all the way home, then *wrestle* with homework. After you watch spacemen *invade* the earth, politicians *attack* each other in speeches, sailors *contend* with the sea, lawyers *defend* criminals, and football teams *fight* to be in a bowl game, you may feel like turning off the TV. Chances are that after such a tiring day, you won't *disagree* with anyone who suggests that it's time to go to bed.

Fight is an everyday word. You won't have to *fight* too hard to find more exciting words to use.

Argue, attack, and *battle* are other good *fight* words.

find (v)

Find means come upon something that is lost or come to know something new. Bess *found* a set of keys on the street. When you *find out* something, you come to know information about it. I finally *found out* what became of my model boat.

Abby finally **found out** what became of her model boat.

discover

Discover means find something for the first time. Whatever is *discovered* has been there before but hasn't been seen or known about. Lewis and Clark *discovered* that the Columbia River leads to the Pacific Ocean. Manufacturers have *discovered* many uses for steel.

detect

Detect means find something that is usually hidden, by carefully searching or watching for it. Johann *detected* a mistake in the violinist's performance.

learn

Learn means find out or come to know something. They are *learning* to speak French.

ascertain
determine

Ascertain and *determine* can mean find out exactly. Through investigations and experiments, scientists have *ascertained* the distances between the planets in our solar system. An eye doctor can *determine* the kind of glasses you might need by testing your eyes.

ANTONYMS: hide (v), forget, lose

160

firm (adj)   *Firm* means not easily moved out of place or out of shape when you use it as an adjective. If a player has a *firm* grip on a bat, it won't slip out of his or her hands. When mud dries in the sun, it becomes *firm*. *Firm* can also mean not easily changed. We say that someone has a *firm* belief in something or takes a *firm* stand on a subject when that person is sure that he or she is right.

hard   We say something is *hard* when it is so strong and stiff that it resists any kind of pressure or force. Maple is a *hard* wood; pine is a soft wood. *Hard* also describes something that is difficult to do. So it is *hard* to spread *hard* butter.

solid   *Solid* means hard, firm, and sturdy. A *solid* board has no holes or cracks in it. Something that is *solid* is not hollow.

Barney's great-grandpa always liked **stiff** collars.

stiff
rigid   *Stiff* and *rigid* mean unbending or not easily moved. They are the opposite of soft, limp, and flabby. Great-grandpa always liked *stiff* collars. Inez's arms and legs felt *stiff* after exercising for a long time. Something *rigid* cannot be bent without being broken. Ice and glass are *rigid*. We also say that rules are *rigid* when they are strictly enforced or hard to obey.

inflexible   *Inflexible* also means firm and not capable of being bent. A hard metal is *inflexible,* but rubber is flexible. We can also say that a person is *inflexible* or has an *inflexible*

firm (adj) continued on page 162 ◗

F

firm (adj) continued from page 161

attitude toward something if nothing can persuade that person to change his or her mind.

steady

Steady means firm in position or in movement. The ship remained *steady* even in the rough seas. The archer took a *steady* aim before shooting the arrow.

immovable

Something is *immovable* if it can't easily be moved out of place. The farmer used a crowbar but still couldn't loosen the *immovable* boulder.

unshaken

Unshaken means firm and not easily shaken or disturbed. If you cannot be bullied into doing something you don't want to do, you remain *unshaken*.

See also *tough*.

ANTONYMS: soft, hollow, limp (adj), flabby, flexible, unsteady, movable

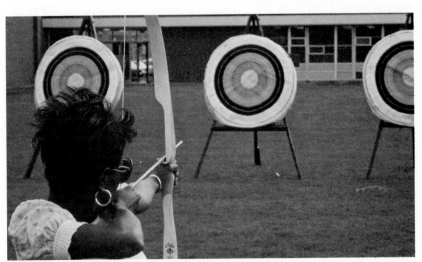

The archer took **steady** aim before shooting the arrow.

firm (n)
A *firm* can be a business that is operated by two or more people. It could be a store or a dry-cleaning plant or a factory or even an airline. A person who finishes law school sometimes joins a *firm* of lawyers.

The Jones brothers formed a **partnership.**

• company
A *company* often is a firm that makes or sells products or services. Our washing machine was manufactured by a *company* in Michigan.

• corporation
A *corporation* is another kind of business owned by one or more persons. The owners act as one united group when dealing with other firms. Many large *corporations* have branch offices in other countries. My grandmother bought stock in a *corporation*.

• partnership
A *partnership* is a legal agreement between two or more people who are owners of a business. When the Jones brothers formed a *partnership,* they each put up ten thousand dollars.

follow
Follow means go in the same direction that something or someone else has gone. If you *follow* the ball with your eyes, you can see where it goes. You can also *follow* a trail or a park ranger through the woods.

chase
Chase means run after someone in order to overtake or catch that person. The cowhand *chased* the stray calves and drove them back to the herd. *Chase* also means cause something to leave. The mouse *chased* the cat out the door.

follow continued on page 164 ▶

F

follow continued from page 163

hunt

Hunt means go after something or someone whose whereabouts are unknown. Jenny *hunted* everywhere for her glasses and finally found them on top of her head. We had to *hunt* all morning before we found the lost dog.

pursue

Pursue means go after someone or something with determination until you are successful. The reporter *pursued* the question and finally got an answer.

track

Track means follow the path of something by watching for clues to its movements. Astronomers *track* the path of a star with a telescope. The sheriff's posse *tracked* the outlaws into the hills.

trail

Trail means follow at a distance, often by using clues such as tracks. We *trailed* the cat to the fish store.

See also *imitate*.

ANTONYMS: lead (v), precede

They **trailed** the cat to the fish store.

Bernie **cheated** Marie out of her piece of cake by eating it when she wasn't looking.

fool (v)   *Fool* means make someone believe that something is true or real when it actually isn't. You may *fool* someone just for fun. People *fool* each other on April Fools' Day.

cheat   *Cheat* means fool or take advantage of a person by doing something he or she doesn't notice. Bernie *cheated* me out of my piece of cake by eating it when I wasn't looking.

mislead   *Mislead* means cause to go in the wrong direction or away from the truth. If you are offered something free and later find that you have to pay for it, someone is *misleading* you. The low price of this motorcycle *misled* me into thinking that it was a real bargain.

trick   *Trick* means fool by cheating or misleading. A mind reader *tricks* the audience.

deceive hoodwink   *Deceive* and *hoodwink* mean give a false impression in order to fool and confuse someone. One person can *deceive* another person by lying or by stretching the truth. The industrial spy *hoodwinked* the other company and stole the perfume formula.

bluff   *Bluff* means fool someone by pretending that you can do something that you really won't or can't. Minnie was *bluffing* when she said she could answer all the questions.

See also *pretend.*

F

foolish   *Foolish* means without sense or judgment. I made a *foolish* mistake on the crossword puzzle. I was *foolish* not to wear boots on a snowy day.

funny
ridiculous   *Funny* and *ridiculous* describe something so foolish it makes you laugh. Something that is strange or unexpected is often called *funny.* Emmet looked very *funny* in his *ridiculous* clown costume.

silly   *Silly* means foolish and ridiculous because of strange ways of talking or strange behavior. The monkeys in the zoo usually do *silly* tricks in their cages.

absurd   *Absurd* means so foolish it doesn't make much sense. It's *absurd* never to admit your mistakes. Gina had some *absurd* dream about becoming invisible.

The **idiotic** horse refused to eat the carrots Lucy brought.

idiotic   *Idiotic* means very foolish and stupid. It would be *idiotic* to jump into the deep end of a pool if you can't swim. The *idiotic* horse refused to eat the carrots I brought.

nonsensical   Something that is *nonsensical* is absurd and meaningless. Gibberish is *nonsensical* talk.

ANTONYMS: reasonable, sensible, wise

force (v)   *Force* means use power or strength to make a person do something. You can be *forced* to do something against your will. Sally's logical argument *forced* me to change my mind. *Force* can also mean make something happen. He *forced* open the locked door. A gust of wind *forced* the sailboat to overturn.

A gust of wind **forced** the sailboat to overturn.

propel   *Propel* means force to move forward or onward. Fuel *propels* jet planes and large boats. Your legs *propel* you when you swim.

require   You can be *required* to do something by law. You are *required* to pass a driver's test before you get your license.

compel   *Compel* means force a person to do something. Opal was *compelled* to clean the basement before she could invite her friends over. The heavy traffic *compelled* us to travel slowly.

coerce   *Coerce* is stronger than compel. You can be *coerced* into doing something by a punishment or a threat. The street gang *coerced* Rico into joining them.

See also *push* (v), *urge.*

167

F

forecast (v)   If you *forecast* that something is going to happen, you announce that it will happen before it does. Often you can *forecast* something after you have analyzed and studied the known facts. A meteorologist, for instance, *forecasts* tomorrow's weather after studying today's weather conditions and weather maps.

A meteorologist **forecasts** tomorrow's weather.

predict   *Predict,* like forecast, means tell of something that will happen in the future. People can often *predict* certain things by using their knowledge and experience. Physicians can usually *predict* the course of mumps because they know how the human body reacts to this disease.

foretell   *Foretell* means tell about something before it happens. A fortune teller says that he can look at your hand and *foretell* your future. It was such a good mystery story that no one could have *foretold* the end.

prophesy   *Prophesy* means foretell future happenings. In Greek and Roman times, certain persons claimed that they were told by the gods to *prophesy.* Even today some people *prophesy* that the end of the world is coming.

anticipate   *Anticipate* means prepare ahead of time for something good or bad. If you know that your mother will be working late, you may *anticipate* a late dinner and eat a snack. *Anticipating* rain, I brought an umbrella to the picnic.

foresee

Foresee means see ahead of time that something is going to happen. No one could *foresee* that the bus would have a flat tire.

warn

Warn means tell someone of possible danger so that he or she can avoid it. You might *warn* your young sister to watch for cars when she is crossing the street.

forewarn

Forewarn means warn a person of danger well in advance. The Farm Bureau *forewarned* farmers of an early frost.

forecast (n)

A *forecast* is the announcement that something is likely to happen or take place in the future. Like the verb, a *forecast* is made after known facts have been analyzed and studied. Light rain or snow is the *forecast* for tomorrow.

prediction

A *prediction* is what has been predicted, or a telling of something in advance. A *prediction* is based on knowledge or experience. As the earliest election returns come in, computers make *predictions* about the outcome.

prophecy

A *prophecy* is a forecast of a future event. It is what you prophesy. People often make *prophecies* about what the world might be like one hundred years from now.

prognostication

A *prognostication* is a prediction. Some people make interesting *prognostications* about world affairs.

See also *warning.*

F

foreign People who are born and reared in one country but later live in another are *foreign* to the country in which they are living. *Foreign* can also mean not belonging or out of place. *Foreign* matter in the eye may be a speck of dirt.

alien *Alien* means strange or different in some way. You could say that one penguin in a flock of ducks is *alien* to the others.

outlandish In ancient times, people traveled very little. When strangers from other countries or lands did appear, wearing their usual clothes and speaking their own languages, they were called "outlanders." So today *outlandish* means unusual or strange because it is foreign or it belongs to another country. The clothing of the people who live in the Arctic would probably seem *outlandish* to natives of a desert.

The clothing of people who live in the Arctic seems **outlandish** to natives of a desert.

extraneous *Extraneous* means not forming an essential part of something, or foreign to it. Racing stripes on a car are *extraneous*. They are not needed to make the car run.

170

external
: *External* means outside of something. His *external* appearance was that of a beast, but he was really an enchanted prince. An *external* force may cause you to do something you did not expect to do. Ants may be the *external* force that causes you to end a picnic suddenly.

See also *odd.*

free (v)
: *Free* means set loose. You can *free* a butterfly from a net or *free* a clogged drain. The lumberjacks *freed* the logs that were causing a jam in the river.

release
: *Release* also means set loose, but without the promise of lasting freedom. A manager may *release* an employee from certain duties so that person may help someone in another department.

rescue
: *Rescue* means free something or someone from danger by quick action. I *rescued* the newspaper from a puddle by grabbing it before it got all wet.

liberate
: *Liberate* means free or set at liberty. Prisoners in some countries are *liberated* when the king or queen pardons them.

emancipate
: *Emancipate* means free a person from slavery or from the control or power of another. Slaves were *emancipated* during the Civil War.

ransom
: *Ransom* means free by paying a price. The captives were *ransomed* by an agreement between the two governments.

See also *save.*

F

friendly

Friendly means acting like a friend. A *friendly* person is good-natured, pleasant, and always helpful. Someone who is *friendly* is not hostile or quarrelsome. That dog is very *friendly* when you speak to it.

kind

Kind means friendly, thoughtful, and considerate. A *kind* person is interested in other people, is willing to help them, and is never cruel.

neighborly

Neighborly really means acting like a neighbor to those who live nearby. But it can also describe anyone who is friendly and kind to others.

sociable

Someone who is *sociable* enjoys being with other people. A *sociable* person likes to entertain people and go to social gatherings.

genial

Genial means cheerful, smiling, and pleasant. A *genial* person puts people at ease and makes them feel welcome. The new student was pleased that everyone was *genial*.

That dog is very **friendly** when you speak to it.

amiable

An *amiable* person is friendly, agreeable, and courteous to others. He or she tries to please others and make them happy. Anita was *amiable* when I asked her to wait for me.

See also *thoughtful*.

ANTONYMS: quarrelsome, cruel, mean (adj), unfriendly, unkind

172

G

gather

Gather means bring something together into one place or group. You might *gather* leaves or *gather* wild flowers on a hike through the woods. *Gather* can also mean come together into one place or group. A group may *gather* around a campfire to toast marshmallows. A crowd often *gathers* if there has been an accident. Clouds *gather* in the sky before a storm. Another meaning of *gather* is put ideas together in your mind. From their conversation, Adam *gathered* that everyone planned to go surfing this weekend.

collect

Collect can be used to mean gather. It is often used when objects are carefully selected and gathered for a definite purpose. You might enjoy *collecting* stamps or antiques. A lawyer *collects* evidence.

harvest

Harvest means gather grain or crops. In the early days, farmers used scythes when they *harvested* their grain crop; now they use large machines.

gather continued on page 174 ▶

In the early days, farmers used scythes when they **harvested** their grain crop.

G

Things **accumulate** when they gather in a heap or pile or in one place.

accumulate Things *accumulate* when they gather in a heap or pile or in one place. Leaves will *accumulate* on your lawn if you do not rake them. Dust *accumulated* in the empty house. My aunt and uncle *accumulated* a fortune by saving and investing their money. Suzanne has *accumulated* a large collection of record albums.

assemble *Assemble* can be used when people gather, or meet together, for a convention or a meeting. Our representatives in Congress *assemble* in Washington to make and pass laws.

congregate *Congregate* is used when people come together and form a crowd. Crowds often *congregate* during a parade. When the excitement is over, the people scatter in different directions.

ANTONYMS: scatter, disperse, separate (v)

gathering A *gathering* is a coming together or a bringing together of something. A *gathering* of corn or wheat or apples is a harvest. A *gathering* of cattle is a roundup. You can probably think of other kinds of *gatherings. A group* is a kind of *gathering.* Look up *group* and see the words listed there.

There are many words for *gatherings* of people. Actually, though, you'll find two kinds in this book.

A *gathering* may be people brought or called together at a certain time for some special purpose. Look up *meeting* to find words for this kind of *gathering*.

People may gather in one place at one time even though they were not actually called together. This kind of *gathering* is a *crowd.* These people may just happen to gather because they are all interested in the same thing at the same time—like swimming at the beach or pool or getting to work in the morning. Look up *crowd* (n) and the words listed in that entry.

Party sounds like a good word (and a good reason) for calling people together. But the word *party* also belongs to another kind of *gathering.* This is a group of people gathered to do something together, like a party of tourists or a political party. To see other kinds of parties or groups of people working or playing together, look at the words listed in the entry *party.*

People may form a group because they all have an interest in one special thing. These groups do not have to be gathered in a certain place, though they usually do have meetings. They may be organized with a president and vice-president and other officers. The members of groups like these may be in different parts of the world, but they are joined by this interest. Look up *club* (n) to find other groups.

Some groups of people working together are listed and explained in the entry *firm* (n).

G

gentle

Gentle means not harsh or rough or mean. A *gentle* breeze makes little ripples on a lake. A harsh wind can cause large waves. A *gentle* person is kind and considerate. He or she is not mean. A nurse is *gentle,* not rough, with patients. Leslie gave me a *gentle* pat on the shoulder. The trainer spoke to the seal in a *gentle* voice.

soft

Soft can mean gentle, not rough or loud. The child's touch was *soft,* not rough. A *soft* light is not too bright or glaring. The sun made a *soft* light in the thick forest. The air feels *soft* after a spring shower. The woman spoke to the baby in a *soft* voice. The music in the background was *soft* and quiet. Satin is a *soft* material.

The **tender** buds pushed through the snow.

tender

Tender can mean delicate and gentle. The *tender* buds pushed through the snow. She gave the sick child *tender* care.

mild

Mild means gentle and calm. A *mild* man does not often lose his temper. Clark Kent is a *mild*-mannered reporter. Winters are *mild* in the South. They are usually harsh in the North. A *mild* flavor is not bitter or sharp.

• moderate

Moderate can mean just right or about in the middle. A *moderate* climate is neither too hot nor too cold. A *moderate* price for five pounds of sugar is a price you'd be willing to pay. An excessive price might make you decide to do without sugar. A *moderate* volume on a radio is neither too loud nor too quiet.

soothing

Soothing means gentle, pleasing, and comforting. Quiet music is *soothing*. The vet's *soothing* touch calmed the frightened horse. Honey is *soothing* to a sore throat.

See also *calm* (adj).

ANTONYMS: harsh, rough, mean (adj), loud, bitter, sharp, excessive, hard, tough

give

Give is an interesting word. You can do many kinds of giving. You can *give* a cheer, *give* a hand, *give* a look, *give* advice. You *give* a gift. You *give* thanks. You *give* a kiss or a smile. If you think about it, though, there are really only three ways to *give.*

First, you can *present* something to someone, of your own free will and, sometimes, with your own hands. In the entry *present* (v) you will find other words for this kind of giving—whether it's something for a birthday, first prize, a Picasso, or whatever a person leaves when he or she dies.

Second, you can *allow* something. You can *give* permission or *give* the right to do something. You may *allow* something to go on or to be, just because you don't stop it or object to it. Look at the entry *allow* and see what this kind of giving includes.

Third, you can *surrender.* You can *give in, give away, give out, give up.* Look up *surrender* (v) and see.

G

gleam (n)   A *gleam* is a dim or faint light. We saw the *gleam* of a car's headlights in the fog. A *gleam* can also be a short thought or idea. The sound of a helicopter brought the survivors a *gleam* of hope.

- flash   A *flash* is a sudden burst of light. A *flash* of light appears and disappears instantly. There was a *flash* of lightning. A *flash* can also be a sudden feeling. With a *flash* of understanding the teacher turned and smiled.

- glint   A *glint* is a tiny flash. When sunlight strikes an airplane, it causes a *glint* of light.

- flicker   A *flicker* is an uneven, wavering light. The dying flames in a fireplace give off *flickers* of light. A *flicker* can also be an undecided feeling. There was just a *flicker* of doubt in her mind.

A **beam** is a shaft of light.

- beam   A *beam* is a shaft of light. A searchlight or a flashlight sends out a *beam* of light.

- glow   A *glow* is a steady, bright light. The *glow* from the fire made the cabin warm. A *glow* can also be a warm feeling. Seeing his first child sent a warm *glow* to his heart.

178

go

One meaning of *go* is "*go* away." You'll find that and similar words in the entry *leave* (v).

Words for *go up* and *go down* are listed in the entries *rise* (v) and *fall* (v).

"*Go* after"—whether you mean chase something or *go along* in a certain direction or hunt for something—is in the entry *follow*.

If you *go along* the street and look as though you don't want anyone to see what you are doing or where you are *going,* words to describe your actions are under *sneak* (v).

If you see someone who looks as if he or she isn't really *going* anywhere, there are *wander* words to describe that person!

The essay entry *move* will send you to some other words that are different ways to *go.* Take a look at them and *move!*

govern

Govern means have and use power and authority over others. A person who *governs* must direct and guide the actions of the people within a state, country, or nation. The President, the Congress, and the Supreme Court *govern* the United States.

control

Control means have power over someone or something. A captain *controls* a ship and the actions of the crew. A pilot *controls*

govern continued on page 180 ▶

G

govern continued from page 179

the plane in the air. A supervisor *controls* operations and workers within a plant or factory. You *control* your temper when you stop yourself from getting very angry.

regulate
curb

Regulate and *curb* mean control. You *regulate* something when you control the way it works. By turning the faucet you *regulate* the amount and temperature of water that comes out. Traffic lights *regulate* traffic. You *curb,* or hold back, something that might get out of control. You *curb* your emotions.

command

You *command* someone when you tell that person what to do. The sheriff *commanded* the outlaw to give up.

rule

Rule means govern with absolute authority. Someone who *rules* makes the laws and then commands his or her subjects to obey them. A dictator or tyrant often *rules* unjustly. The people *rule* in a democracy.

reign

Reign means rule as a king or queen. Queen Elizabeth I *reigned* over England for forty-five years. Queen Elizabeth II began to *reign* in 1952.

Queen Elizabeth I **reigned** over England for forty-five years.

grand

Grand means large in size or impressive in appearance. Many hotels have a *grand* ballroom. The windjammer under full sail was a *grand* sight. *Grand* can also mean wonderful. The clear sky and warm temperature made it a *grand* day for an outing. *Grand* is a sadly overworked and misused word. Wouldn't it be *grand* to give it a rest?

magnificent

Magnificent was used to describe kings, queens, and other rulers who were famous because of their great wealth and heroic deeds. Now it is used to describe anything that is grand or beautiful or that impresses you. You might see a *magnificent* building, a *magnificent* display of jewels, or have a *magnificent* view of the sea. The Grand Canyon at sunrise is a *magnificent* sight.

stately
majestic
imposing

Stately, majestic, and *imposing* are other good words to use instead of grand. They add the meaning that something is dignified and inspiring. The changing of the guard at the parliament in Ottawa is a *stately* sight. Snow-covered mountains can be *majestic.* The judge looked *imposing* as she took the oath of office.

Snow-covered mountains can be **majestic.**

exalted

Someone who is *exalted* is praised or glorified. At one time the Japanese people thought their *exalted* ruler was a god.

lofty

That which is *lofty* is either high in position or very high and good in character. You speak of *lofty* mountains, or a *lofty* deed.

noble

Noble describes someone or something that combines all the qualities of being grand, magnificent in appearance, and majestic. The character of a *noble* person is marked by goodness and kindness.

See also *great, splendid.*

ANTONYMS: humble (adj), lowly, petty, small, trivial

G

grasp (v)

Grasp means get or take hold of. People *grasp* with their fingers, hands, or arms. *Grasping* the hand of another person is a sign of friendship. He *grasped* the railing to keep from falling down the stairs. A sea gull *grasps* fish with its strong beak.

grip
clasp
clutch

Grip, clasp, clutch, are other words for grasping and holding something firmly and tightly. A baseball player *grips* the bat. The boy was *clasping* a rabbit that he had found. The girl *clutched* the kitten and wouldn't let go of it.

grab
snatch

Grab and *snatch* mean grasp something quickly and suddenly. Carl *grabbed* a piece of candy before the box was passed. Denise *snatched* the picture out of my hands before I had a chance to see it.

seize

Seize means take something by force. The detective *seized* the suspect.

ANTONYMS: let go, abandon, release (v)

The detective **seized** the suspect.

great

The largest of the five Great Lakes is Lake **Superior.**

Great can mean big and large. It also means outstanding, well known, and important. People, things, and events may be *great.* A skyscraper is a *great* building, and a cottage is usually a small one. Jane Addams was a *great* American social worker. Electricity was a *great* discovery. People often say *great* when they mean wonderful or very good. The weather is *great* today.

There are a *great* number of other words you could use while *great* takes a rest.

notable

People and their accomplishments are *notable* if they are worth being noticed or are worthy of respect or admiration. Dolly Madison is a *notable* historical figure.

illustrious

Illustrious persons are well known, well liked, and greatly distinguished for their deeds or work. Theodore Roosevelt was not only President, but he was also an *illustrious* soldier, hunter, and author.

superior

Superior means higher in position or greater than something or someone else in size or importance. *Superior* is the opposite of inferior. The largest of the five Great Lakes is Lake *Superior.* A captain is *superior* in rank to a lieutenant.

supreme

Something that is *supreme* is unequaled in size, greatness, or importance. The *Supreme* Court is the highest court in the United States.

great continued on page 184 ▶

G

great continued from page 183

monumental   *Monumental* describes something not only great but also massive in size or importance. A long, well-written book might be called *monumental.* Getting snow off a city's streets after a blizzard is a *monumental* task.

See also *famous, grand.*

ANTONYMS: small, inferior, petty, trivial, unknown

group (n)   A number of people gathered together or having the same interests is a *group.* A band is made up of a *group* of musicians. A *group* can also be a number of objects brought together but regarded as one thing. An album is a *group* of photographs or records gathered in a book. An art collection may be a *group* of paintings gathered by one person or by a museum.

A band is made up of a **group** of musicians.

- kind
- category

Kind and *category* are words for a group of animals, objects, or ideas put together because of common interests or characteristics. An apple is a *kind* of fruit. Some *kinds* of trees do not lose their leaves in winter. These trees are not in the same *category* as those trees that do.

- class

A *class* is a group sharing the same condition. A *class* in school may be a group of pupils of approximately the same age. Some people travel in first *class* on an airplane.

There were dogs of ten different **breeds** at the dog show.

- breed

All animals of a particular *breed* have the same ancestors, and they are all similar in some way. A *breed* can be thought of as a group. There were dogs of ten different *breeds* at the dog show.

- set

A *set* is a group of things of the same kind or a group of things that have something in common. They belong together or are used together—a *set* of twins, a *set* of dishes, a *set* of encyclopedias, a *set* of numbers.

See also *party.*

185

G

Cliff's parents have kept records of his **growth.**

grow

Grow means become bigger, larger, fuller, stronger, or better. You *grow.* Animals and plants *grow.* You can also *grow* something or make it *grow.* We also say that ideas or plans *grow* as they are carefully thought out.

develop
evolve

Develop and *evolve* mean change and grow gradually. Flowers *develop* from seeds or bulbs. Athletes *develop* their muscles by exercising. Things *evolve* over a period of time. It took a week to *evolve* the plans for the weekend retreat. Through the ages, the horse as we know it today has *evolved* from an animal that was no bigger than a dog.

mature
ripen

Mature and *ripen* mean grow and develop completely. Young children *mature* into adult men and women. When fruit *ripens,* it is ready to be picked and eaten.

sprout

Sprout means start to grow. Buds *sprout* from branches. New branches *sprout* from bushes and trees.

age

Age means become older. People *age* through the years. Some cheeses have to *age* before they can be eaten.

See also *advance* (v), *come.*

growth

Growth is the process of growing or becoming bigger. My parents started keeping records of my *growth* as soon as I could stand up against the wall. The farmer watched for signs of *growth* of his crops.

Pollution causes **harm** to lakes and beaches.

harm (n)   *Harm* is the actual pain or suffering or wrong done to someone or something. This is the noun meaning. Expecting *harm* can make you afraid of something. I meant Anna no *harm* when I said I didn't agree with her. Pollution causes *harm* to lakes and beaches.

damage   *Damage* is harm done to something. *Damage* lowers the value or usefulness of something. The tornado caused *damage* to many homes and office buildings.

injury   An *injury* is harm or wrong done to a person or a thing. Sharon didn't receive any *injuries* when she fell during the hockey game.

loss   *Loss* is harm caused by losing someone or something. A person may suffer from the *loss* of a relative. We had only two *losses* during this soccer season. His *loss* of memory was temporary.

See also *misfortune.*

ANTONYM: benefit (n), harmless

191

H

harm (v)

Harm means cause pain or suffering or loss. This is the verb meaning. You may *harm* yourself or *harm* someone or *harm* something. You can *harm* your eyes if you read in poor light. Gossip can *harm* other people. Insects can *harm* a garden.

damage

Damage means lower the value or usefulness of something or harm it. If a car has been *damaged* in an accident, it can often be repaired. The furniture was *damaged* by the fire.

hurt

Hurt means damage something or harm someone. The rain can't *hurt* this old coat. Beverly *hurt* herself when she fell from the tree.

injure

Injure means harm something or someone. Tony *injured* his leg in the skiing accident.

ANTONYMS: repair (v), benefit (v)

The rain can't **hurt** this old jacket.

harsh   *Harsh* means rough or unpleasant. A *harsh* surface is not smooth to touch. The weather can be very *harsh* in winter. A person who is *harsh* is unfriendly, impolite, unkind, and often cruel.

The weather can be very **harsh** in winter.

hoarse   *Hoarse* and *raspy* mean harsh in sound.
raspy   Have you ever heard the *hoarse* croak of a bullfrog? A saw cutting metal makes a grating or *raspy* sound.

husky   A *husky* voice is low and hoarse. It is often caused by a cold or cough.

gruff   A *gruff* voice is deep and harsh and impatient. The umpire yelled "Out!" in a *gruff* voice. A stern or bad-tempered person often speaks in a *gruff* or unpleasant manner. The cashier seemed *gruff* and grouchy.

ANTONYMS: smooth, kind, gentle, mild, polite

193

H

hate (v)

The verb *hate* is a very strong word meaning you don't like something. *Hate* is the opposite of love. Many times people say they *hate* something when they really mean they don't like it. It is better to say that you don't like spinach, for instance, than to say that you *hate* it. But when you are talking about something important enough to feel strongly about, you would probably say that you *hate* it.

dislike

Dislike means disapprove of something because you don't enjoy it or don't find it interesting. It is not as strong a word as hate. Lucy *dislikes* raking leaves.

detest
despise

Detest and *despise* mean almost the same thing. *Detest* means dislike someone or something very much. I *detest* grouchy salespersons. You *despise* someone or something if you feel dislike and refuse to be bothered. I *despise* lies.

scorn

You *scorn* something if you look down on it and think it is not worth your attention. After Ryan had learned to ride his bicycle, he *scorned* the training wheels.

loathe

Loathe means detest. *Loathe* is a very strong word. If you *loathe* something, you look at it with disgust and want nothing to do with it. Glen *loathes* spiders.

ANTONYMS: like (v), love (v), enjoy, admire, appreciate

hate (n)

Hate, as a noun, is a very strong feeling against someone or something. A person may feel *hate* toward someone who is mean.

194

hatred

Hatred can be used in place of hate. *Hatred* is usually followed by *of.* Joy's *hatred of* water skiing grew every time she fell.

dislike
distaste

Dislike and *distaste* are not as strong as hate. Both are the feeling of not liking or enjoying something. *Dislike* can be followed by *of* or *for.* A person may show *dislike of* a movie by walking out of the theater before the movie ends. Hazel's *dislike for* cold weather caused her to move to a warmer climate. *Distaste* may be followed by *for.* People have a *distaste for* things that are unattractive, unpleasant, or disagreeable. He looked with *distaste* at the pile of dirty dishes.

After hurting her thumb, the carpenter had an **aversion** to making beds.

aversion

If you have an *aversion to* something, you don't like it and will try to avoid it. After hurting her thumb, the carpenter had an *aversion to* making beds. Some people have an *aversion to* bugs and creeping animals.

disgust

Disgust is a strong dislike and aversion to something. Something bad or sickening might fill you with *disgust.* I feel only *disgust* when I see people litter the streets.

ANTONYMS: fondness, liking (n), love (n)

195

H

heavy

Heavy is the opposite of light. Something is *heavy* if it weighs a lot. Movers lift and carry *heavy* furniture and *heavy* boxes.

Heavy can also mean more than usual. Then it is the opposite of slight or thin. The *heavy* traffic caused us to be late.

We also call something *heavy* if it is difficult or hard to bear. You can speak of a *heavy* responsibility and a *heavy* duty.

cumbersome

Cumbersome means heavy and awkward, hard to carry or move. The *cumbersome* statue was finally brought into the museum.

ponderous

Ponderous describes something that is not only heavy but very large or massive or dull. Many old pieces of furniture are *ponderous*. Books can be *ponderous*.

weighty

Weighty can mean either very heavy or very serious and important. Packages can be *weighty*. A lawyer's words may be *weighty*. The President delivered a *weighty* speech to the nation.

thick

Thick can describe something that is heavily built or something that is very dense. *Thick* is the opposite of thin. A baseball bat is *thicker* at one end than at the other. It would be hard to push your way through a *thick* crowd. The family of deer disappeared into the *thick* forest.

See also *serious*.

ANTONYMS: light (adj), slight (adj), thin, trivial

They didn't **assist** the photographer much by holding the lights.

help (v)

Help means do something for another person. To *help* someone, you give whatever is needed, or you do whatever is useful. *Help* is the opposite of hinder. A doctor *helps* you when you are sick. He or she gives you medicine that *helps* you get well. A person in trouble may cry, "*Help* me!"

aid

Aid means help by giving relief to someone. The Red Cross *aids* people in an emergency. Our contributions will *aid* scientists in their research.

assist

Assist means work together with someone and help that person do something. We didn't *assist* the photographer much by holding the lights. The clerk *assisted* me in choosing after-shave lotion for my brother.

improve

Improve means help by making something better. Lots of practice *improved* Ida's banjo playing.

encourage

Encourage means help a person by giving that person hope. The coach discouraged me at first, but after seeing what I could do, he *encouraged* me to try out for the team.

benefit

Benefit means do good or be of use to someone. A vacation *benefits* almost everyone.

See also *advance* (v), *protect, support* (v).

ANTONYMS: hinder, discourage, obstruct

197

H

help (n)
The *help* you give someone is what you do or give to meet his or her needs. With the *help* of two girls, the old woman was able to walk.

aid
Aid is also help—something that is needed. With the *aid* of a hammer, Pete opened the suitcase. *Aid* is often used in combination with other words—first *aid,* federal *aid,* visual *aid.*

assistance
Assistance means work done with another person to help him or her do something. Expert *assistance* from the police helped keep traffic away from the scene of the fire.

benefit
A *benefit* is something that helps or improves someone or something in some way. Having beautiful, clean parks is one of the *benefits* of putting trash in the proper containers. Good health is one of the *benefits* of proper food and exercise.

support
Support is the act of helping or upholding something or someone. A young tree may need the *support* of a stick. Her friends' loyal *support* helped Elsie win the election. *Support* can also mean the supplying to someone of whatever he or she needs to live. An elderly parent may depend on a son or daughter for *support.*

service
Service is a small help or convenience of some kind that one person provides for another. Often a *service* must be paid for. *Service* at the new restaurant was slow.

Service at the new restaurant was slow.

relief

Relief is the removal or the lightening of a burden or worry that someone is carrying. *Relief* showed on Darrel's face when he was told that his myna bird had been found. *Relief* also means aid given to needy people in the form of money or other necessities.

ANTONYMS: harm (n), hindrance

hide (v)

Hide means remove from sight. Sometimes you *hide* yourself—if you are playing a game or trying to avoid someone. In a game of hide-and-seek, you may be found after you *hide.* When you bring to light something that has been *hidden,* you reveal it.

They tried to **conceal** the dirty dishes so that they couldn't be seen from the living room.

conceal

You *conceal* something if you purposely hide it or cover it up. We tried to *conceal* the dirty dishes so that they couldn't be seen from the living room. It is no fun playing rummy with you if you don't *conceal* your cards.

hide (v) continued on page 200 ▶

H

disguise

Disguise means hide a person or thing by changing its appearance so it can't be recognized. Lorna *disguised* herself so well for her part in the play that no one knew who she was.

obscure

Obscure means conceal or hide by putting something over or in front of. The big man *obscured* Wayne's view of the movie screen.

The big man **obscured** Wayne's view of the movie screen.

mask

Mask means hide the appearance or true character or feelings of something or someone. We put colorful Japanese lanterns on the lights to *mask* the ugly light bulbs. Her smile *masked* the anger she felt.

veil

Veil means cover or conceal something as if you were covering it with a *veil.* Ursula tried to *veil* her unhappiness by joking.

ANTONYMS: reveal, find (v), show (v), unmask, unveil

history

A *history* is a written account or an explanation of past events. The *history* of motion pictures, for example, begins in 1892 with Thomas Edison's invention of a device called the kinetoscope. Babe Ruth is an important name in the *history* of sports.

Unlike stories, which do not always tell about actual events, *histories* tell about events or situations that have actually taken place and try to explain them. There are several special kinds of *histories,* and the following words describe some of those kinds.

- record

A *record* is a history of facts or events. People keep *records* so that important information won't be forgotten.

- diary
- journal

A *diary* and a *journal* are daily records. Sometime during their lives most people keep a *diary* or *journal,* in which they write about what they are thinking and what they are doing.

- log

A *log* is a record that a ship's captain keeps during a voyage to note the ship's progress day by day.

- chronicle

A *chronicle* is a record of events written down in the order in which they happened. Usually there is no explanation of why certain events occurred as there is in a history.

- biography

A *biography* is the history of a person's life written by someone else. The historian read the ship's log before she began writing a *biography* of the captain.

- autobiography

An *autobiography* is the history of a person's life written by that person. Benjamin Franklin described his childhood in his *autobiography.*

See also *account* (n), *story, tale.*

H

hit (v)

Hit means give a blow or a whack to someone or something. You *hit* a nail with a hammer. You *hit* a tennis ball with a racket.

strike

Strike also can mean hit. You *strike* a xylophone with small wooden hammers. *Strike* is often used to mean other kinds of hitting. A grandfather clock *strikes* on the hour and half-hour. Prospectors *strike* gold when they hit, or come upon, a vein of it in the ground. If a batter in a baseball game *strikes out,* he or she didn't hit anything at all!

slap

Slap means hit with your open hand. If your cousin *slaps* you on the back, he is probably congratulating you for something.

cuff

Cuff means hit or slap, usually gently or in fun. A cat *cuffs* her kittens with her paw.

swat

Swat means hit quickly and hard. You can *swat* a fly with a fly swatter or a folded newspaper.

punch

Punch can mean hit with your fist. Pablo *punches* his pillow when he is angry.

slug

Slug means hit very hard. The heavyweight champion *slugged* the challenger with a right to the jaw.

See also *beat* (v).

A cat **cuffs** her kittens with her paw.

honesty   *Honesty* is acting and speaking truthfully. It is the opposite of deceit and dishonesty. A person shows *honesty* by not stealing, cheating, or lying. Salespersons appreciate your *honesty* if you tell them that they did not charge you enough for an item.

truthfulness   *Truthfulness* means being open with people and not trying to hide anything from them. It means always telling the truth. People are respected for *truthfulness* in their dealings with others.

sincerity   *Sincerity* also means honesty. It is saying what you really feel or doing something you really believe in. I promised in all *sincerity* to do my best.

honor   A person of *honor* is honest and fair. If someone is "held in *honor*," that person is greatly respected. To "uphold the *honor*" of something means to defend its name and good reputation. The basketball victory upheld the *honor* of the team. You give a person your *word of honor* when you promise that you can be trusted to do something.

integrity   *Integrity* is a strong word for honesty. It means honesty and trustworthiness. A person of *integrity* can always be trusted to do what is right and just. That person would never try to deceive anyone or give someone a false impression.

ANTONYMS: deceit, dishonesty, dishonor (n), untruthfulness

H

humble (adj)   *Humble* means not proud. A *humble* person does not boast of personal accomplishments. A *humble* person who is praised for something might answer, "Oh, it was nothing," and really mean it. *Humble* can also mean not of high rank or of great importance. Some great figures in history have come from *humble* beginnings.

meek   *Meek* means humble and not wanting to call attention to oneself. A *meek* person is patient and doesn't try to fight back if someone does something or says something that hurts. The *meek* man said nothing when someone pushed in line ahead of him. *Meek* also can suggest lacking courage. A *meek* person may be timid and not strong. The *meek* committee member didn't want to give an opinion in the meeting.

mild   *Mild* means gentle in nature or behavior. A *mild* breeze is a gentle breeze. A *mild* day is a pleasant one, not too cold and not too warm. People who are meek and *mild* have good natures and may be taken advantage of.

The **meek** man said nothing when someone pushed in line ahead of him.

modest *Modest* means not boastful. A *modest* answer to the question "Do you play the piano?" would be "Yes, I do." An immodest answer would be "Yes, I play beautifully."

lowly *Lowly* means humble or ranking low. "Low" means close to the ground, so *lowly* can mean not very high in rank. A pine tree may be called *lowly* when it is compared to a lofty sequoia.

ANTONYMS: proud, lofty, immodest, haughty

humorous Something or someone *humorous* makes you laugh, or at least want to laugh. A *humorous* tale makes you smile.

amusing *Amusing* means humorous and entertaining. An *amusing* movie may be pleasant and lighthearted, and it probably will make you laugh.

funny If something is *funny,* it may be mildly humorous or very amusing or wildly entertaining. We chuckled over the *funny* antics of the chimpanzees.

witty *Witty* means full of wit or cleverness. A *witty* person is quick to see something funny and make a comment about it. The remarks may be very funny, but some of them can be unkind.

comical If something is *comical,* it amuses you very much, and you can't stop laughing. The clown had such a *comical* expression on her face that we howled with laughter.

ANTONYMS: grave (adj), serious

H

hurry (v)

Hurry means move faster or make something go faster. *Hurry* or you'll miss the bus. *Hurry* is often followed by *up*. *Hurry up* or you'll be late for breakfast.

hasten

Hasten means be quick to go someplace or do something. Margo *hastened* her packing because it was time for her to leave.

The racing car **sped** around the racetrack.

rush

Rush means hurry or go forward very quickly. The ambulance *rushed* the sick child to the hospital. In the days of prospecting, gold miners *rushed* to California. *Rush* can also mean appear suddenly. Tears *rushed* to his eyes when he saw his wrecked model train.

speed

Speed means move fast. It is a stronger word than rush. The racing car *sped* around the race track. A police officer stopped all the drivers who were *speeding* in the school zone.

hustle

Hustle means hurry or move quickly. Father *hustled* the toddlers off to bed. *Hustle* can also mean move onward by pushing or shoving. They *hustled* through the crowd at the airport.

ANTONYMS: dawdle, delay (v), hinder, linger, loiter, slow down

I

idea

An *idea* can be the picture in your mind of something you know, think, or imagine. Some *ideas* are thought out, but, like opinions, they change and are not as firmly held as beliefs. You can have an *idea* of something without ever having seen it. Lisa's *idea* that a walrus looks like a seal is correct. An *idea* can also be a plan to do something. There are books full of *ideas* on what to do around the house on a rainy day.

notion

A *notion* is a vague idea about something. I have some *notion* about how to grow African violets from leaf cuttings. I have a *notion* to go with Jaimie on Friday, but it may be better to go on Thursday.

impression

An *impression* is an idea or feeling you receive from something. If something makes an *impression* on you, it affects you in a certain way. First *impressions* are not always correct. Cliff's *impression* of the city changed after he had been there for a while.

thought

A *thought* can be an idea about something. Books are full of new *thoughts.* What is your *thought* about having a picnic? I had a *thought* about what we might do tomorrow.

concept

A *concept* may be a general or detailed idea of what something is or ought to be like. We all have our *concepts* of happiness and of sadness.

See also *belief, opinion.*

Yumiko had a **thought** about what she might do tomorrow.

I

imaginary   *Imaginary* means not real or not actual or not true. The characters in most comic books are *imaginary* people.

fanciful   *Fanciful* describes something that is created in your mind or that does not really exist. Talking animals are *fanciful* creatures. The story about Winnie-the-Pooh is *fanciful.*

fantastic   *Fantastic* describes something so strange or unheard of that it can't be believed. The idea that a human being would ever walk on the moon seemed *fantastic* a hundred years ago.

unreal   *Unreal* and *fictitious* describe things
fictitious   that are invented or supplied by the imagination. A dream is *unreal* even though it seems very real. "Fiction" means an invented story. So *fictitious* describes anything that is not real or that is not a fact. Most authors use *fictitious* names for the characters in their novels.

ANTONYMS: real, actual, true

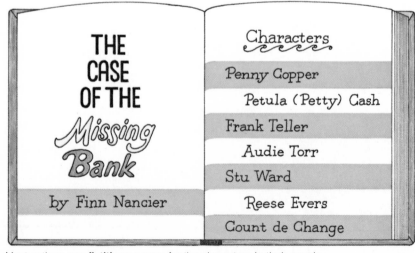

Most authors use **fictitious** names for the characters in their novels.

imagine

Molly is trying to **imagine** how she will look in ten years.

Imagine means see something in your mind. When you *imagine* something, you are letting your mind invent or create ideas. Can you *imagine* how you will look in ten years? *Imagine* can also mean think something is true or something will happen even though you have no proof or reason for thinking so. Since it is Saturday, I *imagine* my friend is golfing at the park. I *imagine* it's going to rain.

suppose

Suppose means think that something is possible. I *suppose* Andrew will make popcorn tonight.

guess

Guess means form an opinion about something when you really don't know much about it. You might *guess* how old someone is or *guess* how much that person weighs. Can you *guess* how tall that skyscraper is?

fancy

Fancy means form a picture of something in your mind. When she was young, Babe Didrikson Zaharias *fancied* herself a great athlete. Sometimes we *fancy* things that really aren't possible. He *fancied* that he was captain of a clipper ship.

realize

Realize means understand something fully and clearly. They *realized* they had made a mistake. Do you *realize* what life would be like if the car hadn't been invented?

believe

Believe means imagine and trust that something is true or real. If a person *believes* in someone or something, it is hard to change his or her mind.

A parrot can **imitate** some of the sounds it hears.

imitate	*Imitate* means try to be like something or someone else. It also means try to make or do something using a pattern or model. Small children often *imitate* the actions of their parents. A parrot can *imitate* some of the sounds it hears.
follow	*Follow* can mean imitate someone else's actions. When you *follow* another person's advice, you act as that person says he or she would act in the same situation.
trace	*Trace* means imitate or follow the lines of something. You *trace* a picture by putting a thin piece of paper over it and following the lines with a pencil or pen.
copy	*Copy* means imitate as closely as possible. A secretary may *copy* a letter for the boss by typing the same words on another piece of paper. A cook may *copy* a famous recipe by cooking a similar dish.

210

duplicate

Duplicate means imitate something exactly. You *duplicate* a key when you have another made just like it. You copy a page from a book when you write down word for word what is printed. You *duplicate* the page if you use a copying machine to make another page that shows the printed words and looks just like the page in the book.

counterfeit

Counterfeit means imitate in order to deceive or give a false impression. The crook was sent to jail because he had *counterfeited* one-dollar bills.

impersonate
mimic
mock

Impersonate, mimic, and *mock* all mean imitate. *Impersonate* is used when an actor takes the part of a character in a play or movie. Colin *impersonated* George Washington. You *mimic* when you imitate the way someone or something talks or acts. We roared with laughter as Sadie *mimicked* a frog. *Mock* is used when you imitate and make fun of a person or thing. It was mean of you to *mock* the way I fell.

important

Important describes something or someone of real value or meaning. An *important* decision is one that could make a big difference in what happens later. Choosing what you will eat for a snack is a trivial decision. *Important* also describes something or someone who is able to influence or change events or opinions. For example, an *important* game is one that decides the championship. A preseason game may be unimportant.

important continued on page 212 ▶

I

important continued from page 211

chief
principal
leading

Chief, principal, and *leading* all describe something or someone of greatest importance. A *chief* usher in a theater tells the other ushers where to stand and what to do. The *principal* character in a story or play is usually the hero or heroine. The *leading* industry of a city is the one for which the city is well known. Automobile manufacture is the *leading* industry of Detroit.

major

Major describes something more important or larger or of more interest than others. The opposite of *major* is minor. Dallas is one of the *major* cities of the United States.

main

Main describes the most important or most obvious part of something. The *main* library is downtown, but there is a branch library near our house. One *main* switch controls the lights all over this building. My *main* reason for going to the theater was to see the star of the show.

The most **significant** clue the detective found was a footprint.

significant

Significant means important because of having some special meaning or reason. The most *significant* clue the detective found was a footprint just below the window. Whether the footprint was big or little was insignificant.

weighty

Weighty can mean that something is heavy because it is so important. The Senate may spend a long time in a *weighty* discussion.

See also *basic, great, large, serious.*

ANTONYMS: unimportant, trivial, minor, insignificant

Theresa **added** one more leaf to her collection.

increase (v)

Increase means become or make larger or greater or more. *Increase* is the opposite of decrease. A crowd *increases* as more people gather, or come together. In 1959, the number of States has *increased* to fifty. A driver can *increase* the speed of a car. Your strength and weight *increase* as you grow older.

add

Add means increase by joining or putting one thing to another. You *add* numbers in math. Theresa *added* more leaves to her leaf collection.

• attach
• annex

Attach and *annex* are other good words to use for increase even though they are not real synonyms. *Attach* means join something to something else. The length of a freight train increases when a caboose is *attached.* A kite increases in weight if you *attach* a tail. *Annex* can mean increase by adding to something that is larger or more important. Hospitals *annex* buildings when more space is needed. A city may *annex* a suburb or surrounding land.

multiply

Multiply means increase in number. Your fears might *multiply* in a scary situation.

extend

Extend can mean make longer or increase in time. If you *extend* your visit with a friend, you stay longer than you had planned.

See also *enlarge.*

ANTONYMS: decrease (v), diminish, divide, subtract

I

inform

Inform means make something known to another person. You can do this by speaking or writing. You told everyone else about the meeting, but you didn't *inform* me. You *inform* someone *of* something. Magazines and newspapers *inform* us *of* recent events.

impart

Impart means share the knowledge you have of something with another person. You might *impart* a secret to a friend. An eyewitness may *impart* valuable first-hand information to a newspaper reporter.

acquaint

Acquaint means inform and familiarize someone else with the facts or details of a situation. The boss *acquainted* Judy *with* the duties and responsibilities of her new job. If you are *acquainted with* another person, you know that person quite well. Notice that you are *acquainted with* someone or you *acquaint* someone *with* something.

notify

Notify means inform, but it also adds the meaning of expecting a response of some sort. Shirley *notified* the post office of her new address and hoped her mail would be forwarded promptly. We were *notified* that the repairs on our car were completed, and that the car could be picked up.

teach
instruct

Teach and *instruct* mean give information or knowledge to another person in order that he or she may learn. You can *teach* people how to do something by simply showing them how or by offering examples, then helping them do it

Edwina **taught** her dog another trick.

themselves. *Instruct* usually means teach by guiding someone through a course of lessons or training, such as a class in school. Edwina *taught* her dog another trick. The class was *instructed* in the proper way to operate a sewing machine. *Instruct* can also mean command. Mr. Sing was *instructed* to appear for jury duty.

ANTONYMS: conceal, misinform

information *Information* is what you learn about something by obtaining the facts. You get *information* by talking with other people or by reading books or by observing and studying something. I went to the library to get more *information* about the American Revolution.

• news *News* is information about recent events. The *news* is reported in newspapers and on television and radio. *News* can also be something you didn't know before. Their triumphant return from the mountain climbing expedition is *news* to me.

information continued on page 216 ▶

I

- intelligence

Intelligence can be secret information. Spies and secret service agents gather *intelligence* about the plans of other countries.

- data

Data are facts and information from which things can be learned. The *data* of past flights are used to prepare for new space missions. The word *data* means more than one fact and should be followed by a plural verb. Are the *data* you have from one experiment enough for you to work with? However, a singular verb is often used. Here is the *data* you asked for.

- knowledge

Knowledge is a general word. *Knowledge* includes all that anyone knows and understands. You gain *knowledge* of things through study, education, investigation, experience, and observation.

inquire

Inquire means search for facts or for truth by asking questions. Some want ads tell people where to *inquire* about renting apartments. Before Mom bought her new car, she *inquired* about several kinds.

ask about

Ask about means inquire. You can *ask about* the price of something, or you can *ask about* someone's vacation plans. If a neighbor *asks about* your grandmother, perhaps he is inquiring about her health because he hasn't seen her for a few days.

question

You *question* someone by asking a series of questions in order to get information. During a job interview, a person may be *questioned* about his or her goals or ambitions.

investigate
Investigate means observe and inquire about something by following a specific procedure. A detective might *investigate* by first checking the scene of the crime. Then he might inquire about the people involved. He might then further *investigate* the suspects by questioning their employers, neighbors, relatives, and friends.

The lawyer for the other side is allowed to **cross-examine** that witness.

cross-examine
If the detective is very suspicious of the answers given by one suspect, he might *cross-examine* that suspect. That means the detective will ask questions which will check the answers the suspect has already given to other questions. In a courtroom after a witness has been examined, or has answered the questions of one lawyer, the lawyer for the other side is allowed to *cross-examine* that witness.

See also *examine.*

ANTONYMS: answer (v), reply (v), respond

I

inspection An *inspection* is made when something is looked at closely. The fire chief made an *inspection* of the old warehouse to see if the building was safe.

inquiry An *inquiry* is a request for information. Grandma received several *inquiries* about the car she had offered for sale.

investigation An *investigation* is a detailed inquiry into a situation in an effort to uncover facts. The *investigation* of the robbery revealed that some of the stolen jewelry had been sold.

probe A dentist may find a cavity by poking a tooth with a pointed instrument called a *probe*. A *probe* can also be a thorough investigation—a poking into a matter to get at the truth. The Senate conducted a *probe* of the pollution of the Great Lakes. A *probe* was made to determine the cause of the accident.

Art's grandma received several **inquiries** about her car.

scrutiny *Scrutiny* is a searching study or inquiry. The *scrutiny* of the riverbank for the missing boat was put off until daylight. *Scrutiny* is also a searching look or a close watch. Before attempting a free fall, the jumpers packed their parachutes under the *scrutiny* of the instructor.

examination An *examination* can be a formal questioning or it can be a test. It can be an inquiry by the police or what doctors do when they take your pulse and listen to your heart.

checkup A *checkup* is any examination or close scrutiny. It is often a medical examination. It is wise to have a *checkup* once a year.

218

instrument   An *instrument* is something you use in order to do something. There are *instruments* for cutting and measuring, drawing and building, cooking and cleaning, farming and gardening. A compass is a very valuable *instrument* to a sailor because it shows direction. Pianos, violins, guitars, trumpets, and saxophones are musical *instruments.* There are many other kinds of *instruments* you may have used or have heard of.

A metronome is a **device** that helps musicians keep time to music.

• tool   A *tool* is an instrument usually operated by hand. A hammer, a saw, and a plane are only a few of the *tools* a carpenter uses.

• implement   The tools that are used in farming or gardening can be called *implements.* Rakes, hoes, and spades are all *implements.* A plow is a farm *implement* used to break the soil before seeds are planted.

• device   A *device* can be an instrument or small machine that has been designed or invented for a special purpose. A car jack is an important *device* to have when a flat tire must be removed from a car. A metronome is a clocklike *device* that helps you keep time to music.

• utensil   A *utensil* is an instrument or container that is usually used in the kitchen. Pots and pans, beaters, and slicers are all *utensils.*

• appliance   An *appliance* is an instrument or device that needs some form of power to operate. A washing machine, a stove, an iron, and a vacuum cleaner are *appliances.*

J

join

Join means put or bring or fasten together. You *join* a club when you become a member and take part in its activities. People may *join* each other for dinner. The Golden Gate Bridge *joins* Marin County and San Francisco. José completed an electric circuit by *joining* the wires. The caller at the square dance directed the people to *join* hands.

combine
unite

Combine and *unite* mean join things to make a new whole. A baker *combines* ingredients to make bread. The states *united* to form a new government.

connect

Connect means join or fasten things together by putting something between them. A walk may *connect* the garage to a house. Ties are used to *connect* the rails of a railroad track. The Isthmus of Panama *connects* North and South America.

link
couple

Link and *couple* also mean join or connect. The girls *linked* arms in order to steady each other as they roller-skated. A steel hook, called a coupling, is used to *couple* two railroad cars.

A steel hook, called a coupling, is used to **couple** two railroad cars.

attach   *Attach* means join one thing to another.
            Lyle *attached* the trailer to his car.

annex   *Annex* means join a thing to something
            else that is larger or more important. A
            country *annexes* territory.

Harry put the vase back together by **gluing** the broken pieces.

cement   *Cement, glue,* and *paste* all mean put or
glue   stick things firmly together by using
paste   something to make them stick. Your dad
            may *cement* flat rocks together to make a
            walk. Harry fixed the vase by *gluing* the
            broken pieces. Will you help my little
            cousin *paste* these paper chains together?

fit   *Fit* means put together parts of the right
            size and shape. Some people enjoy *fitting*
            the pieces of a jigsaw puzzle.

            See also *fasten.*

            ANTONYMS: detach, divide, separate (v)

223

K

know

Know means have knowledge of or information about something or someone. You come to *know* many things by observing what is around you, by reading books, by listening, and by studying in school. Some teen-agers *know* how to cook and sew. Some *know* a lot about sports. I *know* we will have a good time on our trip. My sister *knows* how to speak two languages. Do you *know* that girl? I *have known* her a long time. I *knew* that we could trust her with the secret.

Here are some other words you may use for *know,* even though they aren't really synonyms.

- understand
- realize

Understand and *realize* are good words to use when you know something well or have a clear idea about it. It is wise to ask a question if you don't *understand* something. Do you *understand* how to get to my house? He *realized* that he had better tell the truth about the missing piece of pie. When I tried on my new jacket, I *realized* I had sewed the zipper in upside down.

Is she **aware** that her pen is running out of ink?

- be aware
- recognize

Be aware and *recognize* mean know and admit that something is a fact or that something is true. *Are* you *aware* that your pen is running out of ink? Carla *is aware* of the damage her dog caused when it ran through your garden. The critics *recognized* that the young singer had enough talent to become a star. *Recognize* also means know again. I *recognized* him, even though I hadn't seen him in five years.

• discern
• distinguish

Discern and *distinguish* mean know the difference between things that seem to be alike, and be able to tell them apart or separate them. By the end of the inning, we *discerned* signs of weariness in the pitcher. It isn't always easy to *distinguish* between the right and the wrong thing to say.

• be sure

You can *be sure* about something that you know with certainty. *Are* you *sure* Abraham Lincoln was born in 1809? She *was sure* she had turned off the TV before leaving the house.

See also *imagine, remember.*

By the end of the inning, the batter **discerned** signs of weariness in the pitcher.

L

large

Large describes something that is bigger than usual in size or amount.

extensive
vast

Extensive and vast describe something that fills or covers a large or wide area. It is not limited to one place. The tornado caused *extensive* damage. My spelling was so bad that I had to make *extensive* corrections in my report. Antarctica is a *vast,* ice-covered continent. There is a *vast* difference between my height and yours.

immense
enormous
tremendous

Immense, enormous, and tremendous, all mean very large. *Immense* describes something larger than normal in size or better than usual. The boy has an *immense* appetite for candy. There is an *immense* improvement in her handwriting. *Enormous* and *tremendous* mean shockingly large. Something *enormous* is much larger than you would ever expect it to be. When the polar bear stood on its hind feet, it was *enormous. Tremendous* describes something so large it fills you with awe or terror. A *tremendous* crash of thunder made me jump. Niagara Falls is a *tremendous* sight.

huge
gigantic
mammoth

Huge, gigantic, and mammoth are good words for large. Something *huge* is larger than usual or ordinary in size. The *huge* oak tree fell across our yard, just missing our house. Something is *gigantic* or *mammoth* if it is larger than other things like it. Our rosebush has lots of buds and one *gigantic* blossom. Every time I tried to shoot for the basket, this *mammoth* guard jumped in front of me.

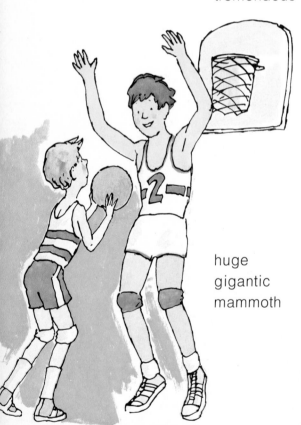

Every time Clay tried to shoot for the basket, this **mammoth** guard jumped in front of him.

226

bulky
massive

Bulky and *massive* mean large in size and often in weight. A *bulky* package may not be heavy, but it is awkward to carry. For example, if you wrapped an open umbrella, you would have a *bulky* package! Something *massive* is not only *bulky* but surprising in size and appearance. A ship is *massive*. Some mountains are *massive* piles of rock.

ANTONYMS: little, minute (adj), slight (adj), small, tiny

last (adj)

Last describes something that comes at the end or is the only one remaining. The *last* flower in the garden is the one that remains after all the others are dead. The *last* day to enter the contest is May 24. If you haven't entered the contest before then, you still have one *last* chance on that day. When the group lined up from shortest to tallest, Joe was *last*.

last (adj) continued on page 228 ▶

When the group lined up from shortest to tallest, Joe was **last.**

Last and these other words cannot always be used in place of each other, but perhaps you can see the differences as you read on.

The **concluding** chapter of the book is very exciting.

- latest

Latest means most recent or newest. The *latest* issue of a magazine is the last one that has been printed so far. The *latest* records are played by disk jockeys.

- final

Final means last, with no more to come, or occurring at the end of something. *Final* exams are taken at the end of the school year. Your *final* word on a subject is the last thing you say about it. His decision was *final* and he refused to discuss it.

- closing
- concluding

Closing and *concluding* mean final or ending or last. In the *closing* paragraph of his letter, Raoul asked his friend to come to visit him next summer. The *concluding* chapter of the book is very exciting.

- conclusive

Conclusive can mean final and true beyond any questioning. *Conclusive* evidence in a trial cannot be proved false. Fingerprints are *conclusive* evidence because no two people have the same fingerprints.

- eventual

Eventual means coming or happening sooner or later. We asked again if we could go to the movies because we hoped Mother's *eventual* answer would be "yes."

- ultimate

Ultimate means last or final or eventual. The *ultimate* goal of our swimming team is to compete in the Olympics.

ANTONYMS: basic, beginning (adj), earliest, first, primary

law

A *law* is a practice that is accepted and required in a community, state, or nation. A *law* is enforced by the police or someone else in authority. Bicycle riders must obey traffic *laws.* Taking someone else's mail from a mailbox is against the *law.*

Here are some words that are not quite synonyms of *law* but have similar meanings.

• rule

A *rule* is a guide for conduct or action. While governments make laws, other organizations have *rules.* Most schools have a *rule* forbidding pupils to run in the halls. If you don't play the game according to the *rules,* no one will want you on the team. Lola has a *rule* she follows: She always treats other people the way she'd like to be treated herself.

• regulation

A *regulation* is a rule that controls a particular group of people very strictly. According to a city *regulation,* food handlers have to pass a health examination. Our organization has so many rules and *regulations,* we can't remember them all.

One city **ordinance** forbids bicycle riding on any main streets.

• ordinance

An *ordinance* is a law passed by a local government to handle a local problem. One city *ordinance* forbids bicycle riding on any main streets.

• act

An *act* can be a law passed by a government. The Stamp *Act* was a law passed by England in 1765 to collect taxes from the American colonies.

L

leave (v)

Leave means go away or move away from. The train will *leave* in an hour. I didn't want to miss the TV show, so I *left* the car races as soon as I could. *Leave* can also mean go away without taking something. Where did you *leave* your book? Did Rose *leave* her sweater behind in her locker?

depart

Depart means leave one place and go to another. We will *depart* for the Smoky Mountains tomorrow morning. One plane *departed* just as another one arrived.

vacate

Vacate means go away from something, leaving no one in it. You *vacate* your chair when you get up and don't sit down again. A family *vacates* a house by moving out and not living in it any longer.

quit

Quit means leave or give up something. She *quit* her job because it no longer interested her. When you *quit* a club, you give up your membership and no longer remain a member.

abandon
desert
forsake

Abandon, desert, and *forsake* mean leave someone or something completely. If you *abandon* a place, you leave and never return. The passengers *abandoned* the sinking ship. If a watchman *deserts* his post, he leaves it unguarded. You *forsake* your friends if they're counting on your help and you let them down.

See also *surrender* (v).

ANTONYMS: stay (v), come, arrive, remain, linger

They **abandoned** the sinking ship.

230

lengthen	*Lengthen* means become or make longer. It is the opposite of shorten. A tailor *lengthens* a coat by letting down the hem. You can *lengthen* a paragraph by adding more sentences. The shadows *lengthened* as the sun dropped lower in the sky.
stretch	*Stretch* means make something longer, usually by pulling it rather than adding to it. You can *stretch* such things as rubber bands, pieces of cloth, material, string, and wire. You might *stretch* your arms and legs if you feel tired. If you *stretch* the truth, you pull it out of shape because you do not tell the facts correctly.

A chameleon can **extend** its tongue beyond its snout.

extend	*Extend* can mean stretch out. You *extend* your hand when you hold it out to shake hands with someone. The highway *extended* from Chicago to Cleveland. A chameleon can *extend* its tongue beyond its snout. *Extend* can also mean lengthen in time. He *extended* his vacation for another week.
draw out continue prolong	*Draw out, continue,* and *prolong* mean make something last a long time or keep something going on so it won't end. Storytellers can *draw out* a story by adding their own ideas. Rosa will *continue* writing her letter after dinner. Medicine *prolongs* our lives. I would have hung up sooner, but my friend kept *prolonging* the conversation.

See also *enlarge, increase* (v).

ANTONYMS: shorten, arrest (v), cut short, stop (v), terminate

231

They had an accidental
meeting.

meeting

A *meeting* is any gathering of several or many people in one place at a certain time. A *meeting* can be large or small, long or short. It is usually planned ahead of time. *Meetings* that are planned usually bring together people with the same interests. Carl and I had a *meeting* to plan our class play. At our club *meeting* we plan to talk about ways to raise money. You can, of course, have an accidental *meeting* with someone if you both just happen to be in the same place at the same time.

• assembly

An *assembly* is a planned meeting, usually attended by a large group of people for the purpose of being informed, being entertained, or making group decisions. At the school *assembly* yesterday we saw a film about fire prevention.

• conference

A *conference* is a meeting in which two or more people exchange views on a subject. Often a *conference* is a regular meeting of people who represent a group or organization. There is no school today because of the teachers' *conference.*

• convention

A *convention* is often an annual meeting to which certain members of an organization are sent to handle the group's business. A meeting of a political party is also called a *convention.*

• council

A *council* is a meeting of a small group of people chosen from a larger group to serve as advisers or consultants. The student *council* met yesterday to discuss the problem of noise in the halls.

244

misery	*Misery* is the state of feeling very sad or unhappy or unwell. Anything unpleasant or troublesome may cause *misery.* The severe flood brought *misery* to the villagers.
suffering	*Suffering* is the pain you experience when you are sick or unhappy. The medicine relieved Nick's *suffering.* You could see the *suffering* on the faces of those poor, hungry children.
distress torment	Worry or anxiety over something can cause *distress* or *torment.* I was in *distress* after losing Grandmother's ring. Remembering the mean things I had said caused me hours of *torment.*
agony	*Agony* is extreme misery and suffering brought about by something that is almost impossible to endure. A toothache may cause a great deal of *agony.*
unhappiness	*Unhappiness* is not as strong as the other words. A slight disappointment may cause you *unhappiness,* but you'll soon get over it.

A toothache may cause a great deal of **agony.**

See also *sadness.*

ANTONYMS: contentment, happiness, joy, pleasure

misfortune	*Misfortune* is anything bad that happens to a person, which causes that person to be physically or mentally upset. Some people think of *misfortune* as just bad luck. Tammy overslept yesterday, and then, to add to her *misfortune,* she forgot her lunch and missed her ride.

misfortune continued on page 246 ▶

M

Eric's sister has **trouble** tying her shoes.

misfortune continued from page 245

• difficulty

A *difficulty* is a problem you find hard to solve. Don's *difficulty* is that he would rather sleep than work.

• trouble

Trouble is difficulty or misfortune. Some *troubles* are big and some are little. Since the accident last week, Dad has had *trouble* with the car. My little sister has *trouble* tying her shoes.

• distress

Distress can be a difficult or painful situation that causes suffering to someone. Ships send out an SOS whenever they are in *distress*. Usually *distress* doesn't last long and probably is not very serious. Losing that scarf caused me *distress*.

• hardship

A *hardship* is something that causes suffering and is very hard to bear. The group of backpackers who were lost in the mountains endured many *hardships* before they were finally rescued.

• ruin

Ruin is the complete collapse of someone or something. My grandpa says that failure to pay even one bill can start any family on its way to financial *ruin*. A building or an object that has been damaged or destroyed may be called a *ruin*.

• disaster

A *disaster* is a terrible misfortune that hits suddenly and often unexpectedly. The apartment fire was a *disaster* for the families who lived there.

See also *harm* (n).

ANTONYMS: blessing, happiness, help (n), pleasure, prosperity, success

246

mix (v)   *Mix* means put together two or more things to make something else. You *mix* flour and water to make paste. A baker makes a cake by *mixing* the ingredients together. Danny *mixed* the chocolate syrup into his milk.

combine   *Combine* means bring or join different things together. If you *combine* yellow and red, you'll get orange. Hydrogen and oxygen *combine* to make water. *Combine* can also be used when people act together. In assembling the baseball team, the coach *combined* players who were good at fielding with players who had good batting averages.

blend   *Blend* can mean mix thoroughly and smoothly. An eggbeater is used to *blend* ingredients for cooking. An artist *blends* two colors to make a third color.

fuse   *Fuse* means blend or join by melting. A soldering iron can be used to *fuse* broken wires. Brass is a metal made by *fusing* copper and zinc.

mingle merge   *Mingle* and *merge* mean mix or come together with something or someone else. At a big party the host usually *mingles* with the guests to see that they are having a good time. Companies or business firms *merge* when they combine to make one firm. Drivers must *merge* quickly into traffic when they enter expressways. The two creeks *merged* to form a river.

ANTONYMS: scatter, separate (v), sort (v)

Left 32, right 8, left 13?

A **combination** of numbers in the right order will open the safe.

mixture   A *mixture* is a product formed by mixing or putting different things or materials together. Cement is a *mixture* of materials such as clay and limestone.

union   A *union* is the bringing together of different things to form a whole. The United States is a *union* of fifty states. A labor *union* is a group of workers who join together to improve working conditions.

combination   A *combination* can be a mixture of anything, such as persons, numbers, or chemicals. A bouquet is a *combination* of flowers. A *combination* of numbers in the right order will open the safe.

fusion   *Fusion* means the joining of two or more things, sometimes by melting. We speak of the *fusion* of wires in an electrical circuit.

merger   A *merger* is a combination of business firms or other organizations.

compound   A *compound* is something formed by putting different parts together. Water is a *compound* of two parts hydrogen to one part oxygen. "Blackboard" is a *compound* of two words.

blend   A *blend* is a thorough mixture. Seasonings are a *blend* of herbs. In a chorus, high and low voices form a *blend* of sounds.

assortment   An *assortment* is a collection of various kinds. An *assortment* of chocolates may include some pieces with hard centers and some with soft centers.

ANTONYM: separation

248

moist *Moist* means slightly wet. Anything that is *moist* is not completely dry. Fresh bread sometimes feels *moist.* Your eyes are *moist* after you cry.

damp *Damp* also means somewhat wet. I used a *damp* cloth to clean my shoes. Please check to see if the clothes on the line are still *damp.*

humid *Humid* describes air that is moist or damp. A city near a river or lake may be *humid* in the summer. A jungle is hot and *humid,* but a desert is hot and arid. Today it was hot, *humid,* and sticky.

rainy *Rainy* means wet with rain. It is usually quite *rainy* in a jungle. A *rainy* day may spoil your plans to go to the fair.

It is usually quite **rainy** in a jungle.

watery *Watery* means containing water. *Watery* paint may be too thin to use.

juicy
succulent *Juicy* and *succulent* mean full of juice or moisture. Certain fruits, vegetables, and meats are *juicy.* A cactus is a *succulent* plant. It can grow in a desert because its leaves and stem store all the water it needs.

ANTONYMS: dry (adj), arid, parched

249

M

move

Move means change position or set in motion. That is a simple definition of a simple word. But did you ever stop to think of all the ways in which things can *move* or be *moved?*

For instance, can you think of anything that can't *move* or be *moved?* Engineers who are building a highway can *move* a hill by having it blown up. Builders can *move* a house from one side of town to the other. People often *move* from city to city. Traffic *moves.* Time *moves.* A clever actor can *move* an audience to laughter or tears.

You probably can't think of many verbs that don't mean *move* or *move* something. You can *move* yourself. *Walk* (v) and *run* (v) are entries that contain several words to describe the way people and animals *move.* Look them up. Also read the entry *go.*

You can *move* something or someone. You might *lift* or *carry, take* or *send, advance* or *change* it. You may *throw* or *catch* it. You can *shake, push, pull,* or *put* many things.

Perhaps you want to *move* a person or a thing to do something. Look up *urge* and *force* (v) for synonyms. If you *move* something or someone in an unwelcome way, you *disturb.*

mystery

A *mystery* is something that has not been explained or cannot be completely understood. My disappearance was a *mystery* to them until they found my note. Scientists are gradually solving the many *mysteries* of space travel.

problem

A *problem* can be anything that you wonder what to do about. It may be a question you can't answer or a situation you are not sure how to handle. That math *problem* has me stumped. My *problem* is fitting my tape recorder into that small space.

He finds the solution to a **puzzle** by putting pieces together.

puzzle

You find the solution to a *puzzle* by putting pieces or words or information together. You are probably familiar with jigsaw *puzzles* and crossword *puzzles.* Sometimes a person is a *puzzle* if you don't understand that person's behavior.

riddle

A *riddle* is a puzzling question that usually requires hard and clever thinking to answer. The *riddle* of the disappearing hat was finally solved. Many children enjoy *riddles* and even buy books of *riddles.*

secret

A *secret* is something that one or more persons know but don't tell to anyone else. *Secrets* are a mystery to those who are left out. If you tell a *secret* to too many people, it won't be a *secret* any more.

N

neat   *Neat* means clean and in order. It can describe anything that isn't messy or sloppy. A *neat* house isn't cluttered with trash or rubbish. *Neat* clothes are not wrinkled or dirty. He has very *neat* handwriting. After she washed the car, it looked *neat* as a pin!

tidy   A *tidy* room is one in which everything is carefully arranged and in its proper place. People who are *tidy* are very careful about how they look and how they do things.

trim   *Trim* means neat, clean, and well fitting. The mail carrier looked *trim* in the new uniform.

orderly   *Orderly* means neat and tidy and in order. If I would keep my room *orderly,* I would never have any trouble finding things. Papers and books are arranged carefully in an *orderly* desk.

shipshape   Something is in *shipshape* condition if it is well cared for. When I finished sweeping the tree house, it looked *shipshape.*

ANTONYMS: messy, sloppy, disorderly, untidy

new   *New* is used in many ways. It is the opposite of old. *New* describes something or someone that has never existed before. A *new* house is one that has just been built. A *new* bud is just beginning to grow.

New also describes something that has never been used or worn before. He bought a *new* suit. My stereo is brand *new.* You

may also do or think of something for the
first time, and this can be called *new.* She
starts her *new* job tomorrow.

current
up-to-date

Current and *up-to-date* mean new and
happening right now. Newscasters report
on *current* events. The automobile is a
current means of transportation. The horse
and buggy are obsolete. The old-fashioned
pictures in the catalog were replaced by
up-to-date ones.

modern
contemporary

Modern and *contemporary* mean happening
or existing at the present time. Many
modern paintings seem hard to understand.
The skyscraper is a *contemporary* form of
architecture. *Contemporary* also means
happening or existing at about the same
time. The opening of the Panama Canal
and the beginning of World War I were
contemporary events.

Many **modern** paintings seem
hard to understand.

recent
late

Recent and *late* mean not long past. They
describe something that has just happened
or has just been made. The whole family
was anxious to get the pictures of our
recent vacation. A *late* copy of a magazine
is more current than a copy from last year.

young

Young describes someone or something
that is not fully developed or mature. A
child is *young.* The mare is guarding her
young colts. *Young* corn is not yet ready to
be picked.

ANTONYMS: old, obsolete, old-fashioned,
antique (adj), mature (adj),
adult (adj), ancient

N

normal
Normal means something that is expected because it fits a standard or custom or rule. For some pupils a *normal* school day begins at 8:30 A.M. and ends at 3:00 P.M. *Normal* means not far from the average. Sometimes the bus driver finishes her route in four hours; at other times it may take her five hours; but the *normal* time is about four and one-half hours.

regular
Regular means arranged or formed according to some standard or rule. A *regular* work week is Monday through Friday.

routine
typical
Routine and *typical* mean ordinary or happening regularly and always in the same way. A *routine* inspection of an automobile must be made at certain times; certain parts of the car are always checked. A *typical* day is one that is about the same as any other day—up in the morning, off to school, back home again, and then back to bed.

A **typical** day is one that is about the same as any other day—up in the morning, off to school, and then back to bed.

natural

Natural can mean normal because of the way something is or the way something acts. It is *natural* for some birds to fly south in the winter. The *natural* dwelling place for a lion is a den.

See also *ordinary*.

ANTONYMS: irregular, abnormal, unnatural

notice (v)

Notice means catch sight of or look carefully at someone or something. Did you *notice* the boy who just passed us? I *noticed* a hole in my jacket, but I tried to ignore it.

Those faces carved on the mountainside are a sight to **behold.**

behold

Behold is an old-fashioned word that means notice something or take a look at something. Those faces carved on the mountainside are a sight to *behold*.

observe

Observe can mean notice or look closely at something. You *observe* the movements of amoebas through a microscope.

note

Note can mean notice or observe with care. A salesperson demonstrating a new vacuum cleaner might say, "*Note* how easy it is to operate." The coach asked us to *note* the correct way to hold a football.

view

View means consider or notice something that is before you. A committee tries to *view* all sides of a problem. The mayor came to *view* the damage done by the storm.

See also *examine*.

ANTONYMS: ignore, overlook, miss (v)

255

object (n)

An *object* is anything you can see or touch. Toys are *objects* to play with. Tools are the *objects* a carpenter uses. A storekeeper displays *objects* on the shelves.

An *object* can also be something toward which an action is directed. It's what someone is working toward. Her *object* in baby-sitting was to earn enough money to go to camp. The *object* of the game is to get your marker home first.

thing
article

Thing and *article* are other words for objects. It's hard to see *things* in the dark. An *article* can be any particular thing. A shirt is an *article* of clothing. The five *articles* I brought with me are missing.

target
mark
bull's eye

A *target* and a *mark* are objects to shoot at. A *bull's eye* is the center of a target. An archer gets more points if the arrow hits the *bull's eye.* When someone hits a *target* in the center or goes right to the point of something, you might say, "You've hit the *bull's eye!*" Some people think it's fun to throw darts at a *target. Target* and *mark* are often used to mean an object, or goal, you are trying to reach. A million dollars is the *target* of the Community Fund drive this year. Last year's drive set a high *mark* for us to aim for this year.

COMMUNITY FUND

— 1,000,000
— 900,000
— 800,000
— 700,000
— 600,000
— 500,000
— 400,000
— 300,000
— 200,000
— 100,000

A million dollars is the **target** of the Community Fund drive this year.

purpose
end
goal

Purpose, end, and *goal* are all objects to be reached or achieved. Her *purpose* in calling was to invite me to the party. Umberto's dream was to be a violinist, and he was working toward that *end.* Dale's *goal* is to become a civil engineer.

256

intent
aim
objective

Intent, aim, and *objective* are other words you can use to mean what you have in mind to do. My *intent* was to warn her, not frighten her. Finding the North Pole was the *aim* of Admiral Peary's expedition. Our *objective* is to save enough money to buy a ten-speed bicycle.

object (v)

If you *object* to something, you argue against it, giving your own idea or opinion. You might *object* to something you oppose, such as stealing, or to something that seems unfair, such as having to go to bed every night at seven o'clock. I *objected* to turning down the stereo, but my neighbors insisted.

Fred **complains** about the food but eats more than anyone.

complain

Complain means tell someone that you are not satisfied with a situation. When you *complain,* you let people know that you are opposed to something, or at least that you are not happy with it. Ruby *complained* to the mechanic that the car was hard to start on cold mornings. Fred *complains* about the food but eats more than anyone.

disagree

Disagree is the opposite of agree. People *disagree* if their ideas or opinions are not the same. Often when people *disagree,* they argue about who is right or who has the better idea. We always seem to *disagree* about which TV programs to watch.

protest

Protest means object strongly to something that happens or doesn't happen. Often a group *protests* by presenting its views in an

object (v) continued on page 258 ▶

O

object (v) continued from page 257

organized manner, either in writing or speech. The citizens signed petitions *protesting* the building of an amusement park on good farm land.

See also *argue*.

ANTONYMS: agree, approve, consent (v)

objection *Objection* is the act of objecting to something that is said or to something that happens. I have no *objection* to wearing boots, but I hate to carry an umbrella. "*Objection* overruled," declared the judge.

complaint A *complaint* is an objection and is usually the result of a person's not being satisfied with a situation. She heard many *complaints* about the way the banquet was handled. I like Victor, but I get tired of listening to his *complaints*.

disapproval *Disapproval* is the opposite of approval. You show *disapproval* by refusing to agree or to accept someone's action or opinion. If you cheat at a game, you can expect *disapproval* from your friends and opponents. When she walked into the room, *disapproval* showed on her face.

When she walked into the room, **disapproval** showed on her face.

protest   A *protest* is an objection to something that you disapprove of or feel is unfair. *Protests* against poor service should not be ignored by the post office. If an umpire's decision during a baseball game seems unfair to one team, that team may play the rest of the game under *protest.*

ANTONYMS: approval, agreement, endorsement

obtain   *Obtain* means get something, usually by putting forth some kind of effort or by paying for it. People *obtain* knowledge and information through reading and studying. After what seemed like weeks of waiting, Rita finally *obtained* her driver's license. If we can *obtain* the necessary tools, we can build a sailboat.

receive   *Receive* means get something that is given, offered, sent, or delivered to you. You may *receive* without putting forth any effort or paying. You *receive* cards and gifts on your birthday. You will *receive* a diploma when you graduate from school. Harold *received* a black eye in the fight.

inherit   *Inherit* means receive something when someone dies. The will indicated that Sara was to *inherit* her grandfather's farm. Also, you may be said to *inherit* something passed on to you from someone who gives it up. Bob *inherited* a coat his brother had outgrown. I *inherited* the job of keeping a record of the bazaar's profits.

obtain continued on page 260 ▶

Delia will **win** first prize if she correctly guesses the number of jellybeans in the jar.

obtain continued from page 259

buy
purchase

Buy and *purchase* mean obtain something by paying for it. He went to the store to *buy* some food for dinner. He *bought* hamburger and buns. *Purchase* is the more formal word. Our family *purchased* a new home. Yoshiko *purchased* a tennis racket.

win

Win means get something in a contest or competition. You may work hard to beat someone, or you may *win* by luck. You will *win* first prize if you correctly guess the number of jellybeans in the jar. Linda *won* a blue ribbon in the sack race.

earn

You *earn* something if you obtain it in return for work or for something you do. She *earns* her allowance by taking out the garbage every day. Many teen-agers baby-sit to *earn* money. Jason *earned* my respect by working hard at his job.

achieve

Achieve means get or obtain something by doing a lot of hard work. She finally *achieved* her goal of becoming a doctor.

ANTONYMS: give, send, give up, forgo, let go, lose, relinquish

odd

Odd describes something that is out of the ordinary. Something might seem *odd* to you if it is different from what you are used to or different from what you would normally expect. You might hear an *odd* noise or see an *odd* sight. It is *odd* that my friend didn't meet me as we had planned.

unusual

Unusual means not common or ordinary or usual. It would be *unusual* to hear a clock strike thirteen.

curious
Curious can also describe something unusual. I found some *curious* antiques in the junk shop. This belt has a *curious* brass buckle on it.

strange
mysterious
Strange and *mysterious* mean odd and hard to understand. He gave me a *strange* look after I bumped into him. The kitten was trying to figure out where the *strange* sound was coming from. I saw a *mysterious* light moving across the sky. Where is this *mysterious* shadow you say you've seen?

queer
funny
Queer and *funny* are often used to describe something odd or strange. Jellyfish have *queer* shapes. A Pekingese is a *funny* little dog with long hair and a pug nose.

quaint
Something *quaint* is odd and unfamiliar because it is old-fashioned. She took many pictures of the *quaint* little town. The square dancers wore *quaint* costumes.

He has that stiff walk **peculiar** to some cowhands.

peculiar
Something *peculiar* is odd or typical of one kind of person or thing, not shared by others. Mary has a *peculiar* way of snapping her fingers. The kangaroo is an animal *peculiar* to Australia. He has that stiff walk *peculiar* to some cowhands.

eccentric
An *eccentric* person acts in an odd or strange way. The *eccentric* old man wore his boots even in dry weather.

See also *foreign, rare.*

ANTONYMS: common, ordinary, usual, familiar, natural, normal, regular

P

part (n)

Any object or idea can be separated or broken up into *parts.* So a *part* is always less than the whole of something. Since there are many ways of dividing something, there are many different kinds of *parts.*

If you drop a mirror, you probably sweep it up in *fragments.* If you eat a piece of cake, you'll have crumbs, or tiny *particles,* left on your plate. If you make a batch of cookies, you may drop *chunks* of dough on a cookie sheet. Look up the entry *piece* for words that mean *parts* of something broken away or taken away from the whole.

When you cut an apple pie into *parts* and give a piece to each member of the family, you are giving each person a *portion.* A *portion* is a *part* meant for a certain person or purpose. A *portion* may also be a definite size or amount. You'll find other good words for this kind of *part* in the entry *portion* (n).

When you think about the *parts* of animals, plants, and people, you probably think of arms and legs, branches, stems, roots, blossoms. Words for *parts* of bodies or systems are listed under *branch* (n).

Just about everything in the world is made up of *parts.* And we have all kinds of words to describe this division. Of course, air, water, and land are the three main *parts* of our earth. But take a look at *zone* (n). You'll see some interesting words that tell how we divide the face of the earth.

party

Party probably brings to your mind pictures of cake and ice cream and presents. But the word has another meaning. A *party* is one or more persons taking part in an activity. The search *party* hasn't come back yet. Which political *party* are you working for?

Other words can be used for different *parties.*

• group

A *group* is a gathering of two or more persons, usually with a common interest. Such a gathering can be either accidental or planned. The angry *group* of people waited five minutes for an elevator. We waited in line for ten hours to see our favorite rock *group.*

• gang

A *gang* is a group of people who work together toward some common goal. Work *gangs* repair railroad tracks. Often *gang* is used for a group that is doing something unlawful or violent. The Jets and the Sharks were rival *gangs* in "West Side Story." Sometimes *gang* is used in an informal way to mean friends. The *gang* is over for pizza tonight.

party continued on page 266 ▸

The **gang** is over for pizza tonight.

P

party continued from page 265

- band

A *band* is a group of people joined for a common purpose and working very closely together. The marching *band* performed all over Europe and the United States. Have you ever seen a *band* of gypsies?

- team

A *team* is a group of people playing or working together to reach a particular goal. A *team* of doctors worked day and night to save her life. Our golf *team* finally won the championship.

- troupe
- troop

Troupe and *troop* are both groups of people. A *troupe* is a group of performers which presents entertainment in a circus or on the stage. A *troop* is a group of members in an organization, such as the Boy Scouts or the Girl Scouts.

perfect (adj)

When something has no faults or defects or errors, you might say it is *perfect*. Homework that is free from any mistakes is *perfect*. But you also use *perfect* to describe anything that is very good or the best of its kind. The swimmer made a *perfect* dive. Today is a *perfect* day. I found the *perfect* gift for you.

The swimmer made a **perfect** dive.

There are many other words that you can use to tell just how *perfect* something is.

flawless

Flawless means free from any faults or defects. A table top is *flawless* if there are no marks or scratches on it. The diamond was valuable because it was *flawless*. The skater's performance was *flawless*, according to the judges.

pure
absolute

Pure and *absolute* mean perfect and not mixed with anything else. *Pure* silver doesn't contain any other material. You tell the *absolute* truth about something when you tell all you know and don't leave out any details or include anything that is false.

excellent
expert

Excellent and *expert* mean very good and very fine. You might read an *excellent* book or have an *excellent* time at the zoo. He had an *excellent* idea for the title of the variety show. An *expert* mechanic is highly skilled and does only the best work. Take your watch to an *expert* watchmaker for repairs. She is an *expert* horseback rider.

Take a broken watch to an **expert** watchmaker for repairs.

ideal

Ideal is even stronger than excellent. Something that is *ideal* is absolutely the very best. It suits the purpose exactly. This is an *ideal* spot for a picnic.

ANTONYMS: defective, imperfect

P

permission

When someone tells you that you are allowed to do something or go somewhere, that person has given you *permission.* A lawyer asks the judge for *permission* to speak in court. If you want to leave your job early, you must get *permission* from your supervisor. I was given special *permission* to paint scenes on a store window at Halloween.

leave

Leave is permission to do something that is usually forbidden. The knights used the phrase "By your *leave,* my lord" when talking to King Arthur. That meant "with your permission" I will do this or that.

Jane's **consent** was necessary before her brother could sell the table tennis set.

consent

If you give your *consent* to help someone with a project, you agree with and approve of the way that person wants to do it. *Consent* is permission, too. My *consent* was necessary before my brother could sell the table tennis set; after all, I owned half of it.

license
permit

A *license* is written permission to do something. So is a *permit.* Both are issued by people who have a legal right to do so. A *license* is needed before a person can practice medicine. A *permit* is issued so that a person can learn to drive a car.

piece

A *piece* is one of the parts into which something is divided or separated. You might have a *piece* of cake or break a glass into *pieces.* A *piece* may also be one item among several like it. A chair, for instance, is called a *piece* of furniture. A platter is a *piece* of china.

particle

A *particle* is a very small part or piece of something. (When you get a *particle* of dirt in your eye, though, it does not feel tiny.) Sand is made up of *particles* of rock. Some people are allergic to the *particles* of dust in the air.

bit

A *bit* is a small piece or amount. A *bit* of food or a *bit* of rest is welcome to one who has worked hard all day. I'd go if I had a *bit* more time to get ready. I have just a *bit* of yellow yarn left. Caroline tore the letter into *bits*.

fragment

A *fragment* usually means a piece broken off of something or an unfinished part of something. *Fragments* of glass were found beneath the broken window. We found Indian arrowheads and the *fragments* of a clay cooking dish at the site. I heard only *fragments* of the conversation.

Chris found Indian arrowheads and the **fragments** of a clay cooking dish at the site.

lump
chunk
hunk

Lump, chunk, and *hunk* are words for pieces that have no certain shape or size. Though the words are synonyms, each is used with some materials but seldom or never with others. You might speak of a *lump* of sugar or a *lump* of coal. You probably wouldn't say a *chunk* or *hunk* of sugar, though. You could call a piece of wood a *chunk* or *hunk;* you would not usually say a *lump* of wood. A *chunk* of meat or candy sounds better than a *lump* of meat or candy. A *hunk* of melon or apple sounds more appetizing than a *lump. A lump* of gold sounds good!

P

plan (n)

A *plan* is a method of doing or showing something. It is also a group of ideas arranged in an order that will make something happen. A *plan* may be written—like a recipe—or it may be drawn—like a floor *plan*—or it may be just an idea in your head about how to get out of doing dishes.

• outline

An *outline* is a written plan that contains only the main points of something. Before writing a book, an author may make an *outline,* setting down the events, in order, from the beginning to the end of the story. It is then easy to follow the *outline* and fill in the details.

• draft

A *draft* may be a written plan, design, or drawing. A *draft* is usually not the final version. An author often writes a rough first *draft* of an article. The first step is to write down everything without paying much attention to details. Later the writer polishes the article and finally checks the spelling and corrects all mistakes.

• diagram
• sketch

A *diagram* and a *sketch* can both be plans that are drawn. They show the main points and give a rough idea of how something will be done or made. A *diagram* would probably look less like a picture than a *sketch* would. A *diagram* of the water system in your house might show lines that represent water pipes coming into the house and going to different small squares, or rooms. On a *diagram,* items are usually labeled. Otherwise you wouldn't recognize

A **sketch** would be a rough drawing.

what they were. A *sketch* would be a rough drawing. A *sketch* of your kitchen would be a quickly and simply drawn picture, showing doors, windows, and appliances. You wouldn't need labels to tell what the artist had drawn.

A **blueprint** is a photographic print of a precisely measured and carefully drawn plan.

• blueprint

A *blueprint* is a photographic print of a precisely measured and carefully drawn plan, especially of a building. The lines are white on blue paper. One way to copy a plan is to make a *blueprint.*

• design

A *design* may be a sketch or plan for something that is to be made, like a *design* for a new car. It can also be a plan to accomplish something. Sometimes a *design* is a secret or evil plan. As soon as my sister finished her piece of cake, I could see she had *designs* on mine.

• scheme

A *scheme* may also be a sly or crafty plan. Often it is a plan that is poorly thought out and unsuccessful. Sometimes it is a plan to get something for nothing or by any means, fair or foul. Uncle Joe had a wild *scheme* for becoming rich overnight.

• plot

A *plot* is a carefully laid out plan to accomplish something—often bad. Police uncovered a *plot* to hijack the truck.

• project

A *project* is a long-range plan for doing something. It requires much thought and effort. During the space program's *Project* Mercury, scientists studied the effects of outer space on humans.

See also *arrangement.*

271

P

plan (v)

Plan means have something in mind or decide on a way to do something. You think out each step you must take to carry out your plan. You may be *planning* to go to college to study law. Or perhaps you haven't *planned* that far ahead.

intend

Intend means have in mind. If you buy a coat, you *intend* to wear it. I *intended* to wash the windows, but I got so interested in this book that I forgot to do them.

arrange

Arrange means plan or prepare and get ready for something. You may *arrange* a picnic by asking each person in your group to bring part of the lunch. Sandra *arranged* to have someone pick her up at the station.

program

Program, nowadays, can mean prepare a machine to give certain information and perform a task. For example, a large store *programs* a computer to figure out and prepare monthly bills. The name and address of each customer and the amounts of the purchases are all fed into the machine. The bill then comes out of the machine, all ready to be mailed to the customer.

Program, nowadays, can mean prepare a machine to give certain information and perform a task.

scheme
plot

Scheme and *plot* usually mean plan something secretly. Through the open window we could hear the boys *scheming* to climb the wall. Rebels are *plotting* to overthrow the dictator.

hatch

You might say someone *hatches* a scheme or plan if that person thinks it up secretly. What crazy scheme is he *hatching* now?

playful *Playful* means full of play or fun. People who are in a *playful* mood are happy and lighthearted and not at all serious. They laugh and joke a lot. Some people become *playful* when it snows. They cannot resist throwing snowballs. The *playful* dog ran off with my shoe.

frolicsome *Frolicsome* means playful, gay, and merry. The *frolicsome* kitten batted the ball of yarn around the room. The *frolicsome* porpoises splashed as they raced around the pool, dived through hoops, and jumped into the air.

frisky *Frisky* means very playful, lively, and high-spirited. It is hard to saddle a *frisky* horse. The *frisky* colts galloped around the corral. The *frisky* goats tried to butt each other with their horns.

The **frisky** colts galloped around the corral.

impish
mischievous *Impish* and *mischievous* mean playful but in a harmful or annoying way. An *impish* person plays pranks and teases other people. According to some folk tales, the *mischievous* deeds of elves caused problems for many people.

ANTONYMS: serious, businesslike, solemn

273

P

pleasant

Pleasant describes anything that pleases you or gives you a good feeling. You might spend a *pleasant* day in the city or take a *pleasant* ride through the countryside. A *pleasant* person is easy to get along with.

agreeable

Something is *agreeable* to you if you like it. Most fruits have an *agreeable* flavor or taste. The coming of spring is *agreeable* to most people. A show or movie can be *agreeable.* They spent an *agreeable* afternoon shopping at the new mall.

pleasing

Something is *pleasing* if it is agreeable and makes you feel good. Anita has a *pleasing* smile. Sitting in front of a fire can be *pleasing* on a cold, wintry day.

delightful

If something is very pleasing and enjoyable, it is *delightful*. It is *delightful* to go to a circus or watch a parade. Our tour through the candy factory was *delightful.*

Sitting in front of a fire can be **pleasing** on a cold, wintry day.

cheerful
cheery

A *cheerful* room is pleasant, sunny, and bright. Someone with a *cheery* disposition is gay and merry and fun to be with. Ernie's *cheery* letter brightened my day.

satisfying

Something is *satisfying* if it fills your need or makes you feel happy and contented. Hearing that your friends enjoyed your recital is *satisfying*. A big sandwich is *satisfying* if you're hungry.

A big sandwich is **satisfying** when they're hungry.

refreshing

Something is *refreshing* if it makes you feel rested and like new again. If you're very tired, a short nap can be *refreshing*. A glass of ice water is *refreshing* on a hot day.

charming
enchanting

Charming and *enchanting* originally meant able to cast a magic spell. Now they are used to mean very pleasant, attractive, delightful, or fascinating. Everyone feels comfortable in your home; you are a *charming* host. There are many *enchanting* stories in this old book.

See also *delicious*.

ANTONYMS: bad, displeasing, gloomy, melancholy (adj), obnoxious, repulsive, sad, unpleasant

275

P

pledge (n)

A *pledge* is your statement that you will do something. You make a *pledge* to a charity when you say you will contribute some time or money to it. An IOU is a *pledge.* Sometimes you have to back up a *pledge* with something. She left a hundred dollars with the salesperson as a *pledge* that she would return and buy the car.

An IOU is a **pledge.**

- promise
- word

When you make a *promise* or give your *word* to someone, that person believes and trusts that you will do what you have said you will do. I gave my *word* that I would be home in time to help her with her math. They made a *promise* never to reveal the secret formula. He did not come over, though he gave me his *word* that he would. Don't make a *promise* that you don't intend to keep.

- vow

A *vow* is a solemn, or serious, promise. When Ella and Phil got married, they made a *vow* to love each other. After spending an unhappy week at camp, she made a *vow* that she would never go again.

- agreement

People reach an *agreement* when they decide that something should or should not be done. The citizens made an *agreement* to keep the city clean. The city officials signed an *agreement* to halt construction of the new city hall.

It's fortunate that this toaster has a one-year **guarantee.**

• guarantee   A *guarantee* is a pledge that a manufacturer makes to the customers. If a product doesn't measure up to a certain standard, the manufacturer's *guarantee* pledges that the product can be returned, repaired, or replaced. It's fortunate that this toaster has a one-year *guarantee.*

• security   *Security* is something a person gives as a pledge to repay what was borrowed. A person who wants to get a loan from a bank might use a car as *security.* If the loan is not paid back, the bank can take the car. If you have to borrow movie money from your dad, you may give him an IOU—your written pledge to pay back the money. Or you may let him have your baseball mitt as *security.*

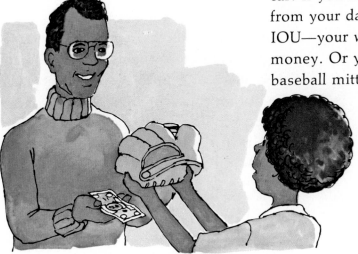

Charlene let her father have her baseball mitt as **security.**

277

polite

Henry was being **courteous** when he held the door open for the woman on crutches.

courteous

well-mannered

• tactful

Polite people have good manners. They show courtesy to others. When we go to Grandma's house, Father always reminds us to be *polite.* It is impolite to interrupt when others are in the middle of a conversation. It is often difficult to be *polite* to someone who is rude.

Courteous means having good manners and being considerate of others. Henry was being *courteous* when he held the door open for the woman on crutches. *Courteous* people wait their turn in line. Rude people push ahead of others or push others out of their way. Kim was very *courteous* in letting me go ahead of her.

Well-mannered means having or showing good manners. *Well-mannered* people know how to act in different social situations. Roy is too *well-mannered* to have slammed the door in your face on purpose.

Tactful means knowing what to do or say in order to keep from embarrassing or hurting someone. It is not really a synonym for polite, but both words mean thoughtful of other people. A *tactful* person who is allergic to chocolate might refuse a piece of cake by saying "No, thank you, but it certainly looks delicious." A tactless person might answer "No, thanks; chocolate cake makes me sick."

See also *thoughtful.*

ANTONYMS: impolite, rude, tactless

poor

Poor means having just a few things or having little or no money. Then it is the opposite of rich or wealthy. Someone who is *poor* can't afford to buy luxuries. A very *poor* person may not have enough to eat.

penniless

Penniless means without any money at all. Losing her purse left the woman *penniless*. He was *penniless* after spending the last cent of his allowance.

bankrupt

A firm or business is *bankrupt* when it hasn't enough money to pay its debts. People with no way of getting money to pay their bills may also "go *bankrupt*." You can "go *bankrupt*" or "be *bankrupt*."

A business is **bankrupt** when it hasn't enough money to pay its debts.

broke

Broke is a slang word people use to mean penniless. I'm *broke* and can't lend you a cent. As with bankrupt, you can "be *broke*" or you can "go *broke*."

needy
destitute

Needy and *destitute* mean very poor and poverty-stricken. Charities help *needy* people who haven't enough money to live on. The fire left the family *destitute*— without clothes, money, or shelter.

ANTONYMS: rich, wealthy, well-to-do

P

portion (n) A *portion* is a part of something. It is usually a part that is of a certain size or amount, or it is the part that is meant for a certain person or purpose. Leon asked the waiter for a double *portion* of dessert. Each week I save a *portion* of my allowance.

share A *share* is a portion meant for one person or contributed by one person. Did you get your *share* of the candy? I was willing to take my *share* of the blame for the accident. The girls did more than their *share* of work in cleaning the yard.

segment A *segment* is a portion clearly marked off or separated from the whole by natural divisions. It is easy to split an orange into *segments*.

section A *section* is a portion made by cutting or dividing a whole. The last *section* of this book is the Index. People pronounce words differently in some *sections* of the country.

unit A *unit* is one thing or one portion of a group that makes up a whole. The parade had ten *units*. Each *unit* was made up of a band and two floats. An apartment is one *unit* of an apartment building. We just finished the third *unit* of this science book.

member A *member* is a part of a group or a body. Our club has five *members*. Is Frank Chin a *member* of the bowling team? Your arms are *members* of your body.

element An *element* is one of the simplest parts that are combined to make a whole. Scientists have found more than one hundred

portion (n) continued

elements in the earth. The *elements* of mathematics mean the simplest rules or principles of mathematics.

fraction

A *fraction* is a portion less than a whole, or a part that has been broken off from something. One-half and one-fourth are *fractions.* Because of the snow, just a *fraction* of the expected audience was present for the piano recital.

Water **power** makes a mill wheel turn.

power

Power is the strength and ability to do or cause something. Everyone has the *power* to think and make decisions. A flying fish has the *power* to glide through the air. An engine furnishes the *power* to move a car. Water *power* makes a mill wheel turn. A queen has the *power* to rule her people.

power continued on page 282 ◗

P

power continued from page 281

authority   *Authority* is the power to tell other people what to do in a certain situation. Parents have *authority* over their children until the children grow up. A police officer has the *authority* to arrest people who break the law.

dominion   *Dominion* means absolute power or supreme authority. Dictators have *dominion* over their people.

command   *Command* is the power to give orders and demand obedience. It can also be the order itself. A captain is in *command* of the ship. The crew had better obey these *commands!*

control   *Control* is the power to direct and keep someone or something in check or in order. A teacher has *control* of a class. You might lose *control* of your temper during an argument.

mastery   *Mastery* can mean the knowledge or skill that makes a person able to use something. Her *mastery* of spelling patterns enabled her to spell all the words correctly.

See also *strength.*

powerful   *Powerful* means full of power or energy to do or to cause something. A *powerful* engine has enough drive and strength to make a heavy truck move. *Powerful* speakers not only have strong, clear voices, but also speak with such confidence and authority that people listen and believe what they say. A *powerful* person may be one who can lift great weights, or one who can lead people and make them obey.

almighty
omnipotent

Almighty and *omnipotent* mean all-powerful or having complete power over everything. Both words are usually used only when someone is speaking of a Supreme Being.

potent
mighty

Potent and *mighty* describe something or someone powerful. A *potent* drug is very strong and is able to combat disease. The cleaning fluid was so *potent* that it took all the spots off the rug. A *mighty* wind is one that is far stronger than an ordinary wind. The lumberjack chopped down the tree with one *mighty* blow of his ax.

The cleaning fluid was so **potent** that it took all the spots off the rug.

forceful

Forceful means full of force or strength. A *forceful* person does everything with much energy and ability. This organization needs a *forceful* leader to keep all the members interested. Mia offered *forceful* arguments for disagreeing with me.

influential

Influential means powerful, or able to affect what others do or think. An *influential* senator can help get a law passed by persuading other senators to vote for it. A newspaper may be *influential* enough to defeat or elect a candidate.

effective

Effective is the weakest of these words for powerful. It means able to produce or cause some desired result. A bright poster is *effective* because it catches the eye of everyone who passes by. A scolding is *effective* if the kittens that have been scolded stop whatever they were doing.

See also *strong.*

ANTONYMS: helpless, powerless, weak

P

powerless

Powerless means without power or strength or force. The sultan was *powerless* after the legion stormed his palace. A person left *powerless* is unable to act. Sometimes a person becomes *powerless* out of fear or fright. Without his magic sword, the knight was *powerless* to fight the dragon.

helpless

Helpless means powerless to help yourself. A tiny baby is *helpless.* The librarian felt *helpless* without his glasses.

defenseless

Defenseless means unprotected and helpless against any kind of danger, harm, or attack. When the oar was swept away, the canoeist was *defenseless* against the rushing water. A dog without teeth is *defenseless.*

A dog without teeth is
defenseless.

weak

Weak means lacking power or strength. It is the opposite of strong. Sickness can make a person feel *weak.* The radio picked up a *weak* signal from the lost plane. *Weak* lemonade has too much water in it.

ANTONYMS: strong, healthy, powerful

practice (v)

Practice means do something over and over so that you become skilled at it. You have to *practice* if you want to be an expert cook, a safe driver, a fine musician.

drill

Drill means teach something or learn something by saying or doing it over and over until it can be done almost without thinking. Joan's sister *drilled* her on the multiplication tables. The marching band was *drilling* on the field.

practice (v) continued

exercise

Exercise means strengthen something by using it over and over. He *exercises* his muscles by running two miles every day.

• train
• develop
• repeat

Train, develop, and *repeat* are not really synonyms of practice, but they have related meanings. *Train* means prepare for something by drilling for it or being instructed. The speed skater *trained* for six months for the competition. *Develop* means make something change gradually or grow. Gretchen's cold *developed* into pneumonia. You can *develop* your muscles by exercising every day. *Repeat* means say or do something again or many times. They practiced their dance steps by *repeating* them twenty times.

The speed skaters **trained** for six months for the competition.

precious

Precious means having a high value or price. You would not want to lose something that is *precious*. A diamond is a *precious* stone. Your eyesight is *precious*. A picture of someone you love may be *precious* to you even though it is worth nothing to anyone else.

precious continued on page 286 ▶

precious continued from page 285

Some people have some old sneakers that are **dear** to them.

expensive
costly

Expensive and *costly* mean high-priced—maybe higher than a thing is worth. An orchid is one of the most *expensive* flowers you can buy. Heating and lighting the huge mansion was very *costly*.

dear

Dear is sometimes used to describe things that cost a lot because they are scarce. Fresh vegetables are *dear* in winter; they may be cheap in summer. *Dear* also means well loved and valued. You may have a *dear* friend or some old sneakers that are *dear* to you. Grace is my *dearest* friend.

valuable

Valuable can mean important, useful, or worth a lot of money. This ring is a *valuable* piece of jewelry. A stethoscope is a *valuable* instrument to a doctor. People keep their *valuable* papers in a safe place.

priceless

Priceless describes something very precious and valuable because no price would be large enough to pay for it. A *priceless* object cannot be replaced. Happiness is *priceless*. The original Declaration of Independence is *priceless*.

prized
cherished

Something that is *prized* or *cherished* is highly valued and cared for. The dealer would not sell us any stamps from his *prized* collection. Grandmother's most *cherished* possession is her silver teapot.

See also *rare, special.*

ANTONYMS: cheap, inexpensive

present (n)
A *present* is something that is freely given without any payment for it. You may get flowers as a *present* when you're sick.

gift
A *gift* is a present. The blanket that I knitted was my *gift* to the new baby.

contribution
donation
A *contribution* and a *donation* are gifts, usually of money, given to a fund or an organization that puts them to good use. The American Cancer Society uses *contributions* for research. *Donations* to the poor may be clothing, food, and money.

offering
The contribution a person makes to a church is sometimes called an *offering*. If two friends quarrel, one might send the other a gift as a peace *offering*.

grant
A *grant* is a present—usually money—given to a person or an institution for a particular reason. *Grants* are given to students so they may continue their education. He received a *grant* to study in France. The *grant* enabled the university to build a new science building and a library.

favor
A small or inexpensive gift given away is called a *favor*. Every guest at a party may receive a *favor* to take home.

legacy
A *legacy* is something given in a will. It may be money or a valuable possession. These pearls are a *legacy* from my aunt. A *legacy* can also be anything received from the past. Independence is America's *legacy* from the founders of the country.

P

present (v)

Present means give something to someone—usually in a formal way. The children *presented* a bouquet of wild flowers to their teacher on her birthday. She was delighted to receive it. Alex *presented* his ideas on the benefits of the space program to the rest of the class.

contribute
donate

Contribute and *donate* mean give money to a fund that is being collected, or give help to a charity or an organization. Everyone was asked to *contribute* to the fund. He *donated* a dollar. Have you *donated* any clothes to the clothing drive?

grant

Grant is a formal way of giving something that is requested or desired. Mother *granted* me permission to stay overnight at Anna's house. Will you *grant* me this favor?

award

Award means present something that is deserved or earned. He was *awarded* five gold medals for placing first in the swimming competition.

He was **awarded** five gold medals.

bequeath

Bequeath means give or leave something to someone in a will. He *bequeathed* all his property to his children.

ANTONYMS: receive, withhold, get, take back, withdraw

pretend

Pretend means give a false impression or make something appear to be true when it is not. Sometimes people *pretend* to be

288

pretend continued

better at something than they really are. My six-year-old brother *pretends* he's old enough to drive a car. She *pretended* that she had finished her chores, even though she hadn't. He *pretended* that someone else had broken the window.

make believe play
Make believe and *play* can mean pretend to be someone or something else. Some children may *make believe* they are the characters in a book. I taught my dog to roll over and *play* dead. An actor *plays* many different parts on stage.

act
Act means pretend. It usually refers to actors taking the parts of characters in a play or movie. My sister has *acted* in three community plays. *Act* also means pretend to feel something you don't feel. Try to *act* interested in what the speaker is saying. Jody is trying to *act* pleased about the results of the class election.

feign
Feign means give a false appearance. You might have to *feign* a look of surprise when you get a gift if you've peeked at it beforehand. I *feigned* sleep when my mother opened the door, but I had a book under my blanket.

She **feigned** sleep when her mother opened the door, but she had a book under her pillow.

simulate
Simulate means make something act or look like something else. For making movies, fans are used to *simulate* strong wind.

See also *fool* (v), *imitate*.

289

P

promise (v)   *Promise* means give your word to someone. I *promised* to go to the dance with Ted. The tailor has *promised* that my coat will be ready today.

agree   *Agree* means promise to go along with someone else's idea or to do what that person does. You might *agree* to play tennis with your friend even though you'd rather go swimming. They *agreed* to meet at the movie at twelve o'clock. Miriam *agreed* to wait for me if I was late.

swear   *Swear* can mean promise that something is true. When someone is put under oath, that person has to *swear* to tell the truth. When the President of the United States takes the oath of office, he *swears* he will defend the Constitution.

pledge
vow   *Pledge* and *vow* mean make a solemn, or serious, promise. You might *pledge* never to do something again. You often *pledge* your allegiance to the flag. The widow *pledged* a thousand dollars to her church. The children *vowed* to keep their meeting place a secret.

protect   *Protect* means save from harm or injury. A crystal *protects* the face of a watch from being damaged. A heavy coat or jacket *protects* you from cold weather. Welders wear goggles to *protect* their eyes.

guard   *Guard* means watch over something and protect it from danger. A watchdog *guards* its master's house. Sentries were posted to *guard* the entrances to the castle.

protect continued

defend
Defend means protect against whatever danger or attack is present. He *defended* himself by using judo. A public defender is a lawyer who *defends* someone accused of a crime.

shield
screen
Shield and *screen* mean protect against something by putting up or having a barrier in between. Sunglasses *shield* your eyes from the sun. The knight wore a suit of armor to *shield* himself from attacks. The tall apartment building *screens* the sunlight from our house. The mother lion placed her cubs in the tall grass to *screen* them from the approaching hunter.

The knight wore a suit of armor to **shield** himself from attacks.

shelter
harbor
Shelter and *harbor* mean protect by offering a covering or a safe place. A tent *shelters* campers from the cold night air. An inlet *harbors* a boat. It is against the law to *harbor* someone the police are looking for.

keep
Keep means watch and take care of something. Mother *keeps* a vegetable garden. It can also mean prevent someone from having or doing something. The fence *kept* the rabbits out. Try to *keep* from catching cold.

ANTONYMS: endanger, expose

P

proud

Proud people are extremely pleased with themselves, with what they have, or with what they have done. You may be rightly *proud* of some things—*proud* of your parents or *proud* of your brother or sister. You should be *proud* of your country and your school. If you've worked hard and long to accomplish something, you certainly can be *proud* of that. But sometimes you can be too *proud,* and then there are other words to describe you.

haughty

Haughty describes people who act as if they are better than other people, either because of birth or position. Such people are often called "stuck-up." Cinderella's stepsisters were *haughty* toward her.

vain

Vain describes people who are very proud of their appearance and who want others to notice how great or beautiful they are. A *vain* boy may stop to look in every mirror (or shop window!) he passes to admire himself.

A **vain** boy may stop to look in every mirror (or shop window!) he passes to admire himself.

conceited

Conceited people have far too high an opinion of their own worth. They are so pleased with themselves that they hardly think about anyone else. We thought the new girl was *conceited* because she never spoke to anyone.

egotistical

Egotistical comes from the old Latin word "ego," which means "I." An *egotistical* person thinks and talks about himself or herself almost all the time. Practically every third word is "I" or "me."

smug

Smug people are well satisfied with themselves or with something they can do or have done. Almost anyone can be *smug* once in a while. If you are the only one in class who knows the answer to a question, you may feel *smug.* You can be *smug* one minute and humble the next. A *smug* person can be just as unpleasant as a haughty or conceited person is, but usually smugness doesn't last a lifetime, while haughtiness and conceit probably will.

ANTONYMS: humble (adj), modest

pull (v)

Pull is the opposite of push. *Pull* means move an object closer to yourself or move it in the direction you are going. Some objects are easier to *pull* than others. It would not take as much effort to *pull* an empty wagon as it would to *pull* one filled with bricks. And if you accidentally put your hand in boiling water, you would *pull* it out very quickly. Some teeth are harder to *pull* than others. If a drawer is warped, you may not be able to *pull* it open.

pluck
pick

Pluck and *pick* mean pull quickly using just your fingers. A butcher *plucks* chickens by pulling off the feathers. A guitar player *plucks* the strings on the guitar. You can *pick* apples or pears from trees.

jerk

Jerk is a good word to use when you mean pull quickly and suddenly. The rider at the rodeo *jerked* his hat down on his head as the horse started to run and buck.

pull (v) continued on page 294 ▶

P

A violinist **draws** a bow across the violin strings.

pull (v) continued from page 293

yank

Yank means pull hard and fast. You might *yank* open a drawer that is stuck. First my big sister politely asked me to move; then she *yanked* me out of her chair.

tug

Tug means make a number of short, hard pulls. If you *tug* at something very heavy or immovable, you might be able to move it only a short distance or not at all. Little children sometimes *tug* at adults' clothing to get their attention.

draw

If you *draw* something, you pull steadily and firmly. An archer *draws* a bow. A violinist *draws* a bow across the violin strings. The carriage was *drawn* by eight horses.

drag

You may *drag* an object if it is either too heavy or too clumsy to carry. You pull it along the ground—usually very slowly. A small child might *drag* a large stuffed animal across the floor. A lumberjack *drags* heavy logs. If you are extremely tired, you may *drag* your feet when you walk.

haul

Haul means pull something large or heavy for a long distance. Trucks and trains are used to *haul* many things. The truck *hauled* the oranges from Florida to Cleveland.

tow

Tow means pull something behind by using ropes, chains, or bars. You usually *tow* something that could move by itself. You wouldn't *tow* a rock or a building. The tugboats *towed* the freighter to the dock.

ANTONYMS: push (v), shove (v)

push (v)   *Push* means move an object away from yourself. It also means move or make something move forward or backward or out of the way by force. It is the opposite of pull. You may *push* open a stuck door. You *push* a button on a vending machine to obtain the kind of food you want. He *pushed* his way to the head of the line. I was sorry I *pushed* her into the pool.

nudge   *Nudge* and *poke* mean push lightly. You
poke   might *nudge* someone with your elbow to get his or her attention. The pony *nudged* my pocket with its nose, trying to find another lump of sugar. She *poked* me in the ribs. We say that busybodies *poke* their noses into other people's business.

prod   *Prod* can mean push with something sharp or pointed. The farmer *prodded* the mule with a stick. *Prod* can also mean make a person do something by urging that person over and over. Rico had to be *prodded* into joining the volleyball game.

shove   *Shove* means push roughly. People often *shove* each other when they get on and off a crowded bus. *Shove* can also mean push something along a surface. Jerry *shoved* the table across the floor.

drive   *Drive* means push onward, or make something or someone go or move or do something. Farmers *drive* their cattle across a road. A strong wind will *drive* a sailboat. A practical joke might *drive* you to tears.

push (v) continued on page 296 ▶

R

• reflect

Reflect isn't a synonym of remember, but it can be used when you think carefully about things that you remember or things which have taken place in the past. My uncle often *reflects* on his boyhood in Montana.

ANTONYM: forget

repair (v)

Repair means put in good condition again. We *repair* things that are broken, damaged, or run-down. Sheryl sent for an electrician to *repair* the light. The hole in the fence has to be *repaired*.

fix

Fix is the word used most often to mean repair. The leak in the roof has to be *fixed*. My sister helped Dad *fix* the flat tire. Can you *fix* a broken chair?

mend

Mend means put something back into shape or in working order again. You can *mend* a torn page with tape. Dave *mended* the iron pot by welding the broken pieces together. A rip in a sleeve can be *mended* with a needle and thread.

The knees of Barbara's jeans need to be **patched.**

patch

Patch means put a piece of material over a hole, a tear, or a worn spot. We *patch* old clothes. The knees of Barbara's jeans need to be *patched*.

restore

Restore means put something back in its original condition. Part of the city of Williamsburg has been *restored* to look the way it did before the Revolutionary War. Staying in bed when you are sick helps *restore* your health.

ANTONYMS: break (v), destroy, tear (v)

report (v)   *Report* means give an account. You might *report* on something you have done or seen or heard or read. A newscaster *reports* on the news and weather. The secretary *reported* that all members were present at the meeting. A serious automobile accident has to be *reported* to the police.

• relate   *Relate* can mean tell or report something. Gus *related* some of his adventures in the West.

• narrate   *Narrate* means tell a story. A person *narrated* the play as the puppets performed.

• recite   *Recite* means read something out loud or repeat something from memory. When Marvin's grandfather was in school, he had to *recite* the Gettysburg Address.

• reveal
• divulge   *Reveal* and *divulge* mean make known something that has been hidden or kept secret. The bookcase opened to *reveal* a secret passage. The outlaw in the western movie would not *reveal* where he had hidden the stolen money. The spy *divulged* very important information to the enemy. True to her promise, she never *divulged* the secret.

The bookcase opened to **reveal** a secret passage.

R

request (v) *Request* means ask for something or ask someone to do something. You might *request* directions or *request* help in finding your way if you are lost. We were *requested* to leave our boots in the hall when we entered the apartment. My friend *requested* a favor from me, and I didn't refuse. Grandmother *requested* a cup of tea.

beg *Beg* means ask for something over and over again. Irma *begged* for another chance to prove she was not afraid of heights. Flo *begged* her friend to go with her to the play. Dave *begged* me to let him feed my puppy.

beseech *Beseech, implore,* and *plead* mean beg
implore firmly and seriously for something. I
plead *beseech* you to listen to me. The citizens *implored* the town council to use the land for a park instead of a parking lot. I *pleaded* with my brother to let me play his records.

coax *Coax* means ask and persuade someone to do what you want. Martin *coaxed* me to go to the movies by offering to pay my way. We finally *coaxed* the frightened kitten to come out from under the couch.

demand *Demand* means ask for something and insist that you get it. The judge *demanded* order in the court. The customer *demanded* to know why the bill was so high. Our coach *demands* that we get eight hours of sleep each night.

ANTONYMS: refuse (v), decline (v)

306

result (n) Something that happens because of an action may be called the *result* of that action. I fell while I was practicing gymnastics. As a *result,* I have a sprained ankle. The candidate won the election as a *result* of the hard-fought campaign. Many people were forced to leave their homes as a *result* of the flood.

outcome An *outcome* is also the result of something —or the way it comes out. The *outcome* of this year's World Series was hard to predict. If someone goes on and on telling a very long story, you might become impatient and say, "What's the *outcome* of this story?" I was surprised by the *outcome* of the bobsled race.

end The *end* of something can be the outcome. The *end* of a cake-baking venture could be a disaster if you don't stick to the recipe.

consequence *Consequence* means the result of something that happens or exists. A cold room was the *consequence* of leaving the window wide open all day. If you do something bad, you must take the *consequences.* This means that, because of what you've done, you must accept whatever happens. I suffered the *consequences* of having walked in the rain without an umbrella; I caught a cold.

effect *Effect* also means result. One *effect* of a stuffy room may be a sleepy class. What *effect* does eating too much ice cream have on you? What is the *effect* of the drought on the corn crop?

One **effect** of a stuffy room may be a sleepy class.

307

R

right

"Where have you been? Everyone else has been here for an hour. We were wondering what had happened to you!" Bill said as Lisa, Karen, and Roger entered.

"We got lost," Karen announced.

"We were all *right* until we got to the square," explained Roger. "Then Mom made a *right* turn—"

"That wasn't the *right* turn to make!" Bill interrupted him with a laugh. "At the square the *right* turn to make would be left."

"Then those directions you gave us weren't *right*," Lisa put in.

"I'm really sorry," replied Bill. "But at least everything turned out all *right*. Let's get something to eat."

This little scene is not very dramatic, but it does show how a word like *right* can have several different meanings and many synonyms. When *right* means the opposite of left, it is a definite direction. You won't find any synonyms for that. But when *right* means the opposite of wrong, you'll find many shades of meaning. If you are looking for the *right* answer or the *right* time, look under *correct* (adj), the opposite of incorrect.

Many people have trouble finding the *right* thing to say or do in some situation. Some people discover (often too late) that their clothes are not *right* for a certain place or that their behavior is wrong for some occasion. Perhaps they wore shorts and dirty sneakers to a meeting when everyone else looked clean and shining. Perhaps they giggled when they should have been serious. Synonyms for this kind of *right* are under *appropriate* (adj).

If you think some of the rules at school are *right* but some may be wrong, or if you feel that the punishment for disobeying a rule or law is *right* or wrong, you can look for those shades of meaning in the entry *fair* (adj).

Suppose someone handed you three one-dollar bills and told you that two of them were counterfeit. Suppose the person then said, "If you pick out the *right* one, you may spend it." You can find other words for the *right* dollar bill under *real.*

If you ever try to describe something that is just *right* in every way—something that couldn't be better—for those words turn to *perfect* (adj).

Bread dough **rises.**

rise (v)

Rise means go or move in an upward direction. People, animals, and things can *rise.* You *rise* when you get up from a chair. You *rise* every morning when you get out of bed. Your voice *rises* when it gets higher or louder. It falls when it gets lower or softer. And your spirits *rise* when something good or exciting happens. A kite will *rise* in the sky on a windy day. Smoke from a fire *rises.* Bread dough *rises.* Prices *rise.* A hill *rises.* The sun *rises* in the East and sets in the West.

rise (v) continued on page 310 ▶

R

Here are some other words that mean *rise* which can be used more precisely.

soar
Soar means fly at a great height or fly upward. Birds and airplanes *soar* in the sky. A ball will *soar* in the air if you hit it hard.

ascend
Ascend means gradually rise or move upward. Smoke *ascends* from a chimney. An airplane *ascends* when it takes off. It descends when it lands. A climber may *ascend* to the top of a hill or *ascend* to the peak of a mountain.

mount
Mount means go up. You *mount* the stairs or *mount* a ladder. But you also *mount* a horse when you get up on it.

ANTONYMS: fall (v), set (v), descend

rough
Rough is the opposite of smooth and of soft. It is used in many ways. We call a road *rough* when it has many ridges and bumps on it. A piece of wood that hasn't been sanded is *rough.* Coarse material like sandpaper is *rough.* When the wind makes waves on the ocean, we speak of a *rough* sea. Frank snagged his sweater on a *rough* spot on the desk. The hiker twisted an ankle on the *rough* trail.

uneven
Uneven means not smooth or straight or level. A plowed field is *uneven.* A hem on a dress is *uneven* if it is crooked and makes the dress shorter in some places than in others. The bedspread was *uneven*—longer on one side of the bed than on the other.

The mountain path is **rugged** and hard to walk on.

stormy	*Stormy* is used to describe rough weather. A *stormy* sea has huge, crashing waves. Sometimes if a person's life has been rough and unhappy, that person is said to have had a *stormy* life.
craggy jagged	*Craggy* and *jagged* describe rough, uneven, hard surfaces. Rocks, cliffs, and mountain chains are *craggy* or *jagged.* A *craggy* reef can cause much damage to a ship that hits it. You might cut yourself on a *jagged* piece of glass.
rugged	A *rugged* terrain or stretch of land also has a rough surface. The mountain path was *rugged* and hard to walk on. *Rugged* periods of time, like the Great Depression of the 1930s, are harsh and difficult.

See also *rude.*

ANTONYMS: smooth, soft, even, straight, level (adj)

311

R

rude

Rude describes something that is unfinished or undeveloped. A *rude* hut is a small building that has little more than four walls and a roof.

Rude can also mean lacking in manners, because of carelessness or ignorance. When you are invited to a friend's house for dinner, it is *rude* to be late.

uncivilized

Uncivilized means not civilized. People living on an island that is cut off from the rest of the world may be considered *uncivilized* by certain people. People who live differently tend to think that the way they do things is better and more mannerly and correct. Therefore, *uncivilized* has come to describe actions that seem rude and wrong. I thought it was *uncivilized* of them to wear no shoes to my party.

crude

Crude means unpolished or unrefined. *Crude* oil is oil as it comes from the ground, before it has been processed in any way. Once it has been refined, it is no longer *crude* oil. People are *crude* if they are unrefined in their relationships with others. His *crude* way of inviting us to the party was "Well, you're invited, too, if you really feel you have to come."

rough

Rough means not gentle. When *rough* is applied to a person, it usually describes someone who hasn't been around people very much and doesn't know how to act with others. According to some people, cowhands who live mostly on the range may have *rough* ways of speaking.

impolite

Impolite people have bad manners. They are not careful of the way they treat others. Sara was *impolite* when she took all the candy before anyone else could get a piece.

ill-mannered
unmannerly

Ill-mannered and *unmannerly* describe people who are impolite. Sometimes it is embarrassing to eat in a restaurant with Barry because he is so *ill-mannered.* It is *unmannerly* to start eating before everyone is seated.

It is **unmannerly** to start eating before everyone is seated.

discourteous

Discourteous means not considerate of others. The librarian told the group that it was *discourteous* to be so noisy in the library.

disrespectful

Disrespectful means lacking honor for someone or something. It is *disrespectful* not to stand when "The Star-Spangled Banner" is played at a stadium.

ANTONYMS: civilized, refined, gentle, courteous, genial, mannerly, polite, respectful

R

ruin (v)

Ruin means damage something so completely that it can't be repaired or fixed. An object that has been *ruined* has lost all its value or usefulness. The floods in Italy *ruined* many priceless paintings. Moths *ruin* good woolen clothes by eating holes in them. Gwen's plans for camping will be *ruined* if it rains tomorrow.

wreck

Wreck means ruin, usually by breaking or smashing. An iceberg can *wreck* a ship. Two cars were *wrecked* in the collision on the expressway.

destroy
demolish

Destroy and *demolish* are used when something is smashed to pieces or pulled down. An earthquake and fire once *destroyed* almost an entire city. Many buildings have to be *demolished* before the new highway can be built.

Many buildings have to be **demolished** before the new highway can be built.

spoil

Spoil also means ruin something so that it can't be used. An early frost *spoiled* the farmer's crops. Milk will *spoil* if it is not kept cold.

See also *harm* (v).

ANTONYMS: repair (v), fix (v), build, construct

314

run (v)   *Run* means move fast and steadily. An animal *runs* by taking steps so long and so rapid that at one point of each step all its feet are off the ground. An engine *runs* well if all of its parts move steadily and smoothly. Water or some other liquid *runs* if it moves steadily along some route or in some direction. I poured too much milk, and it *ran* down the outside of the glass onto the table.

gallop   A horse can run in several different ways
lope   and at different speeds. It runs fastest
trot   when it *gallops,* using springy, leaping steps. It *lopes* when it runs with long steps in an easy, steady, fairly fast motion. It *trots* when it moves just a little faster than walking. These words are often used to describe ways a person can run.

race   *Race, sprint,* and *jog* are three kinds of
sprint   running that people often do. You *race* if
jog   you go very fast, usually to beat someone else to a goal. You can *race* to beat a time limit too. Betty *raced* me to the end of the block, but I won. You'd better *race* to the post office before it closes, or you won't get a stamp. If you run as fast as you can for just a short distance, you are *sprinting.* The bell rang as I turned the corner, so I *sprinted* the rest of the way. If you run slowly, just to be running and not to get somewhere in a hurry, you *jog.* You can get a lot of exercise if you *jog* for half an hour every morning.

run (v) continued on page 316 ▶

run (v) continued from page 315

R

flow
Liquid *flows* when it runs steadily. Blood *flows* through veins and arteries.

operate
When an engine runs, it is *operating*. Our lawn mower *operates* on electricity. The big presses *operate* all night to print the morning newspaper. The elevator has been *operating* perfectly since it was repaired.

The big presses **operate** day and night to print magazines.

flee
You *flee* if you run away from some danger or some unpleasant situation. People *flee* from a burning house. When the burglar alarm went off, the bank robber tried to *flee* in a truck.

escape
If you get out and run away from some place where you have been shut or locked up, you *escape*. Animals sometimes *escape* from the zoo. Grandpa's canary *escaped* when he opened the door of its cage.

abscond
If you run away or leave home secretly to avoid being arrested or captured, and then hide, you are *absconding. Abscond* is often followed by *with.* The day before the bank officials came to check the books, an employee *absconded with* a million dollars.

S

sad

Sad means not feeling happy or pleased or glad about something. People feel *sad* when they lose things or when something bad happens. When my pet rabbit ran away, I felt *sad* and lonely. They were *sad* when they heard the news of the tragedy. Sue becomes very quiet when she's *sad.*

unhappy

Unhappy means sad and not cheerful. Not being included in the basketball game hurt Kay's feelings and made her *unhappy.* Al was *unhappy* when the picnic got rained out.

mournful
sorrowful

Mournful and *sorrowful* mean full of sadness and grief for something. The nation was *mournful* over the death of its leader. One kind of dove is called a "mourning dove" because of its *mournful* call. We knew something was wrong when we saw the *sorrowful* look on Tad's face.

downcast
depressed

Someone who is *downcast* or *depressed* feels sad and discouraged about something. You might feel *downcast* or *depressed* when things don't turn out the way you want them to. Jackie was *downcast* after her puppy ran away. When he didn't get the paper route, Neil was *depressed* for weeks.

gloomy
blue

Gloomy and *blue* mean low in spirits. A person can feel *blue.* And a dark, rainy day can make someone feel *gloomy.*

melancholy

Someone is in a *melancholy* mood when that person is sad and thoughtful. Some music can put you in a *melancholy* mood.

sad continued on page 318 ▸

miserable

Miserable means very sad or unhappy. A cold can make a person feel *miserable*. *Miserable* can also describe something that makes someone feel sad or unhappy. On a *miserable* day nothing goes right.

ANTONYMS: happy, pleased, glad, cheerful, excited, gay, lively, merry

On a **miserable** day, nothing goes right.

sadness

Sadness is a feeling you have when you are sad and unhappy. There was much *sadness* at the zoo when the baby elephant hurt its leg. When they moved to another town, the children experienced *sadness* at leaving their friends.

sorrow

Sorrow is a feeling you have when you are sorrowful or grief-stricken. The people of the United States were filled with *sorrow* when President Kennedy was killed.

melancholy

Melancholy means a feeling you have when you are sad and thoughtful. Pat couldn't explain the feeling of *melancholy* that seemed to weigh him down.

gloom

Gloom is a lowness of spirits. Joyce was the picture of *gloom* as she watched her friends go off to camp.

woe
: *Woe* is deep sadness or grief or suffering. The illness of his dog caused him *woe*. *Woe* is also used, at times, to mean great distress. My cousin is learning the *woes* of being a baby-sitter.

despair
: *Despair* is a loss of hope in something or someone. People who are in *despair* have lost confidence in themselves or in others. She was in *despair* when she found it was her best friend who had made fun of her.

See also *misery*.

ANTONYMS: happiness, gladness, hope (n), expectation, hopefulness

safe (adj)
: *Safe* is the opposite of dangerous. *Safe* means free from danger or harm or risk. You should always put your valuables in a *safe* place. Water is tested to see if it is *safe* for drinking.

secure
: *Secure* means safe or free from fear, anxiety, or uneasiness. Dad felt *secure* after locking all the doors. If something is *secure,* it won't break, collapse, or fall. It won't be lost or stolen. Before climbing the ladder, Eve made sure it was *secure* against the building. The square knot is *secure;* it won't slip.

protected
: *Protected* means kept safe from danger. Your basement is a *protected* place to stay during a tornado. Forest preserves, state parks, and national parks are *protected* areas where animals are safe from hunters.

safe (adj) continued on page 320 ▶

safe (adj) continued from page 319

A **harmless** snake is not poisonous.

snug

Snug means safe and comfortable. We sometimes think of a small and cozy room as being very *snug.* The baby was *snug* and warm in the crib.

harmless

Something is *harmless* if it causes no harm or injury. Plastic scissors are *harmless* because they are not sharp or pointed. That dog barks a lot, but it is really *harmless.* A *harmless* snake is not poisonous.

ANTONYMS: dangerous, poisonous, risky, hazardous, precarious, unsafe

satisfy

If something *satisfies,* it does whatever you need or expect it to do. A bag of jellybeans *satisfied* my craving for sweets. He can't seem to *satisfy* his piano teacher, no matter how hard he tries. She couldn't join the club because she didn't *satisfy* its age requirement.

answer

Answer means satisfy or fill the needs of something. The invention of the sewing machine *answered* the need for mass production of clothes. If you can't find a screwdriver, a nail file will *answer* the purpose.

please
gratify

Please and *gratify* mean give pleasure or satisfy. A vacation in the country would *please* Mother. It always *gratifies* my grandparents to receive a letter from me. My aunt was *gratified* to hear that we had enjoyed her homemade jam.

appease

Appease means gratify completely by doing whatever is necessary to please someone.

To *appease* my brother, I promised to help him wash the car.

content

Content means satisfy to some degree, but not by meeting every wish or desire. An ice-cream cone will *content* Nelson for a while. *Content* also means limit your wishes or actions. We should try to *content* ourselves with what we have.

save

Save is the opposite of throw away and spend. *Save* means hold on to something. You might *save* a souvenir from a trip. People often *save* things that they may need later. You *save* your allowance if you don't spend it. You sometimes can *save* time by taking a shortcut.

Save also means treat something carefully. You will *save* your eyes if you always read in a good light.

Save can mean protect something or someone from harm or danger. Firefighters *save* burning buildings if they can. Doctors *save* lives.

save continued on page 322 ▶

People might **save** a souvenir from a trip.

321

S

save continued from page 321

keep

Keep is a good synonym for save. Did you *keep* the book I gave you? The captain *kept* the ship from capsizing during a typhoon.

economize

Economize means use things carefully and not waste them. We *economize* when we don't squander our money.

accumulate

Accumulate can mean save gradually. You can *accumulate* a lot of money by saving regularly.

store

Store means save for a later use. Our family *stored* our furniture in a warehouse until the apartment was ready.

conserve
preserve

Conserve and *preserve* mean keep something safe or keep something from being used up. We speak of *conserving* forests, wildlife, and other natural resources. Scuba divers must *conserve* their oxygen supply. You *preserve* certain foods by canning them or by keeping them in a refrigerator or freezer.

rescue

Rescue means save someone or something from danger or destruction. The Coast Guard *rescued* the dog that was trapped on the ice in the middle of the lake.

See also *free* (v).

ANTONYMS: throw away, spend, discard, squander, destroy, let go

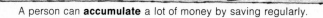

A person can **accumulate** a lot of money by saving regularly.

Janet **professed** her belief in
unidentified flying objects.

say

pronounce

profess

swear

When you *say* something, you express a
thought by using spoken words. What did
you *say* to Uncle Howie when you saw
him? It is possible for *say* to be used in
other ways—What does the clock *say*?
What has Aunt Marilyn *said* in her letter?
The sign *says* "Danger." The look he gave
me *said* more than any words he could *say*.

For finding synonyms, though, *say* is used
in this book to mean speak in words.

Pronounce means say carefully or solemnly.
A judge *pronounced* sentence on the thief.
The minister *pronounced* them husband
and wife in the wedding ceremony.

Profess means say freely and clearly that
you believe something. You *profess* loyalty
to your country. Janet *professed* her belief
in unidentified flying objects.

The word *swear* can mean say solemnly or
promise something. Do you *swear* to tell
the whole truth and nothing but the truth?
He *swore* he'd do better next time. I could
have sworn I knew the girl sitting across
from me on the bus.

While *pronounce, profess,* and *swear* are
good synonyms for *say,* you would
probably never use them instead of *say*
when you are writing a conversation that is
set off by quotation marks. The rest of the
synonyms for *say,* listed on the next page,
may well be used for any kind of writing
you are likely to do.

say continued on page 324 ▶

S

state

State means say. Mario *stated* his name and address when he ordered the tools. "I'll wait here," the woman *stated* firmly.

declare

Declare means say publicly or seriously. Donald Bloomfield *declared* his candidacy for the Senate. "I'm going to ski only on the beginners' slopes," *declared* Nate.

mention

Mention means say something to refer or call attention to something. Mother *mentioned* that it was getting late. I heard someone *mention* my name in the elevator. "Don't forget the pickles," Jean *mentioned* as she went out the door.

comment

Comment means state your opinion on something. Lots of people *commented* on my oil paintings. "Your shirt is dirty," *commented* Vince.

murmur
mutter

Murmur and *mutter* both mean make a low sound that is hard to hear, or say words that are hard to understand or distinguish. Mother was *murmuring* softly to the baby, hoping the child would fall asleep. Carol *murmured* something in my ear, but I only understood half of what she said. The bus driver *muttered* angrily under his breath. The boy *muttered*, "I'll get even with you." Jane walked by, *muttering* to herself.

repeat

Repeat means say again or say over and over. You can *repeat* what you have said or *repeat* what someone else has said. He had to *repeat* his name three times before I could understand it. Don't *repeat* the secret I told you.

scare (v)
Scare means fill with sudden fear. If something *scares* you, you might scream. If you're "*scared* stiff," you might not be able to move at all. Hearing strange sounds in the middle of the night *scares* me.

Someone who is "**scared** stiff" might not be able to move at all.

frighten
Frighten is another word for scare. Is Edgar *frightened* by the dark? The growling dog *frightens* everyone who walks by.

startle
Startle means scare and surprise. If something *startles* you, you might move away or jump back quickly. The sudden clap of thunder *startled* me.

alarm
Alarm can mean make afraid and worried because of some possible danger. The approaching storm *alarmed* the sailors.

intimidate
cow
bully
Intimidate, cow, and *bully* mean force a person to do something out of fear. People can *intimidate* others by threatening them. Our pile of snowballs *cowed* the enemy in the snow fort across the street. The older girls thought they could *bully* us into leaving the pool.

Bully also means pick on or tease someone younger or weaker than yourself. The kids upstairs started to *bully* the new boy.

terrify
terrorize
Terrify and *terrorize* mean cause great fear, panic, or terror. The fire in the barn *terrified* the horses. The tiger had been *terrorizing* the villagers for weeks.

ANTONYMS: calm (v), comfort (v), quiet (v), soothe

325

The crowd **scattered** when the rain began to come down.

scatter

Scatter means throw things here and there, often not caring where they land. At one time farmers *scattered* seeds by hand over a field. You might *scatter* things all over your room when you are looking for something.

Scatter also means separate or cause to go in different directions. A gust of wind will *scatter* leaves over a yard. The crowd *scattered* when it started to rain.

strew

Strew means cover an area by scattering things over it. You might *strew* your desk with books. The floor was *strewn* with the baby's toys.

spread

Spread can mean scatter or distribute. News *spreads* if it reaches many different people. An infection or disease may also *spread*.

disperse

Disperse means cause a group of people to break up and go off in different directions. The police tried to *disperse* the crowd that had gathered near the burning building. The fans *dispersed* after the game.

dispel

Dispel means scatter or drive away. The hot sun *dispelled* the rain clouds. The good news *dispelled* her worries.

squander

Squander means scatter or throw away foolishly money or something else. The inventor *squandered* his money and time on many worthless ideas.

See also *throw* (v).

ANTONYMS: gather, collect

326

see

Bob: My aunt can *see* with her tongue.
Bill: That's silly. What can she *see* with her tongue?
Bob: She can *see* if the soup's hot.

See means take in or receive by using your eyes. But we use the word in many more ways. You can *see* who's at the door. You can just *see* yourself leading a parade. Some folks *have seen* better days. You might suddenly *see* what someone has been trying to teach you. If you begin a project, you should *see* it through.

See and *look* or *look at* are almost synonyms. But actually when you *look,* you have to move or direct your eyes toward something. So before crossing a street, you *look* both ways. You can *see* out of the corner of your eye. You can *see* things without directly *looking at* them.

In this book you will find entries dealing with four different ways to *see.* Under *look* (v) are words for directing your eyes toward something. *Examine* and words listed there mean *look at* closely to learn, understand, or test something. *Notice* (v) has words for *seeing* and taking note of what you *see.* *Watch* (v) includes words for following the action of something—like a game—as well as words for carefully *seeing* that things are all right or that nothing will happen. *Look up* these entries. *Notice* the shades of difference in meaning. *Examine* your speech and writing to *see* how precise you can be. But *watch* it!

S

send

Send means cause something or someone to move from one place to another. It is the opposite of receive. You may have received more valentines than you *sent.* Your mother may *have sent* you on an errand. You can *send* a football flying through the air if you kick it hard.

mail

Mail means send someone a letter or a postcard or a package through the post office. After you *mail* a letter, it is transported by train or truck or plane. A letter carrier then takes it to the address of the person you sent it to.

deliver

Deliver can mean send to a destination. The pizza we ordered will be *delivered* in ten minutes. Do you know anyone who *delivers* newspapers after school?

truck
ship

Truck and *ship* mean send something aboard a truck or a ship. Farmers *truck* their produce all over the country. Some foreign nations *ship* their goods to the United States. *Ship* is also often used to mean send by any means at all. Please *ship* at once the plants and seeds we ordered. (You don't care how they are sent.)

dispatch

Dispatch means send off. A teacher might *dispatch* a student with a note for the principal.

transmit

Transmit means send a message or a signal from one place or one person to another. Telegraph operators *transmit* messages. When you talk to someone on the phone, your voice is *transmitted* over a wire.

Telegraph operators **transmit** messages.

drive You *drive* someone or something when you make the person or thing go to another place. You can *drive* away some noisy birds or *drive* off a vicious dog. You *drive* a ball when you hit it hard and send it a great distance.

See also *carry.*

serious If something is *serious,* it is important and must not be treated lightly. A *serious* problem or decision may need a lot of thought.

Serious also describes something that is not humorous or amusing. Jenny gave a very *serious* speech about the economy.

Serious can describe people who are deeply concerned with and interested in important matters. When it comes to doing something about pollution, Bob is *serious.*

Serious also means having great importance because of some possible danger or harm. You might hear of someone being in *serious* condition in a hospital.

Other words are better to use than *serious* for some of these meanings.

sober *Sober* can mean serious and thoughtful. The television announcer gave a *sober* comment on the day's news. A *sober* person is one who is sensible, levelheaded, and hard-working.

serious continued on page 330 ▸

S

A **grave** or **solemn** ceremony is very formal and impressive.

grave
solemn

Grave and *solemn* mean serious and dignified. A *grave* look on your friend's face might tell you that something is bothering your friend. A *grave* or *solemn* ceremony is very formal and impressive. The girls made a *solemn* promise never to reveal their secret meeting place.

thoughtful
earnest

Thoughtful and *earnest* describe people who think things over carefully and are serious about what they do. They don't rush into things or make hasty decisions. There was a *thoughtful* look on the man's face as he read the letter. Toshio is *earnest* about wanting to go to college.

important

Important is the opposite of trivial and frivolous. Something is *important* if it means a lot to someone and has great worth or value. We speak of making *important* decisions, meeting *important* people, and remembering *important* dates.

See also *heavy*.

ANTONYMS: flighty, trivial, frivolous, lighthearted, minor

shake (v)   *Shake* means move up and down or back and forth. You can *shake* something, or something may cause you to *shake.* You might *have shaken* a bottle of salad dressing before you poured it over your salad. Perhaps you *shook* sand out of your shoe after a day at the beach. You might *shake* your head instead of answering "no." People *shake* hands when they are introduced to each other. People or animals might *shake* if they are afraid. The whole stadium seemed to *shake* from the roar of the crowd.

The whole stadium seemed to **shake** from the roar of the crowd.

tremble
shudder
shiver

Tremble, shudder, and *shiver* mean shake without meaning to, because of fear or excitement or cold. You might *tremble* if you saw a huge grizzly bear coming toward you. People may *shudder* when they see or think of something awful or terrible. He *shuddered* at the thought of being left alone in a deserted house. People *shiver* when they are cold.

shake (v) continued on page 332 ◗

331

S

quiver

Quiver means shake or tremble slightly. A child's lip may *quiver* just before he or she begins to cry. Leaves on a tree *quiver* when a breeze moves them.

quake

Quake means shake violently. An explosion can make the ground *quake.* We were *quaking* with fear as we waited for the hurricane to turn inland.

sway
rock
vibrate

Sway, rock, and *vibrate* are all good words to use when something or someone moves or is caused to move back and forth or from side to side. You *sway* when you lose your balance and lean first in one direction, then in the other. Ernie *swayed* after getting off the ride at the carnival. Trees *sway* during a storm. A boat *rocks* on stormy waters. You might *rock* a baby to sleep. Something *vibrates* when it shakes rapidly. You might feel the whole house *vibrate* when a heavy truck passes.

Trees **sway** during a storm.

shape (n)   Everybody and almost everything has a *shape.* The *shape* of a thing is its outward appearance, its length, width, and thickness. The *shape* of a carrot is different from the *shape* of a beet. A globe has the same *shape* as a ball. Myra's grandfather gave her a locket in the *shape* of a heart.

form   The *form* of something can be the way its parts are put together or arranged. Cookies baked in the *form* of lions, tigers, and elephants are called animal crackers. In a fairy tale you may read about a prince being changed into the *form* of a frog.

figure   *Figure* is another synonym for shape. Some weather vanes have the *figure* of a rooster. I saw the dim *figure* of a man in the fog.

outline   An *outline* is a line that shows the outer shape of something. When children color, they sometimes begin by tracing along the *outline* before they color the picture completely.

silhouette   A *silhouette* is an outline that has been filled in with a dark color. You can make a *silhouette* by cutting out a shape from black paper and placing it on a light background. That distant tree makes a lovely *silhouette* against the sky.

• profile   Your *profile* is what you look like from the side. When drawing the *profile* of a face, an artist may draw only an outline or draw every feature that can be seen from just one side—one eye, one ear, and so on.

See also *plan* (n).

shape (v)

A blacksmith **forges** tools and horseshoes on a heavy iron anvil.

Shape means give a shape or form to an object or to some material. You can *shape* clay, wood, paper, metal, plastic, mud, and even snow in many ways.

mold

Mold can mean shape something with your hands. People *mold* clay into different figures. It can also mean shape something using a mold—a hollow frame or container. When certain liquids are poured into a mold, they take the shape of the mold as they harden. You can *mold* gelatin into many different shapes.

model

Model can mean shape using a plan or pattern. It often means copy something else. The boy *modeled* a horse out of clay. This building is *modeled* after an ancient temple.

forge

Forge means shape metals by heating and hammering them. A blacksmith *forges* tools and horseshoes on a heavy iron anvil.

bend

Bend is the opposite of straighten. *Bend* means shape by turning, curving, or twisting something. The plumber had to *bend* the water pipes.

fit

To *fit* something, you shape it to the right size. Jill cut the wallpaper to *fit* around the window.

form

Form means shape or mold something. You can *form* letters out of pipe cleaners. A gym class may *form* a circle to do exercises.

See also *create*.

ANTONYM: straighten

shelter (n)   A *shelter* is something that covers or protects. Peggy used a box as a *shelter* for the baby chicks. Our only *shelter* against the rain was a newspaper. A *shelter* is also a place that protects. People wait in the *shelter* at the bus stop when the weather's bad.

- protection   *Protection* can refer to anything that protects or keeps from harm or injury. Vaccine is a *protection* against disease.

- shield   A *shield* is a protection against something harmful. Knights carried *shields* to protect themselves from enemy swords. Asbestos suits worn by firefighters are *shields* against the smoke and flames.

- sanctuary
- refuge   *Sanctuary* and *refuge* mean protection or shelter from danger or distress. Sometimes the United States gives *sanctuary* to people who have fled their own country. A wildlife *sanctuary* is a place where wild animals may live and not be hunted. The flood victims were given *refuge* in the school auditorium. The farmer built a bird *refuge* so that birds could stop and feed on their way south.

- dwelling   A *dwelling* is a house or a place of shelter. After a week of camping in the woods, I was glad to sleep in a comfortable *dwelling*.

- harbor   A *harbor* is a protected area of water where ships may anchor safely. Sometimes *harbor* is used to mean any safe place. The stray dog found a safe *harbor* on a farm.

S

shining

Shining describes something that gives off or reflects light. A *shining* object has a bright appearance, like the *shining* sun. Many trophies are made of *shining* silver. *Shining* can also mean very smart or outstanding. Someone is a *shining* athlete if that person performs well in sports.

radiant

Radiant means glowing or shining brightly. The sky was *radiant* as the sun rose above the hills. Someone who looks very happy can be called *radiant*. Abe had a *radiant* smile on his face when he won the state spelling bee.

lustrous

Lustrous can be used to describe a shining and glossy surface. A wood table can be kept *lustrous* by dusting and polishing. Alice's horse has a *lustrous* coat.

sparkling
twinkling

Sparkling and *twinkling* describe an unsteady light. *Sparkling* means sending out sparks or quick bursts of light. Some fireworks give off *sparkling* light. *Sparkling* snow covered the branches. A *twinkling* light seems to flash on and off. On a clear night you can see hundreds of *twinkling* stars. The *twinkling* lights of the cabin shone through the forest.

shimmering
glimmering

Shimmering and *glimmering* mean shining faintly and softly. The sailboat glided across the *shimmering,* moonlit waters. The *glimmering* wings of the airplane disappeared into the clouds.

ANTONYMS: dark, dim (adj), dull

The sailboat glided across the **shimmering,** moonlit waters.

336

A salesperson may clean a rug to **demonstrate** how a vacuum cleaner works.

show (v)

Show can mean cause something to be seen. You may want to *show* your new watch to a friend. By frowning, people may *show* that they are displeased with something. *Show* also means explain or make something clear. You might *show* someone how to make something.

display
exhibit

Display and *exhibit* mean show things in a way that draws the attention of other people. A store manager tries to *display* merchandise attractively so that people will want to buy it. Artists *exhibit* their work at art fairs.

demonstrate

Demonstrate means show how something is done. A salesperson may clean a rug to *demonstrate* how a vacuum cleaner works.

signify

Signify means show or make something known by a sign or a signal or a certain action. Senator Torres *signified* disapproval of the bill by voting "nay."

reveal

Reveal also means make something known. But you *reveal* things that have previously been concealed or things that should be hidden. The engineer *revealed* plans for the new shopping mall. I promised never to *reveal* the secret.

illustrate

Illustrate means make something clear by pictures or examples. The pictures in your thesaurus *illustrate* the meanings of words. Geography books are *illustrated* with maps and diagrams.

ANTONYMS: conceal, hide (v)

337

S

show (n)   A *show* is something presented for people to see or view. People who like animals would enjoy going to a horse *show* or a dog *show*. Someone who gets angry in front of others may put on quite a *show*. Josh was too sick to attend the farm *show*.

display   A *display* is something arranged to be viewed. Many stores have *displays* of merchandise in their windows. Barry set up a *display* of ancient arrowheads.

exhibit   An *exhibit* is something shown or put on view. You can see an *exhibit* of farm products or an *exhibit* of farm equipment at a county fair.

exhibition
exposition   An *exhibition* and an *exposition* are shows usually open to the public. The museum has an *exhibition* showing circus life in the 1800s. The World's Columbian *Exposition* was held in Chicago in 1893.

performance   A *performance* can be a play or some other form of entertainment. We saw the dancer's last *performance* before she retired from the stage. Lydia and Ron decided to go to the 8:00 *performance*.

spectacle   A *spectacle* is also a show. We usually think of a *spectacle* as being an unusual or exciting show. The *spectacle* of fireworks is always breathtaking.

Often *spectacle* is used to mean behavior that is not appropriate or acceptable. People who lose their tempers can "make *spectacles* of themselves."

338

shrink

Shrink means become or make smaller. The hot water *shrank* my wool sweater. Everyone noticed that the roast *had shrunk* while it was cooking.

contract

Contract is the opposite of expand. When something *contracts,* it becomes smaller. Pipes expand during the summer heat and *contract* in the winter cold. The pupil of your eye expands in the dark and *contracts* as light strikes it.

compress

Compress means make something smaller or make it occupy less space by pressing, squeezing, or flattening. You *compress* air when you pump it in a bicycle tire. You *compress* a handful of snow to make a snowball.

condense

Condense can mean become or make something more firmly packed. Dave *condensed* into one box the magazines that were scattered all over the floor. *Condense* can also mean write or say something in fewer words. A book reviewer *condenses* a story by leaving out details.

deflate

Deflate is the opposite of inflate. It means release the air or gas from something. If you *deflate* a balloon, it will collapse.

If someone **deflates** a balloon, it will collapse.

shrivel

Shrivel means shrink by drying up. Under direct sunlight grapes *shrivel* into raisins. A flower *shrivels* if it is broken from its stem and can't get water.

See also *decrease* (v).

ANTONYMS: expand, inflate, swell (v)

339

It wasn't really funny when Nick accidentally **shut** Joe **in** the closet.

shut (v)

Shut means move something into place in order to stop up an opening. *Shut* also means move something into place to stop something or somebody from coming in or going out. It is the opposite of open. You might *shut* your door if you don't want to be disturbed. You *have shut* your eyes when you go to sleep. You *shut up* when you stop talking. I lost my key and was *shut out* of the house. It wasn't really funny when Nick accidentally *shut* me *in* the closet.

close

Close means shut off an opening or a passage. You *close* a box when you put a lid on it. Karen *closed* the corral gate after exercising the horses. The street was *closed* to traffic during the parade.

suspend

Suspend means stop or shut off something for a certain time. The U.S. government *suspends* mail deliveries on national holidays. *Suspend* also means shut someone out for a period of time. A club might *suspend* a member who doesn't obey the rules.

confine

Confine means shut in. Inmates are *confined* to prisons until they have served their sentences.

exclude

Exclude means shut out. A window shade *excludes* light. You *exclude* people from an activity when you don't let them join in the fun. Anyone with mumps is confined indoors, and all visitors are *excluded.*

ANTONYMS: open (v), admit, include

shy

Shy means timid and uneasy in the presence of others. It also means easily frightened. *Shy* people do not have confidence in themselves. They feel uncomfortable being with and talking to other people—especially strangers. *Shy* people may have a hard time making new friends. Jeff was too *shy* to try out for the chorus. Some animals are *shy* of people.

bashful

Bashful describes a person who is shy and easily embarrassed. My little brother was too *bashful* to say hello.

modest

Modest people are not vain or conceited. *Modest* persons would rather praise other people's accomplishments than call attention to their own.

coy

A *coy* person just pretends to be shy. Some of the guests thought Alice was shy, but her friends knew she was just *coy.*

ANTONYMS: vain, conceited, confident, daring (adj)

sign (n)

A *sign* is something that stands for, represents, or points out something else. There are many kinds of *signs.* There is a stop *sign* at an intersection. A store may have a *sign* in its window. A robin may be the first *sign* of spring.

• symbol

A *symbol* is usually an object that stands for something else. The eagle is a *symbol* of the United States. The American flag is also a *symbol* of the country.

sign (n) continued on page 342 ▶

S

• signal

A *signal* can be a warning sign or a sign that alerts us to something. A flashing red light can be a *signal* that tells you to stop at a railroad crossing.

• gesture

A *gesture* is a sign made by moving some part of your body—usually your head, arms, or hands. Putting a finger to your lips is a *gesture* that says be quiet.

• symptom

A *symptom* can be a sign that a person is sick. A sore throat and a runny nose could be *symptoms* of a cold.

• token

A *token* is a sign or symbol of something. It is usually an object which substitutes for, or gives proof of, some thought, feeling, or thing. You may give someone a gift as a *token* of your friendship.

• omen

An *omen* is a sign of something that may happen in the future. People who are superstitious think that breaking a mirror is an *omen* of seven years of bad luck.

• badge

A *badge* is a small sign that someone wears. A *badge* may show that a person is a member of a certain group or organization. A *badge* may indicate that the person wearing it has done some outstanding deed or deserves special respect. Scouts work hard to earn merit *badges*. A police officer wears a *badge*.

• emblem

An *emblem* is a badge. Most organizations have *emblems*. The *emblem* of the Olympic games is five interlocking circles.

See also *warning*.

A flashing red light can be a **signal** that tells you to stop at a railroad crossing.

silent	*Silent* means without any sound or noise. A *silent* person is not talkative. You are asked to be *silent* in a library. The class was *silent* while Enrique spoke.
quiet	*Quiet* means without much noise or commotion. Mom and Dad wanted to spend a *quiet* evening at home after a busy day at their offices.
still	*Still* means silent and motionless. The air is *still* when there isn't any wind. There wasn't a ripple on the *still* pond.
noiseless	*Noiseless* means with little or no noise. Chess is a *noiseless* game, but you wouldn't call football *noiseless*.
dumb speechless mute	*Dumb, speechless,* and *mute,* all mean unable or unwilling to speak. Animals are *dumb.* Some people are *speechless* when something frightens, shocks, or surprises them. Millie was *speechless* when she saw the washed-out bridge ahead. Chuck remained *mute* instead of admitting his mistake. Some people who are deaf and *mute* can learn to speak.

ANTONYMS: talkative, restless, boisterous, loud, noisy

simple	*Simple* means not hard or difficult to do or understand. It doesn't take very long to solve a *simple* problem. It's *simple* to ride a bike, once you learn how. Jo's directions to her house were so *simple* that I had no trouble following them.

simple continued on page 344 ▶

S

simple continued from page 343

easy

Something is *easy* if it takes just a little work or effort to do. Some books are *easy* to read. It's *easy* to make a cake from a cake mix. It's *easy* for a stranger to get lost in a big city.

effortless

Effortless means needing little strength, energy, or thought. Something can become *effortless* through practice. Riding a horse seems *effortless* for an experienced rider. Putting all the names in alphabetical order seemed *effortless* by the time Craig got to the "R"s.

Riding a horse seems **effortless** for an experienced rider.

uncomplicated

Uncomplicated means simple and not at all confusing. If the instructions on a hobby kit are *uncomplicated,* they are easy to figure out.

plain

Plain means clear and obvious. The moral of that fable is as *plain* as day. It is *plain* to see that Harvey has the measles.

ANTONYMS: hard, difficult, complex, complicated, intricate

skillful	*Skillful* means able to do something well. The most *skillful* students displayed their pottery in an exhibit.
able capable	*Able* and *capable* mean skillful. They often suggest that someone can do something exceptionally well and often quite easily. Because he was such an *able* pilot, he successfully landed the crippled plane on the road. Alice is *capable* of playing three instruments.
ingenious	*Ingenious* means skillful in inventing or discovering things. Thomas A. Edison was an *ingenious* scientist. The light bulb is an *ingenious* invention.
clever cunning	*Clever* and *cunning* mean skillful in a quick or crafty way. Aunt Ellen did not expect Rose to give such a *clever* answer to the riddle. The fox is a *cunning* hunter.
dexterous handy	*Dexterous* and *handy* describe people with the ability to use their hands well. A dentist has to be *dexterous*. A *dexterous* typist is constantly in demand. Mom and Dad are *handy* at fixing things around the house.

ANTONYMS: unskillful, awkward, clumsy, stupid, unable

A **dexterous** typist is constantly in demand.

S

slant (v)

Something *slants* if it doesn't extend in a straight line up and down or in a straight line across. For instance, your handwriting *slants* when your letters do not go straight up and down. The roof of a barn *slants*. The legs of a stepladder *slant*.

slope

Slope is usually used in place of slant when you speak of the ground or land. *Slope* means slant gradually. A hill *slopes* toward its base. The winding path *sloped* toward the river.

lean

If something *leans,* it isn't standing or placed straight up. You might *lean* to one side if you lose your balance. But you wouldn't say you are slanting to one side. You can *lean* your back against a wall or *lean* a ladder against a building. Someone with a sprained ankle may *lean* against you to walk.

list

A boat *lists* when it leans in one direction. A sudden shift in the wind can make a sailboat *list*.

tip

Tip means slant or cause something to slant and possibly overturn. Maria *tipped* over the glass of water.

tilt

Tilt also means slant or cause to slant. A table will *tilt* if the legs are uneven. A seesaw *tilts* as it moves up and down.

incline

Incline means slant or bow, but it is more formal. The driveway *inclines* away from the house. You might say you *incline* your head when someone whispers in your ear.

slender   *Slender* describes something that is narrow and not wide. An arrow has a *slender* shaft. A *slender* person is not fat or stout.

thin   *Thin* can mean slender and not heavy or thick. Plywood is made by pressing and gluing *thin* sheets of wood together.

slim
slight   *Slim* and *slight* can mean slender and sometimes small and unimportant. You can keep *slim* by exercising. There is only a *slim* chance that it will snow. A *slight* person doesn't weigh much. I have a *slight* headache.

fine   *Fine* can mean very thin. I like to use a pen with a *fine* point.

tenuous   *Tenuous* can describe a long piece of rope or thread or wire that is or looks extremely thin. We watched breathlessly as the circus performer inched across the *tenuous* high wire.

See also *thin.*

ANTONYMS: wide, fat, stout, heavy, thick, coarse, broad

People watched breathlessly as the circus performer inched across the **tenuous** high wire.

S

sneak (v)   *Sneak* means go or move in a secret or sly way. He *sneaked* into the kitchen and ate a piece of cake when I wasn't looking.

slink   *Slink* means sneak away in order not to attract attention. I saw one boy *slink* around the corner as a crowd gathered in front of the broken window. The cat *slunk* through the front door and disappeared behind the sofa.

prowl   *Prowl* means sneak about looking for something. Wild animals *prowl* through the woods in search of food. The girls *prowled* around the Western ghost town.

lurk
skulk   *Lurk* and *skulk* can mean move in a secret way or try to keep out of sight. I thought I saw two figures *lurking* in the shadows. The fox *skulked* through the farmyard toward the chicken house.

slip   *Slip* can mean move quickly and quietly. You might *slip* in or *slip* out of a room without being noticed. They *slipped* quietly through the door. Karen *slipped* into line behind Donna without being seen.

sound (n)   A *sound* is something that you hear. It may be loud, like a jet taking off, or it may be as quiet as a whisper. Some *sounds* are pleasant—a bat hitting a ball (when your team is up), hot dogs sizzling over a fire, your dentist telling you that you have no cavities. There are unpleasant *sounds*, too—a siren, a growl, an alarm clock that wakes you. Did you hear that whirring *sound* coming from my bike?

• noise

Noise can be any sound, but especially it can be a loud and irritating sound. A vacuum cleaner makes a lot of *noise.* When people gather in large groups, they often make *noise.*

A vacuum cleaner makes a lot of **noise.**

• murmur

A *murmur* is a soft sound that is hard to hear. Often it is a continuous sound. You have to listen closely to hear the *murmur* of the trees on a windy day. *Murmur* can also be a low, grumbling complaint. The *murmur* of the crowd soon exploded into angry shouts.

• rumble

A sound that is low-pitched and continuous is called a *rumble.* Just one *rumble* of thunder sent my cousin Katie scurrying under the bed. A *rumble* of dissatisfaction spread through the audience when the singing group failed to appear.

• roar

A *roar* is the loud, deep cry of a wild animal such as a lion. People sometimes make sounds like *roars* when they are angry or in pain. Mr. Martinez's *roar* rang in our ears when he yelled at us for spilling paint on his lawn. A *roar* is also used to mean other loud, low sounds, as the *roar* of an engine or the *roar* of the wind.

ANTONYMS: quiet (n), silence

S

speak

Speak means make sounds, usually words, with your voice. You can *speak* loudly or in a whisper. Some people *speak* two languages. You can *speak* on a subject and *speak* to an audience. When you command a dog to *speak,* it usually barks.

utter

Utter means make a sound or speak. Herbert *uttered* a cry when his sister jumped out from behind a tree. The witch *uttered* some magic words over her bubbling pot.

The witch **uttered** some magic words over her bubbling pot.

express
voice

Express and *voice* mean say what you think or show your feelings. Carmella *expressed* her opinion in a letter to the editor of the magazine. The man's smile *expressed* his thanks. The chairperson asked if anyone wanted to *voice* an objection.

talk

Talk means utter words or speak. Usually you *talk* to someone who listens. People who are *talking* to each other are probably sharing opinions or information.

discuss

Discuss means talk about something in order to explore a subject or reach a decision. You talk about the points for and against some action—then decide on a solution. We *discussed* our plans for collecting bottles, cans, and newspapers.

See also *say.*

350

People speak of someone showing a **special** interest in music.

special	*Special* means different in some way from what is common, ordinary, or usual. We speak of someone having a *special* talent for art or of someone showing a *special* interest in music. Our *special* friends are the ones we like best.
individual particular	*Individual* and *particular* mean belonging to only one person or thing. This artist has an *individual* style of painting that identifies her work. Follow these *particular* directions for baking bread at high altitudes.
unique	Something *unique* is special because it is the only one of its kind. The Capitol is a *unique* building, though many other buildings are modeled after it.
exceptional extraordinary	*Exceptional* and *extraordinary* are used when someone or something is very special and out of the ordinary. He just ate an *exceptional* dessert. The solution to the crime in this mystery story is *extraordinary*.

See also *odd, precious, rare.*

ANTONYMS: common, ordinary, usual, general, average, familiar

S

splendid

Splendid means outshining all others in excellence or beauty. A *splendid* display of colors and shapes can be seen in a kaleidoscope. The United States team made a *splendid* showing in the tennis match.

A **splendid** display of colors and shapes can be seen in a kaleidoscope.

gorgeous

Gorgeous is a synonym for splendid, especially to describe a splendid display of color. It was a *gorgeous* sunset; fiery reds and yellows lit up the sky.

glorious

Glorious means splendid and delightful. A *glorious* morning is one that is crisp and clear, sunny and sparkling.

wonderful

magnificent

Wonderful can mean excellent or splendid or marvelous or astonishing. *Magnificent* means exceptionally fine and strikingly beautiful. Both are very tired words. They should be saved to describe things that are very good. I saw a *wonderful* display of dinosaur skeletons at the museum. Pascu thinks the new skyscraper is *magnificent*.

superb

Superb means of the highest possible degree of excellence. A *superb* book is one that is so beautifully written and so enjoyable that you hate to put it down.

ANTONYMS: dull, ordinary, plain (adj)

spot (n)

A *spot* is a small area that stands out from the things around it because of the way it is colored or the way it feels. Some dogs and cats have *spots*. People with measles have *spots* on their skin. Sometimes we think of a *spot* as something that doesn't belong on a surface. Artists wear smocks so they won't get *spots* on their clothes.

There were **blotches** of paint on the floor near the wall.

mark
: A *mark* can be a spot. You can make scuff *marks* on a floor if you don't pick up your feet as you walk.

stain
: A *stain* is a soiled spot. You can get grass *stains* on your clothes if you sit on the grass.

speck
blotch
: A *speck* is a small spot or mark. A *blotch* is larger than a speck. My glasses were covered with *specks* of dust. There were *blotches* of paint on the floor near the wall that had been painted.

smudge
: A *smudge* is a blurry spot caused by smearing or rubbing. You're likely to get *smudges* on a piece of paper if your hands are dirty.

blot
: We often use *blot* to mean an ink stain. A leaky pen will make *blots* on your paper.

flaw
: A *flaw* is a small spot or weakness in something that may make it break. A bubble in a piece of glass could be a *flaw.* If you had a sweater made of yarn that was not twisted correctly in one place, there would be a *flaw.* If the weak part of the yarn broke, you would have a hole in the sweater.

blemish
: A *blemish* is a spot or a flaw that shows on the surface of something but doesn't weaken the object or keep it from being used. A scratch on a table top is a *blemish.* A bruise on a peach is a *blemish,* but the peach can still be eaten. Some people who eat a lot of chocolate get *blemishes* on their skin.

S

start (v)

Start means begin. When you take the first step, you *start* walking. A telephone may *start* ringing just as you come in the door. School *starts* in the fall.

There are many words to use for the ways different things *start.*

spring
sprout

Spring and *sprout* mean start to grow. A stream may *spring* from a rock or from the side of a hill; it grows bigger until it becomes a river. A small town *has sprung* up where the two railroads meet. Buds *sprout* on trees; plants *sprout* from seeds in the ground.

A small town **has sprung** up where the two railroads meet.

launch

Launch means give something a start. A boat is *launched* when it is put into the water. A rocket is *launched* when it is pushed off the ground. A person can *launch* a new venture or career.

open

Open can mean begin something. The library *opened* a new branch on our street. The interviewer *opened* the conversation with a question. A new hamburger stand is *opening* tomorrow.

Companies **introduce** new products by giving away free samples.

introduce

Introduce can mean bring in or start something new. You *introduce* a new topic into a discussion when you change the subject. You *introduce* a new idea when you present it to other people to consider. Companies may *introduce* new products by giving away free samples.

establish
found

Establish and *found* mean bring into existence or start building something. Both words add the meaning of making something that will last for a long time. Schools and colleges are *established*. Plymouth Colony was *founded* by the Pilgrims in 1620.

commence
inaugurate
initiate

Commence, inaugurate, and *initiate* are all rather formal words that mean begin. You might *commence* exercising with twenty-five pushups. A football game *commences* with the playing of "The Star-Spangled Banner." *Inaugurate* adds the meaning of begin with some ceremony. The United States *inaugurates* a President every four years at the beginning of a term of office. The inauguration ceremony usually takes place on the steps of the Capitol. You *initiate* something when you take the first steps of an action and you expect the action to continue a long time. Ben Franklin *initiated* many improvements in Philadelphia's postal service.

See also *create.*

ANTONYMS: close (v), complete (v), conclude, end (v), finish (v), stop (v)

S

stop (v)

There are many, many ways to *stop* something.

In a story a Dutch boy *stopped* a hole in the dike by putting his finger in it. A truck can *stop* traffic by spilling a load of hay on the highway. You can *stop* your dog from running away by holding its leash. Mother *stops* the newspaper delivery when the family goes on vacation. One team *stops* another by winning the game.

People can *stop* doing something. I *stopped* running when the bus turned the corner. Please *stop* making me laugh. I *stopped* calling her "aunt" years ago.

Things can *stop* too. Rain *stops*. A train *stops*. A clock *stops*.

If you want to *stop* traffic, look up *block* (v).

If you want to *stop* a ball, look up *catch* (v).

If you want to *stop* the noise coming in through the window, look up *shut* (v).
If you want to *stop* doing something, look up *end* (v).

story

A *story* is a series of events or incidents; it is written or told to entertain people. We usually think that *stories* tell about things that never happened, but authors do write *stories* about true events. Small children enjoy hearing bedtime *stories* before they go to sleep. Betty liked to read adventure *stories* like "Kon-Tiki."

There are many other kinds of *stories.*

• anecdote

An *anecdote* is a very short story that usually tells of an amusing or interesting event. There are many *anecdotes* in the life of a famous person. The story of Benjamin Franklin flying his kite is an *anecdote.*

• romance

A *romance* is a story about an imaginary hero and the hero's heroic deeds and adventures. A famous *romance* is the story of King Arthur and his knights of the Round Table.

Often **mysteries** tell of a detective trying to solve a crime.

• mystery

A *mystery* is a story in which the ending is uncertain or unknown. Often *mysteries* tell of a detective trying to solve a crime.

• novel

A *novel* is a long story. There are usually many characters and a lot of action in a *novel.* Even when the people and situations in a *novel* are imaginary, or fictitious, they may seem very real to the reader.

See also *account* (n), *history, tale.*

strength

If you have *strength,* you can do things that are very hard and that require a lot of effort. It takes *strength* to lift weights.

power

Power is another word for strength. A football player needs *power* to run with the ball and get past the tacklers.

energy

Energy is the power to do something. With a burst of *energy,* the runner crossed the finish line.

strength continued on page 358 ▶

S

force

Force is strength or energy to do something. The *force* of the wind nearly knocked me to the ground. The five of us used *force* to break down the door and rescue the cat. The great *force* of the water caused the dam to break.

vigor

If you do something with *vigor,* you do it with all the force you have. Grace mowed the lawn and painted the fence with *vigor.* The candidate conducted the campaign with great *vigor.*

might

Might is unusually great strength. There are many ancient myths about the *might* of Hercules. Roger pushed the stalled car with all his *might.* It took all my *might* to unscrew the lid from that jar.

See also *endurance.*

ANTONYM: weakness

strong

Strong means having a lot of strength or power or force. It is the opposite of weak. A *strong* person is able to carry heavy objects. A *strong* wind can damage trees and homes. Someone who has been sick for a long time is not very *strong.* Sheryl's argument during the debate was so *strong* that I had to agree.

vigorous

Vigorous means having or using much strength and energy. A *vigorous* person is strong and energetic. Someone with a *vigorous* mind thinks quickly and clearly. A *vigorous* plant is one that is growing well. *Vigorous* exercise can be tiring.

stable
sturdy

Stable and *sturdy* mean strong and firm. Something that is *stable* is not likely to break or give way. The workers made sure the scaffolding was *stable* before stepping on it. Something that is *sturdy* is firm and solid and well built. A *sturdy* chair or table will not wobble.

The workers made sure the scaffolding was **stable.**

sound

Something that is *sound* is in good condition. A toy is *sound* if it has not been damaged or broken. You are *sound* if you are healthy and well.

muscular
brawny

A *muscular* or *brawny* person has big, strong muscles. Wrestlers are usually *muscular* and *brawny*.

wiry

Wiry really means like wire. When you say people are *wiry*, you mean that they are thin but strong. Long-distance runners usually have a *wiry* build.

See also *powerful, tough.*

ANTONYMS: weak, flimsy, puny

359

S

substitute (v)   *Substitute* means put something in the place of something else. The recipe called for butter, but I *substituted* margarine. When our teacher was sick, another teacher *substituted* for him.

replace   *Replace* means fill or take the place of something. If you lose someone's pen, you should *replace* it with another one. The actor who *replaces* another actor in a play is called an understudy. I *replaced* the record I had broken.

change   *Change* can mean substitute. You can *change* wet clothes for dry ones. I *changed* places with Brett so that he could see better. Can you *change* a five-dollar bill for five one-dollar bills?

exchange   *Exchange* means trade or give something in return for something else. If you buy something on sale, most stores won't let you *exchange* it. You *exchange* letters with people when you write to them and they write back to you.

switch   *Switch* means change or substitute. The train *switched* to another track. I *switched* desserts with my little sister while she wasn't looking.

shift   *Shift* means change the position or direction of something. Drivers *shift* gears in their cars when they want to back up. If you're carrying a load of books in one arm and they become too heavy, you could *shift* them to your other arm. When the wind *shifted*, the clouds blew away.

succeed

Succeed is the opposite of fail. *Succeed* means do well or turn out well. Your plans for something *succeed* when nothing stops or interferes with them. My cousin *succeeded* in catching a large trout. Did the search for the lost dog *succeed?*

achieve

Achieve means succeed in doing or getting something that is very difficult or takes a lot of effort. She *achieved* her goal of becoming a doctor. Yoshio *achieved* fame as a writer.

prosper

Prosper can mean succeed financially or make lots of money. A company usually *prospers* if it has a product that people want to buy.

flourish
thrive

Something *flourishes* or *thrives* when it succeeds or does well. Inez and Carl's vegetable garden is *flourishing.* My parents' business *flourished* after they started advertising their products. Most plants *thrive* if they get enough water and sunshine.

See also *win* (v).

ANTONYM: fail

Inez and Carl's vegetable garden is **flourishing.**

S

sudden

Sudden means happening very fast. It is the opposite of gradual. We all fell forward when the bus came to a *sudden* stop. I was awakened by a *sudden* clap of thunder. Jack has had a *sudden* change of plans—he wants to leave tomorrow.

quick

Quick means fast. Some action that is *quick* may not last very long, like a *quick* trip to the store. I took a *quick* look at my notes before the test.

unexpected

Unexpected can mean sudden. Something that is *unexpected* also has not been thought of ahead of time or prepared for. Yesterday there was an *unexpected* drop in temperature. We had *unexpected* company, but we had enough food for everyone.

hasty

Hasty means quick and hurried. A *hasty* decision is not carefully thought out. Since we were going to be in Boston for only a weekend, we had to make a *hasty* tour of the Freedom Trail.

abrupt

Abrupt means sudden and often very unexpected. There was an *abrupt* end to our telephone conversation. Watch out for an *abrupt* bend in the road.

There was an **abrupt** end to our telephone conversation.

instant
immediate

Instant and *immediate* mean quick and without delay. It doesn't take long to prepare *instant* rice. There is an *immediate* need for more hospital volunteers.

See also *fast* (adj).

ANTONYMS: gradual, expected, deliberate, unhurried

suddenly

Suddenly tells how fast something happens or is done. The roller coaster stopped *suddenly.* The synonyms for *suddenly* have meanings similar to the meanings for the synonyms of sudden.

The roller coaster stopped **suddenly.**

unexpectedly
: The phone rang *unexpectedly* in the middle of the night. I ran into Beth *unexpectedly.*

hastily
: Linda didn't think about the question and answered *hastily.* You'll be sick if you eat too *hastily.*

abruptly
: The road ends *abruptly. Abruptly* the judge banged the gavel and called for order.

instantly
: They stopped talking *instantly.* The room was *instantly* silent.

immediately
: Josh *immediately* volunteered to help paint the room. Come home *immediately* after the track meet.

See also *fast* (adv).

ANTONYMS: gradually, deliberately, unhurriedly

363

S

suffer

Suffer means have pain or grief or misfortune or loss. Ira is *suffering* from a cold. I don't think I can *suffer* another disappointment. A business will *suffer* if it is poorly managed.

• experience

Experience means go through or live through something. You *experience* many things—both pleasant and unpleasant. You may *experience* sadness when your best friend moves out of town. But you will *experience* happiness when your friend comes back for a visit.

undergo

Undergo means suffer or experience something, usually painful or unpleasant. It is not pleasant to *undergo* an operation. Pony Express riders *underwent* many hardships to deliver mail to Sacramento.

Pony Express riders **underwent** many hardships to deliver the mail.

bear
tolerate

Bear and *tolerate* can mean put up with something. It is hard to *bear* an insult. Jan *bore* her disappointments without complaining. The hotel manager would not *tolerate* any pets in the rooms.

364

Bev **hinted** that she wanted a new catcher's mitt for her birthday.

endure   *Endure* means suffer or put up with for a long time without giving in. I can't *endure* this noise another moment!

See also *allow*.

suggest   *Suggest* means offer an idea or a thought. Mel *suggested* that we go swimming, and we all agreed. Emilio *suggested* hamburgers and potato salad for the picnic.

Suggest can also mean call to mind. Thunder and lightning *suggest* a storm. The color yellow *suggests* warmth and happiness to Russ.

hint   *Hint* means suggest something in an indirect way. The baby-sitter *hinted* that she was hungry by continually turning her eyes toward the refrigerator. I *hinted* that I wanted a catcher's mitt for my birthday.

imply   *Imply* means suggest or mean something without saying it directly. George *implied* that I could have done better. Alice *implied* that I had been on the phone too long when she said, "Isn't your ear tired?"

insinuate   *Insinuate* means suggest something that is often unpleasant or unkind. Denise *insinuated* I wasn't telling the truth, but I really was. Joe *insinuated* I was a weakling just because I dropped the barbell.

propose   *Propose* means offer an idea or a plan for consideration. They *proposed* going horseback riding when the weather cleared up. Bill *proposed* marriage to my older sister.

S

suggestion
A *suggestion* is something mentioned for consideration. Every member of the family had a *suggestion* for the name of the sailboat. The motor club gave us several good *suggestions* for our trip. Jenny's *suggestion* is to use posters to advertise the school project.

proposal
A *proposal* is a suggestion to do something. The residents accepted the mayor's *proposal* to construct a new city hall.

hint
A *hint* is an indirect suggestion. Hal gave me a *hint* that helped me solve the riddle. The children begged me for a *hint* as to where the things for the treasure hunt were hidden.

implication
An *implication* is something suggested indirectly. I was not accused of cheating, but the *implication* was certainly there.

insinuation
An *insinuation* can be an unpleasant suggestion. Your *insinuation* that the election was dishonest is ridiculous! I refused to listen to the *insinuations* Norman was making about my friend.

advice
When you ask for people's *advice,* you want to know what they think about something or what they think you should do about something. The Cabinet gives *advice* to the President. The campers had problems because they didn't follow the ranger's *advice* about equipment.

support (v)   *Support* is used in many ways. It can mean hold something up. Steel beams or columns can be used to *support* the roof of a building. Your legs *support* you when you stand. *Support* also means help and assist. You should *support* your friends when they need you. You can *support* candidates for office by working in their campaigns.

prop   *Prop* means use an object to support something. You can *prop* a ladder against a wall or *prop* a rake against a fence. If you are tired, you might *prop* your head by putting your hand under your chin.

bear   *Bear* means support the weight of something. The walls of a house *bear* the weight of the roof. A person in a high position *bears* the burden of many responsibilities.

defend   *Defend* and *uphold* mean support and fight
uphold   or argue in favor of something. Soldiers *defend* their country. You *defend* a friend's reputation when you speak well of your friend. The Supreme Court *upheld* the decision of the lower courts.

maintain   *Maintain* means keep something in good condition. Jessie *maintained* the beautiful finish on her antique car by polishing it every weekend. *Maintain* also means support or uphold the claim that something is true. The suspects *maintained* that they had been at home the night of the robbery.

Jessie **maintained** the beautiful finish on her antique car by polishing it every weekend.

support (v) continued on page 368 ▶

367

S

surround
Surround means go or be completely around something. Water *surrounds* an island. A fence may *surround* a house or a garden. When the President of the United States makes a public appearance, he is always *surrounded* by members of the Secret Service. The pirates *surrounded* and then captured the ship. When the rock group stepped off the plane, they were immediately *surrounded* by cheering fans.

encircle
Encircle means make a circle around something. The girl carefully *encircled* the phone number in her telephone book. A bicycle path *encircled* the park.

enclose
Enclose means close in or shut in on all sides. A high wall *enclosed* the palace. The horses were *enclosed* in the corral. You can *enclose* words in parentheses.

encompass
Encompass means surround completely. A moat *encompassed* the medieval castle. Darkness *encompassed* the forest.

A high wall **enclosed** the castle.

T

take (v)

The first meaning of *take* is to get possession or control of something. You *take* an object someone hands you. You *take* the change a store clerk hands you.

Think for a moment, though, of just a few ways people use this valuable word. They *take* a walk or *take* a vacation or *take* a chance. They *take* medicine, *take* sides, *take* pleasure. You can *take* a partner, *take* your choice, *take* your time. You can *take* a bus, *take* notes, *take* your temperature. Sometimes you have to *take* a detour. Have you ever *taken* a snapshot or piano lessons or *taken* books to the library? Did you ever start something that *took* longer to finish than you expected?

There are many more ways to use *take.* And after you have thought of all of them (if you can), you might begin thinking of *take on, take off, take in, take out, take up, take down, take back, take over.*

In this book you'll find other words for *take* under five different entries: *carry, catch* (v), *choose, grasp* (v), *obtain.*

tale

A *tale* may be an account about something or someone. A *tale* may be told to amuse the reader or listener but can also teach a lesson. The characters in a *tale* are imaginary, and their actions are often exaggerated. There are many *tales* about talking animals, magic spells, fairies, wizards, and witches.

tale continued on page 374 ▶

T

• folk tale
• fairy tale

A long time ago *folk tales* were told in almost every country; they were passed on by word of mouth. Most people could not read or write, so the storytellers were popular figures who told tales to people of all ages. Sailors and traders carried these tales to many different countries. Stories of magical creatures, such as fairies and elves, became known as *fairy tales.*

• myth

Myths are tales that have come down to us from the ancient past. Many *myths* tried to explain certain facts of nature. One Greek *myth,* for example, explained the rising and setting of the sun as the god Apollo driving a fiery chariot across the sky.

One Greek **myth** explained the rising and setting of the sun as the god Apollo driving a fiery chariot across the sky.

• legend

A *legend* is a tale that is usually based on something true. But it is probably exaggerated, and it cannot be proved. Stories about Davy Crockett are called *legends.*

• fable

A *fable* is a tale that teaches a lesson. In a *fable* animals often talk and act like human beings. "The Tortoise and the Hare" is a famous *fable* by Aesop.

See also *account* (n), *history, story.*

tame (adj) *Tame* usually describes animals that are not wild or animals that have been trained to be gentle and obedient. Some of the animals that perform at a circus are *tame.* *Tame* also describes something that is not very exciting, lively, or spirited. A *tame* movie may not have much action.

domesticated A *domesticated* animal is tame and used to living near people. Farm animals such as cows, horses, and pigs are *domesticated.* So are dogs, cats, and white mice.

docile *Docile* means easily handled or managed. Farmers can drive *docile* cows home from the pasture. It is easy to saddle a *docile* horse. *Docile* people do what others ask or want them to do. Mrs. Ortiz never minds taking Miguel shopping with her because he is a *docile* baby.

quiet A *quiet* person or animal is gentle. When it was sleeping, the fierce lion looked as *quiet* as a kitten.

subdued *Subdued* means quiet or toned down. A *subdued* light or color is soft and not bright. When you speak in a *subdued* voice, you are not noisy or loud.

insipid *Insipid* can mean tame, flat, and colorless. An *insipid* remark is not witty or clever. That book was *insipid,* and I feel I wasted my time reading it. Tasteless food is *insipid.*

ANTONYMS: wild, unruly, fierce, bright, noisy, loud, stubborn

375

T

task

A *task* is a certain amount of work that has to be done. Mowing the lawn is a *task;* so is washing the dishes. The girls helped their father with the *task* of putting up a new fence. Josh was given the *task* of cleaning the attic.

job

A *job* can be any work you have to do. Painting something that is large can be quite a *job.* Betty was given the *job* of baby-sitting when her parents went out. My older sister was lucky to find a summer *job.*

Painting something that is large can be quite a **job.**

chore

A *chore* is a regular task or job. Some *chores* may include setting the table, taking out the garbage, and making the beds every day. Some of Grandfather's *chores,* when he was young, was to chop wood, milk the cows, and collect eggs from the henhouse.

assignment

An *assignment* is a task assigned or given to do. Homework is an *assignment.* The story a reporter writes is an *assignment.* His *assignment* during the charity drive was to collect old clothes.

duty

A *duty* is a task that you should do or are required to do. A police officer has the *duty* of enforcing the laws. It is the *duty* of every citizen to pay taxes. It is also the *duty* of every citizen to keep the streets free from litter.

See also *work* (n).

tell

Here is a small word that *tells* a lot. *Tell* means give knowledge or information to someone else through speech. Of course, *tell* can be some way you communicate without speech too. The fingerprints will *tell* who did it. You can *tell* by the buds on the trees that spring is coming. Jill could *tell* by looking at us that we were having a good time. I can *tell* you don't believe a word I've said. My cousin has learned to *tell* time. The broken vase and my guilty look *told* the whole story.

In this book words for *tell* are grouped by the ways something can be *told.*

Ways to *tell* what has already happened are listed under *announce.*

Ways to *tell* what is going to happen are listed under *forecast* (v).

Ways to *tell* secrets or give out knowledge may be found under *inform.*

Ways to *tell* what someone wants to know or should know are under *answer* (v) and *explain.*

Ways to *tell* a story or *tell* how something happened are listed under *report* (v).

Ways to *tell* someone what to do are under *command* (v).

Ways to *tell* someone what you think, are listed under *advise* and *suggest.*

Ways to make words and sounds will be found under *say* and *speak.*

T

thin

Thin can describe both people and things. When *thin* is used to describe a person, it means the opposite of fat or plump. A *thin* person doesn't weigh much. When *thin* describes an object, it means the opposite of thick or heavy. It would be dangerous to skate on *thin* ice. This soup is very *thin.* This paper is so *thin* that you can almost see through it.

A chick looks **scrawny** right after it leaves the shell.

lean

Lean is the opposite of fat. It is often used to describe meat that has little or no fat. Even a piece of *lean* meat may have some fat around the edge.

skinny
scrawny

Skinny and *scrawny* mean too thin. A *skinny* person is usually underweight. We gave the *scrawny* dog a biscuit. Chicks look *scrawny* right after they leave the shell.

gaunt

Someone who has been sick for a long time may look *gaunt. Gaunt* means thin, pale, and feeble. Barry's face looked *gaunt* for weeks after he got out of the hospital.

emaciated

An *emaciated* person or animal is exceptionally thin and bony. By the end of the hard winter the buffaloes on the prairie were so *emaciated* that they could hardly stand.

weak
diluted

Weak and *diluted* mean made thinner by adding water or another liquid. *Weak* coffee doesn't have much flavor because it is too watery. If you put ice cubes in your milk, it will be *diluted* when they melt. Some canned soups are already *diluted,* so you don't have to add water.

flimsy

Flimsy means light and thin. It describes things, not people. It is the opposite of strong and firm. *Flimsy* can describe something that is poorly made or that will not stand up under wear. A piece of *flimsy* material is likely to tear easily.

See also *slender.*

ANTONYMS: fat, plump, thick, heavy, strong, firm (adj), husky, stout

think

Think means form an idea in your mind. There are different ways to *think.* You may sit back and relax and *think* about the marvelous time you had at a party or on a trip. Words for this kind of *thinking* are in the entry *remember.*

You may lean your chin on your hand and stare out the window and *think* about the moon and the stars and about what life would be like out there. This kind of *thinking* has synonyms under *imagine.*

Perhaps you are *thinking* hard about something you're going to do in the future. Look for this kind of word under *plan* (v).

If you have the hard kind of *thinking* to do before you can make up your mind about something, look up *decide.*

Words for the very hardest way to *think*—the *thinking* that wears you out because it is so important and serious—are listed under *consider.*

If you are sure about something and don't have to *think* at all, look up *know.*

T

throw (v)

Throw means use your hand and arm to make something move through the air. In winter you might *throw* snowballs. Louella *threw* her books on the floor. Where have you *thrown* your coat?

Here are different ways to *throw*.

toss
cast

Toss and *cast* mean throw lightly. We *tossed* a coin to see who would go first. Please *toss* me my pencil. We say that a boat *tosses* when it is thrown about by waves. We *cast* our fishing lines into the water. Rudy *cast* a pebble at the lily pad.

pitch

Pitch means throw something at a target. Our neighbors like to *pitch* horseshoes. Nancy *pitched* a ball of paper into the wastebasket.

sling

Sling means throw something or swing something without letting go of it. You can *sling* stones. The skater *slung* a sweater over her shoulder.

fling
hurl

Fling and *hurl* mean throw forcefully, not always caring where the object goes. Lionel stormed into the room and *flung* his jacket on the floor. You would *hurl* things that weigh a lot. The laborers *hurled* the bags of cement to the ground as they unloaded the truck.

tough

Tough means strong or hard or difficult to pull apart. Something that is *tough* can be bent without being broken. It is not brittle. A rope can be *tough*. A *tough* steak is hard to cut and chew. It is not tender.

tough continued

Tough also means able to endure great strain. People are *tough* if they are physically strong and healthy. The pioneers had to be *tough*.

Tough can also mean difficult to change or move or wear down. *Tough* opponents in a sport are hard to beat; you won't find them easy to face.

firm

Firm means steady and not easily moved. You should build a pier on *firm* supports. My mom was *firm* in her decision not to raise my allowance. The storekeeper said the price was *firm;* he couldn't let me have the baseball bat for less.

sturdy

Sturdy means strong and firmly built. It can be the opposite of fragile. It takes *sturdy* legs to walk ten miles. The roses in our garden look *sturdy* this year. Randy should wear *sturdy* shoes when he goes hiking through the woods.

durable

Durable describes something that can last a long time because it is tough or strong and doesn't change. Blue jeans are made of *durable* cloth. If you have a *durable* friendship, you are lucky.

stubborn

Stubborn means hard to change. *Stubborn* people seldom give up easily. Grandma was *stubborn* in her demand that we all come to her house.

See also *strong.*

ANTONYMS: brittle, tender, easy, fragile, soft, weak

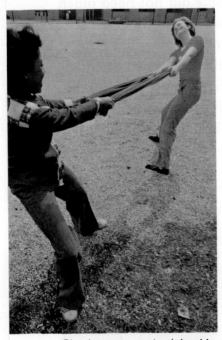

Blue jeans are made of **durable** cloth.

T

training

Nancy can't play golf as well as she used to because she's out of **practice.**

- practice

- exercise

- development

- drill

Training is the things you do when you prepare for something. A swimmer's *training* might include swimming for many hours, trying out different strokes, learning to breathe correctly, and learning how to increase speed. A nurse's *training* is the period in which a nurse learns how to care for sick people, then actually cares for them as a student nurse.

Practice is the doing of something over and over again in order to do it easily or well. There is an old expression that *practice* makes perfect. It takes a lot of *practice* to play a musical instrument well. Nancy can't play golf as well as she used to because she's out of *practice.*

Exercise is like practice. It is physical or mental training. Athletes need *exercise* in order to build strength and endurance.

Development means a series of changes that take place during growth. *Development* of an athlete's muscles is most important. The railroads were responsible for much of the *development* of the United States.

Drill is training in doing something. Fire *drills* prepare you to act correctly in an emergency. A marching band goes through *drills* until it can carry out its formations without mistakes.

U

unclean *Unclean* describes anything that is soiled, spotted, or stained. It is the opposite of clean and pure.

dirty *Dirty* means covered with dirt, mud, grime, or dust. Please clean your *dirty* shoes and then polish them.

soiled Something that is *soiled* is unclean and needs to be washed. A white shirt or blouse becomes *soiled* easily.

filthy *Filthy* means very dirty. The boat was so *filthy* that she had to scrub it before she could paint it. The children's knees were *filthy* from playing.

The children's knees were **filthy** from playing.

slovenly *Slovenly* and *untidy* mean not clean or
untidy neat. People who are *slovenly* don't care how sloppy and dirty their clothes are or how messy they look. Cary looked *slovenly* because his shirt was torn and dirty and his hair was uncombed. *Untidy* people are often careless and sloppy about their appearance and their work. An *untidy* room may have papers and toys and clothes scattered over the floor, with nothing in place.

ANTONYMS: clean (adj), pure, neat, tidy, unsoiled

387

U

urge

Urge means push someone into action or make someone do something. Our teacher *urged* us to see the science exhibit. I *urged* my dog to follow by pulling on its leash.

spur
goad

Spur and *goad* really mean urge an animal onward. You can *spur* a horse forward by poking it with your heels or with spurs attached to your boots. A farmer *goads* a mule into motion by hitting it with a stick or whip. *Spur* and *goad* can also be used to mean urge a person on. The thought of being late *spurred* Clarence to hurry. Angie *goaded* me into playing my guitar.

arouse
excite

Something *arouses* or *excites* you when it stirs up your feelings and causes you to do something. A speaker might *arouse* anger in an audience. Don't *excite* the dog.

prompt

Prompt means urge. The producer *prompted* the newscaster to finish the news report within two minutes. Whatever *prompted* you to say you'd sell tickets?

See also *force* (v).

The producer **prompted** the newscaster to finish the news report within two minutes.

388

useful   *Useful* means being of use. A compass is *useful* to a sailor. A pencil with a sharp point is *useful,* but one with a broken point is useless. Road maps are *useful* on a long trip. Scissors are *useful* for cutting paper. Gail's idea was *useful* to the people on the committee.

helpful   *Helpful* means being of help. A flashlight is *helpful* in the dark. With a weak battery, a flashlight is ineffectual. The truck driver was *helpful* in fixing my flat tire. I was helpless until he came along.

handy   *Handy* describes something that saves trouble and is easy to use. A dishwasher is *handy* when there are a lot of dishes to do. A can opener is a *handy* tool in the kitchen. The bus is *handy* to take to school because it stops right in front of my house.

He doesn't care how old that car is, it is still **serviceable.**

serviceable   *Serviceable* describes something that is useful because it gives good service and does what it is expected, or supposed, to do. I don't care how old that car is, it is still *serviceable.* This old suit is out of style, but it is still *serviceable* for everyday wear.

valuable   *Valuable* means serviceable and useful and desirable to have. A spare tire is *valuable* in case of a flat tire. Mrs. Inada would be a *valuable* worker in any politician's campaign. *Valuable* has the added meaning of worth. Gold, oil, and diamonds are considered to be *valuable.*

ANTONYMS: useless, ineffectual, helpless

389

V

visible

Visible means easily seen. Something that is *visible* is not hidden or concealed. The stars are *visible* on a clear night. Ice is *visible* on the flower.

noticeable

Noticeable describes something that attracts attention. There is a *noticeable* crack in that bowl. Something bright or colorful would be more *noticeable* than something dull and drab.

conspicuous

Conspicuous describes something so different or out of place that it attracts attention. A girl wearing a hoop skirt would be *conspicuous*. *Conspicuous* also means very easily seen. The No Smoking sign was put in a *conspicuous* place in the front of the bus.

Ice is **visible** on the flower.

apparent

Apparent means clearly visible, easy to understand, or obvious. The hole in that coat is very *apparent.* Toward the end of the game it became *apparent* that our team would win. *Apparent* can also describe something that seems to be real or true though it is not. The *apparent* size of a distant object may be about half its actual size.

evident

Evident means clearly visible and obvious. As the sky became darker, it became *evident* we were going to have rain.

See also *clear* (adj).

ANTONYMS: hidden, concealed, inconspicuous

W

walk (v)

Walk means move or go on foot. You *walk* when you raise one foot at a time and step forward. You always have one foot on the ground when you *walk*. You can *walk* at a slow pace or a fast pace, but never as fast as when you run.

Here are other words that describe how people *walk*.

stroll
saunter

Stroll and *saunter* mean walk slowly, leisurely, and happily. You may *saunter* along the beach. Or you may *stroll* through a park on a summer evening.

prance

Prance means walk with a springing movement. Horses often *prance* when they are in a parade. Little children sometimes *prance* when they're feeling happy and gay.

march

March means walk steadily with a certain rhythm, often in step with others. The band *marched* down the street. When the new toaster I'd bought wouldn't work, I *marched* right back to the store with it.

strut
swagger

Strut and *swagger* mean walk in a proud or boastful way, holding your head up high. The drum major *struts* in front of the band. The bully *swaggered* down the street because he knew we were watching.

shuffle

If you *shuffle,* you walk without raising your feet completely off the ground. You drag them. An extremely tired person may *shuffle* along the street.

walk (v) continued on page 392 ▶

W

warning

A *warning* gives advance notice of something or tells of possible danger or harm. A *warning* enables people to prepare for or avoid something. A buoy in a channel is a *warning* to sailors of hidden rocks or shallow places. The weather bureau issued a storm *warning* early this evening.

A buoy in a channel is a **warning** of hidden rocks or shallow places.

advice

Advice is information that warns or helps a person in some way. You may seek your parents' *advice* when you're troubled or not sure about something. It is helpful to follow the *advice* of people who have solved the same problems you face.

admonition

An *admonition* is advice about something a person should do or about something a person has done incorrectly. The police officer gave the couple an *admonition* about crossing the street in the middle of the block.

forewarning

A *forewarning* is a warning that is given well in advance. The early frost was a *forewarning* of a long winter.

hunch

A *hunch* is a feeling or suspicion that something will happen or that something is true. Usually there is no real reason for having a *hunch.* I had a *hunch* it would rain on my birthday.

foreboding

Foreboding is the feeling of something bad to come. It is a stronger feeling than a hunch. My sense of *foreboding* increased when the telephone rang at midnight.

sign

A *sign* can be a warning. A No Trespassing *sign* warns people to stay off private property. The black clouds were a *sign* of an approaching storm.

signal

A *signal* is something that puts a person on the alert, often for danger. A yellow light is a *signal* that the traffic light is going to change from green to red. The driver used the turn *signal* before turning the corner.

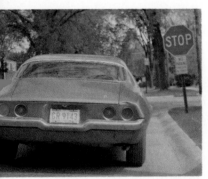

The driver used the turn **signal** before turning the corner.

alarm

An *alarm* is a warning of danger. Alonzo sounded the fire *alarm* when he saw smoke.

symptom

A *symptom* can be a warning of some illness. Aching all over is sometimes the first *symptom* of the flu.

See also *sign* (n).

Dad **watched** the spaghetti so that it wouldn't boil over.

watch (v)

Watch means look at something. You *watch* your favorite show on TV. Spectators *watch* a hockey game that has lots of action. *Watch* can also mean look for something or someone. You might *watch* for signs of rain if you're planning a picnic. I *watched* for the letter carrier.

Watch also means keep a close eye on something or someone. A baby-sitter *watches* young children while their parents are not at home. Dad *watched* the spaghetti so that it wouldn't boil over. I *watched* the time because I didn't want to be late.

observe

Observe means watch or look at closely. You can *observe* the stars through a telescope. The growth of a plant is easy to *observe.*

guard

Guard means watch and protect. Stores hire people to *guard* the merchandise against shoplifters. I was afraid of the huge collie that *guarded* our neighbor's house.

tend

Tend means watch over and care for. We say that a lioness *tends* her cubs when she protects them from dangerous animals. A nurse *tends* sick patients.

oversee

Oversee means watch and direct an activity. A supervisor *oversees* the work of employees.

See also *notice* (v), *protect.*

ANTONYMS: disregard, ignore, overlook

398

weak

Weak means lacking strength. You may feel *weak* if you haven't had breakfast. You could be *weak* if you've been sick for a while. A *weak* voice is not loud enough to be heard easily. A *weak* board is not strong or sturdy. A *weak* excuse is one that is not good or believable.

feeble

Feeble means lacking strength. Some people may become *feeble* as they get older. Barb made a *feeble* attempt to move the heavy chair.

flimsy

Flimsy means not strongly made or not well put together. This chair is very *flimsy;* it broke when I sat on it. A *flimsy* story doesn't have much of a plot.

frail

Frail means physically weak. A *frail* person can become ill easily. *Frail* also means easily broken. The smaller, *frail* blossoms were knocked off the tree during the hailstorm last week.

fragile
brittle

Fragile and *brittle* mean weak and easily broken. Something *fragile* is delicately made and must be handled with great care. A spider's web is *fragile,* but it is strong enough to trap a fly. Something *brittle* is easily broken, cracked, or snapped because it is not tough. It is stiff and cannot be bent. Icicles are *brittle.* Paper becomes *brittle* with age.

See also *powerless, thin.*

ANTONYMS: strong, sturdy, tough, healthy, husky, stout

W

wealth

Wealth means a large amount or supply of something. *Wealth* is the opposite of poverty. People of *wealth* have many valuable possessions. *Wealth* includes a person's money and property. Natural resources are part of a country's *wealth.* An encyclopedia has a *wealth* of information.

money

Money is what is used in buying and selling. What something is worth may be measured in terms of how much *money* it costs or how much *money* someone is willing to pay for it.

property

Property is what a person owns. If you buy and pay for something, it becomes your *property.* A person's *property* may include a house and the land on which it is built, furniture, clothes, and money. People sometimes put up fences to keep strangers off their *property.*

riches

Riches is another word for wealth, though it is not so often used. The *riches* of our earth should be conserved.

treasure

Treasure is wealth that is stored up or collected. Pirates' buried *treasure* is being discovered in sunken ships in the Pacific Ocean.

abundance

An *abundance* is a great supply or quantity of something. Our cherry trees had an *abundance* of blossoms.

ANTONYM: poverty

Pirates' **treasure** is being discovered in sunken ships.

400

wild　　　*Wild,* when it describes animals, means not tame or domesticated. Lions, giraffes, and elephants are *wild* animals. *Wild* also means not cared for or cultivated. *Wild* flowers grow in fields and forests. The explorers went into the *wild,* mountainous region. People who lose their tempers or become very angry sometimes act *wild.* You may say you are *wild* about something you like very much.

furious　　*Furious* means wild and angry. You may be *furious* at yourself if you make a silly mistake. Mom and Dad were *furious* when they saw my sister scribbling on the wall. Wind that whips blinding snow ahead of it is *furious.*

violent　　*Violent* means wild. The moose became *violent* when we surprised it as it was eating. *Violent* can also describe something that is strong or forceful—like a *violent* storm or a *violent* sea.

untamed　　*Untamed* means not controlled or not tame. An *untamed* animal is hard to control. It hasn't been trained to be obedient or gentle.

savage　　A *savage* or *ferocious* animal is wild and
ferocious　fierce and dangerous. When the *savage* grizzly bear invaded the campsite, it ripped the tents. The *ferocious* lion tried to claw its trainer.

ANTONYMS: tame (adj), domesticated, timid, gentle, docile, harmless

401

W

win (v)   *Win* means gain victory or success. A bowling team *wins* when it has the highest score. Two dozen people entered the pie-baking contest, but Dick *won*.

succeed   You *succeed* when you do what you set out to do. The runner *succeeded* in jumping the hurdles without knocking any over. Mrs. Levine's new business is *succeeding*.

triumph   *Triumph* means gain a victory or rejoice after a victory has been won. The ancient Romans *triumphed* over the Greeks. The whole city *triumphed* when the home team won the pennant.

prevail   *Prevail* means win against great odds or because of greater strength. Jack *prevailed* against the giant.

See also *beat* (v), *conquer, defeat* (v), *obtain*.

ANTONYMS: lose, give

Jack **prevailed** against the giant.

402

wisdom

Very intelligent boys and girls of twelve may be called "wise beyond their years," but they do not possess *wisdom*. Wisdom is gained only after years and years of experience. People who have *wisdom* are intelligent and farsighted. They make good decisions based on what they know. They understand even the most complicated situations because of their broad experience and their ability to think things out. Grandmother displayed her *wisdom* when she advised me to get a good education.

These other words are related to *wisdom* but are not synonyms. They may have the precise meaning you're looking for in certain situations.

• insight

Insight is the power to look into a situation with understanding. People who have *insight* catch the real meaning or feeling of something. If something is bothering your brother, you might wish you had an *insight* into his problem so that you could help him. I told Mom I'd take the dog out for a walk before bedtime, but she had the *insight* to know I just wanted to avoid going to bed so early.

• sense

Sense is an ability to judge and make good decisions. It's also the ability to act appropriately in any situation. I hope you have enough *sense* to lock the cage after you feed the hamster.

wisdom continued on page 404 ◗

W

• judgment

Judgment adds training and experience to sense. You need *judgment* when you have to make a choice between two actions or objects. My *judgment* told me we wouldn't have time to see both Washington, D.C., and Jamestown on our vacation.

• knowledge

Knowledge is all the things you know or the state of knowing something well. To my *knowledge* he hasn't left the house all day. Because of Masumi's vast *knowledge* of science, everyone comes to her with questions.

• reason

Reason is the power to think things out in an orderly way. All my *reason* wasn't enough to figure out how Jane knew I'd borrowed her ring while she was away.

• understanding

Understanding is the ability to see things clearly and to see someone else's point of view. Mike's *understanding* of young people and their problems made him an ideal youth counselor.

ANTONYM: foolishness

wise

Wise means having knowledge or not foolish. It describes someone who understands people and situations well and uses good judgment in dealing with them. You would be *wise* to get plenty of sleep the night before a ten-mile hike.

• smart

Smart means alert, bright, or intelligent. It is the opposite of stupid. Rick was *smart* enough to figure out that we wanted him to buy us some pizza.

It is hard for Dottie to be **understanding** when her little brother breaks things.

• understanding

Understanding describes someone who is considerate of others and has kind feelings toward them and their problems. It is hard to be *understanding* when your little brother breaks things that belong to you.

• sensible

Sensible means having or using good sense or judgment. Some people are *sensible* almost all the time; others, not very often. Looking in both directions when crossing a street is *sensible*.

• levelheaded

Levelheaded means sensible and not easily upset. It is important to be *levelheaded* during an emergency.

• reasonable

A *reasonable* person is one who is sensible and not hard to get along with. If something is *reasonable*, it is fair and just. If a librarian asks you to be quiet in the library, she is making a *reasonable* request. An unreasonable request would be to ask you to make no noise at all.

Sometimes *reasonable* means not extreme. A *reasonable* price is one that is not too high. Paying fifty cents for a small package of gum is unreasonable.

ANTONYMS: foolish, unwise, stupid, unreasonable, absurd

W

work (n)

Work is the doing or accomplishing or making of something. It is sometimes the opposite of play. What some people think is *work* may be considered play by others. Washing windows is hard *work* for some people. It may take a lot of *work* to come up with an idea for my book report.

labor

Labor is strenuous work or work that takes a lot of strength. The piano movers were exhausted by their *labor.* Machines have taken much of the backbreaking *labor* out of farming.

toil

Toil is long and tiring work. After days of *toil,* the bird finally completed its nest.

drudgery

Drudgery is unpleasant or dull or very monotonous work. Practicing the piano is *drudgery* to Wanda because she has no interest in music. She thinks that taking out the trash every day is pure *drudgery.*

She thinks that taking out the trash every day is pure **drudgery.**

effort

Effort can mean demanding or difficult work. Sometimes it takes a lot of *effort* to get up in the morning. Eddie put a lot of *effort* into getting his model plane done in time for the contest.

activity

Activity can refer to work that is done over a long period of time. One *activity* of the committee is the planning of the new blood-donor program.

See also *action, task.*

work (v)

Work, when used as a verb, is sometimes the opposite of play. Mom *works* in a factory. When she comes home, she rests or relaxes. I *worked* hard all day.

Work can also mean run. Does your sewing machine *work?* It *works* well now that the parts have been oiled.

labor

Labor means work hard and long. The construction workers *labored* to complete the building on time.

toil

Toil means work even harder and longer. The farmers were completely exhausted after they had *toiled* in the field all day.

operate

Operate means work or make something run. My radio doesn't *operate* very well when the batteries are low. Dennis *operates* an elevator in the office building.

perform
function

Perform and *function* mean do or carry out something or act as something. Doctors *perform* operations. A rock can *function* as a hammer.

See also *act* (v).

ANTONYMS: play (v), rest (v), relax

W

worried

Worried means filled with fear or doubt about something. You may be *worried* about something that has happened or perhaps something you think might happen. If you're *worried* about someone, you fear that something bad may happen to that person. Elio was *worried* about making the swimming team. My grandmother is always *worried* when our family goes camping. She thinks camping is dangerous.

concerned

If you're *concerned* about something, you are interested in it and worried about it. My father is *concerned* about our local government. He's afraid the wrong person will be elected mayor.

troubled
disturbed

Troubled and *disturbed* mean upset or uneasy. After seeing a horror movie, you might fall into a *troubled* sleep. You might feel *disturbed* if you lost a friend's book.

nervous

Nervous means uneasy and even jumpy. If you're a *nervous* person, a loud noise may cause you to jump in your chair. *Nervous* people find it hard to relax.

A loud noise may cause a **nervous** person to jump.

anxious
: *Anxious* means extremely uneasy or fearful. As early as September, settlers in the Northwest Territory became *anxious* about the coming of winter.

frantic
: When people become *frantic,* they are so worried and excited that they do not think clearly. If a small child is lost in a store, the parents may become *frantic.* Instead of asking a clerk for help, they may run around the store calling the child's name.

    See also *eager.*

    ANTONYMS: calm (adj), easy, unconcerned, untroubled, undisturbed

worry (v)
: One of the earliest meanings of *worry* was "snap at, tear, or bite, especially the throat." When a puppy grabs a slipper with its teeth, chews it, shakes it back and forth, and growls at it, the puppy is *worrying* the slipper. So *worry* means pull at something or disturb it or shake it over and over. Something that *worries* you shakes your thoughts and disturbs your mind continually. The problem of finding safe places to dump garbage *worries* the town council.

annoy
: *Annoy* means worry or disturb someone over and over. Usually the things that *annoy* people are small and unimportant. What *annoys* me most about my little sister is that she asks so many questions.

worry (v) continued on page 410 ▶

Y

yearning   *Yearning* means the feeling of wanting or needing something. Have you ever had a *yearning* to join a circus?

desire   A *desire* is a yearning or a wish for something. Sean has a *desire* to travel.

longing   A *longing* is a deep desire or yearning for something presently out of your reach. I have a *longing* to live in Alaska.

craving   A *craving* is usually a yearning for some kind of food. Do you ever get a *craving* for popcorn?

thirst   *Thirst* can mean simply a desire for something, or it can mean a yearning for something to drink. Fern has a *thirst* for detective stories.

Fern has a **thirst** for detective stories.

hankering   *Hankering* is a perfectly good informal word to use when you have a mild yearning for something. Eleanor and Ron have a *hankering* for some deep-sea fishing.

liking   If something is to your *liking,* it pleases you and you may want to have it—if you don't have it already. If you have a *liking* for horses, you probably read books about them and go to horse shows.

taste   If something suits your *taste,* you like it. Many people have a *taste* for hot dogs.

• preference   A *preference* is the liking of one thing better than another. Freda has a *preference* for foreign-made cars.

yell (v)   *Yell* means speak loudly and forcefully. You may *yell* if you're in trouble and need help. You might also *yell* if you get excited over something or are furious at someone. People sometimes *yell* when they are hurt or frightened.

• call   *Call* and the rest of the words in this entry are related to yell but are not synonyms. *Call* means raise your voice so that someone who is far away can hear you. Golfers *call* "Fore" if they think a ball may hit another player. I *called* to Florence, but she didn't hear me.

• cry
• bawl   *Cry* and *bawl* can mean either call or weep loudly. The man *cried* "Help!" when his wallet was stolen in the crowd. The little boy *bawled* when he lost his family at the amusement park.

• exclaim   *Exclaim* can mean cry out in pleasure or surprise. "How good to see you again!" Aunt Marilyn *exclaimed* when she saw me getting off the train.

• howl   *Howl* means cry loudly for a long time. Coyotes *howl* at night. Nancy *howled* with laughter at the comedian.

• whine
• whimper   *Whine* and *whimper* mean speak in a low, complaining voice or make a low sound. Small children sometimes *whine* when they want their own way. Dogs *whine*. A puppy *whimpers*. Babies may *whimper* if they are sleepy.

yell (v) continued on page 414 ◗

Y

yell (v) continued from page 413

• shout

Shout means yell at the top of your voice. People *shout* when they're at a football game. Mary *shouted* "Fire!" when she saw the smoke in the hall. I *shouted* good-by to my friend as the train pulled out of the station.

• scream
• screech
• shriek

Scream, screech, and *shriek* are all good words to use for yell. They mean make a sharp, shrill sound. Some people *scream* when they see a snake. The tires of a car will *screech* if the car stops suddenly. They *shrieked* in fear when they visited a haunted house in the amusement park.

• clamor

Clamor means make a lot of noise. The zoo animals *clamor* for their food at feeding time.

• bellow
• roar

Bellow and *roar* can be used to mean make a loud, deep sound or noise. Wild animals *bellow* and *roar,* but we also say people and things *bellow* and *roar.* "Hurry up and help me clean the garage," Roscoe *bellowed.* The audience *roared* with laughter. The train *roared* out of the tunnel.

ANTONYM: whisper (v)

The train **roared** out of the tunnel.

Z

zone (n)

A *zone* is a particular part of something or a particular place. The earth's surface is divided into five parts or *zones*. Most of the United States is in the North Temperate *Zone.* Streets and highways are divided into traffic *zones.* The streets surrounding a school make up a school *zone.* You are not allowed to park in a no-parking *zone.* Zip Codes on letters and packages indicate the postal *zone* to which they are being sent.

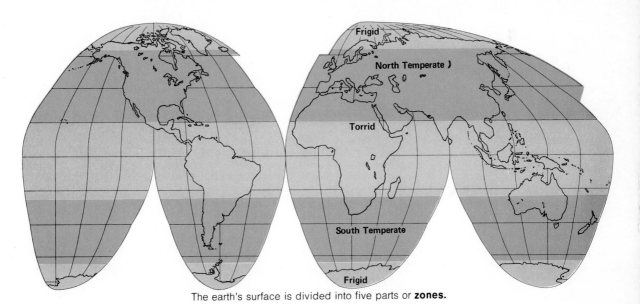

The earth's surface is divided into five parts or **zones.**

• division

Division and the rest of the words in this entry are related to zone but are not synonyms. A *division* is one of the parts into which something can be divided. States, cities, and counties may all be called *divisions* within the United States. Some businesses have several *divisions.*

zone continued on page 416 ▶

Z

- district

    A *district* can be a division within a country or city. We speak of farming, mining, and business *districts.* There are also school *districts* and police *districts.*

- area

    Area may mean the amount of ground space that something takes up. Or it may mean a place—either large or small, open or enclosed—that is set aside for a special purpose. A plain is a large *area* of level grass-covered land, usually used for farming or grazing. The room in your home where you eat dinner may be called a dining *area.* The space where cars can be left is called a parking *area.* A playground is an outside play *area.*

- region

    A *region* is a large area. The area surrounding the North Pole is called the Arctic *region.* A desert is a barren *region.*

- belt

    A *belt* can be a region where certain crops are raised. We speak of the South as being the cotton *belt* and of the Midwest as being the wheat *belt.*

- tract

    A *tract* is a stretch of land. A prairie is a *tract* of level or rolling grassland. The factory bought a *tract* of land next to the railroad.

INDEX

A LIST OF ALL THE WORDS IN THIS BOOK

A

abandon **leave** (v) 230
abandon **grasp** (v) 182
abbreviate **decrease** (v) 110
abdicate **surrender** (v) 371
ability 20
able **skillful** 345
abnormal **normal** 254
abrupt **sudden** 362
abruptly **suddenly** 363
abscond **run** (v) 315
absolute **perfect** (adj) 266
absurd **foolish** 166
absurd **wise** 404
abundance **wealth** 400
abundant **rare** 300
accelerate **advance** (v) 30
accelerate **decrease** (v) 110
acceptable **disagreeable** 120
accomplishment 21
account (n) 22
accumulate **gather** 173
accumulate **save** 321
accurate **correct** (adj) 98
achieve **obtain** 259
achieve **succeed** 361
achievement
    accomplishment 21
achievement **conquest** 91
acquaint **inform** 214
act (v) 23
act (v) **pretend** 288
act (n) **action** 24
•act (n) **law** 229
action 24
action **battle** (n) 52
active 26
activity **action** 24
activity **work** (n) 406
actual **real** 301
actual **imaginary** 208

add **increase** (v) 213
add **decrease** (v) 110
•addition **branch** (n) 62
adjust **correct** (v) 99
admire 27
    See also **love** (v) 241
admire **hate** (v) 194
admit **agree** 32
admit **allow** 36
admit **shut** (v) 340
admonish **advise** 31
admonition **warning** 396
adore 28
    See also **love** (v) 241
adult (adj) 29
adult (adj) **new** 252
advance (v) 30
    See also **move** 250
advance (v) **block** (v) 59
advertise **announce** 41
advice **suggestion** 366
advice **warning** 396
advise 31
    See also **tell** 377
age (v) **grow** 186
agile **active** 26
agony **misery** 245
agree 32
agree **promise** (v) 290
agree **argue** 45
agree **object** (v) 257
agreeable **pleasant** 274
agreeable **disagreeable** 120
agreement 33
•agreement **pledge** (n) 276
agreement **objection** 258
agreement **quarrel** (n) 298

aid (v) **help** (v) 197
aid (v) **block** (v) 59
aid (n) **help** (n) 198
aim (n) **object** (n) 256
alarm (n) **fear** (n) 157
alarm (n) **warning** 396
alarm (v) **scare** (v) 325
alert (adj) 34
alibi **defense** 112
alien **foreign** 170
•alliance **club** (n) 80
allow 36
    See also **give** 177
allow **block** (v) 59
almighty **powerful** 282
alter **change** (v) 75
amaze **surprise** (v) 368
amazement **surprise** (n) 370
ambush (v) **attack** (v) 48
amiable **friendly** 172
amplify **enlarge** 138
amuse 37
amusement 38
amusing **humorous** 205
ancient **new** 252
•anecdote **story** 356
anger 39
•annex (v) **increase** (v) 213
annex (v) **join** 222
announce 41
    See also **tell** 377
annoy **worry** (v) 409
annoy **amuse** 37
•annoyance **difficulty** 116
answer (v) 42
    See also **tell** 377
answer (v) **satisfy** 320
answer (v) **inquire** 216
answer (n) 43

NOTE: Each page listed in this Index is the page on which the entry begins.
•Identifies related word.

C

D

create 100
    See also **make** 243
•creation **invention** 220
•creek **branch** (n) 62
crisp **breakable** 67
crooked **dishonest** 121
cross-examine **inquire** 216
crow (v) **brag** 61
crowd (n) 101
    See also **gathering** 174
crude **rude** 312
cruel **friendly** 172
cruel **thoughtful** 380
•cry (v) **yell** (v) 413
cuff (v) **hit** (v) 202
cumbersome **heavy** 196
cunning **skillful** 345
curb (v) **govern** 179
curb (n) **edge** (n) 131
curious 102
curious **odd** 260
current (adj) **new** 252
custom **habit** 188
cut (v) 103
cut (v) **decrease** (v) 110
cut short **lengthen** 231

damage (v) **harm** (v) 192
damage (n) **harm** (n) 191
damp **moist** 249
danger 105
dangerous **safe** (adj) 319
daring (n) **bravery** 63
daring (adj) **shy** 341
dark 106
dark **shining** 336
•data **information** 215
dawdle **hurry** (v) 206
deadline **limit** (n) 235
deal (n) 107
deal (v) **trade** (v) 384
dear **precious** 285
debate (v) **argue** 45
deceit **honesty** 203
deceitful **dishonest** 121
deceive **fool** (v) 165
decide 108
    See also **think** 379
decide **choose** 78
decision 109
declare **say** 323
decline (v) **request** (v) 306
decrease (v) 110
    See also **make** 243
decrease (v) **increase** (v) 213
decrease (n) **growth** 186
deed **accomplishment** 21
defeat (v) 112
defeat (n) **conquest** 91
defective **perfect** (adj) 266
defend **protect** 290
defend **support** (v) 367
defend **attack** (v) 48
defense 112
defense **answer** (n) 43
defenseless **powerless** 284

definite **clear** (adj) 79
definite **dim** (adj) 118
deflate **shrink** 339
deflate **enlarge** 138
delay (v) **block** (v) 59
delay (v) **hurry** (v) 206
delectable **delicious** 114
deliberate **sudden** 362
deliberately **suddenly** 363
delicate **breakable** 67
delicate **delicious** 114
delicious 114
delight (v) **amuse** 37
delight (n) **amusement** 38
delight (n) **happiness** 189
delightful **delicious** 114
delightful **pleasant** 274
deliver **send** 328
demand (v) **command** (v) 85
demand (v) **request** (v) 306
demolish **ruin** (v) 314
demolish **build** 68
demonstrate **show** (v) 337
deny **allow** 36
depart **leave** (v) 230
depart **come** 82
dependable **dishonest** 121
depleted **exhausted** 145
depressed **sad** 317
descend **fall** (v) 151
descend **rise** (v) 309
describe **explain** 146
desert (v) **leave** (v) 230
design (v) **create** 100
•design (n) **plan** (n) 270
desire (v) **want** (v) 395
desire (n) **yearning** 412
despair (n) **sadness** 318
despair (n) **happiness** 189
despise **hate** (v) 194
destitute **poor** 279

destroy **ruin** (v) 314
destroy **build** 68
destroy **create** 100
destroy **repair** (v) 304
destroy **save** 321
detach **join** 222
detect **find** (v) 160
determine **decide** 108
determine **find** (v) 160
detest **hate** (v) 194
detest **enjoy** 138
develop **build** 68
develop **grow** 186
•develop **practice** (v) 284
development **growth** 186
•development **training** 386
•device **instrument** 219
devoted **loyal** 242
dexterity **ability** 20
dexterous **skillful** 345
dexterous **clumsy** 81
•diagram (n) **plan** (n) 270
dialogue **conversation** 95
•diary **history** 200
die **live** (v) 237
differ **agree** 32
difference **agreement** 33
difficult 115
difficult **convenient** 94
difficult **simple** 343
difficulty 116
•difficulty **misfortune** 245
digress **wander** 393
diluted **thin** 378
dim (adj) 118
dim (adj) **clear** (adj) 79
dim (adj) **shining** 336
diminish **decrease** (v) 110
diminish **increase** (v) 213

direct (v) 119
direct (v) **command** (v) 85
dirty **unclean** 387
disagree **argue** 45
disagree **object** (v) 257
disagree **agree** 32
disagreeable 120
disagreement **quarrel** (n) 298
disagreement **agreement** 33
disappear **come** 82
disapproval **objection** 258
disapproval **agreement** 33
disapprove **agree** 32
disarrange **disturb** 122
•disaster **misfortune** 245
disbelief **belief** 57
discard (v) **save** 321
•discern **know** 224
discontented **comfortable** 84
discourage **help** (v) 197
discourse **conversation** 95
discourteous **rude** 312
discover **find** (v) 160
•discovery **invention** 220
discuss **argue** 45
discuss **speak** 350
discussion **conversation** 95
disguise (v) **hide** (v) 199
disgust (n) **hate** (n) 194
dishonest 121
dishonesty **honesty** 203
dishonor (v) **admire** 27
dishonor (n) **honesty** 203
dishonorable **dishonest** 121
dislike (v) **hate** (v) 194
dislike (v) **enjoy** 138
dislike (n) **hate** (n) 194
disloyal **loyal** 242
disorder **arrangement** 46
disorderly **neat** 252
dispatch (v) **send** 328
dispel **scatter** 326

disperse **scatter** 326
disperse **gather** 173
displace **disturb** 122
display (v) **show** (v) 337
display (n) **show** (n) 338
displeasing **pleasant** 274
displeasure **amusement** 38
dispute (v) **argue** 45
dispute (v) **agree** 32
dispute (n) **quarrel** (n) 298
dispute (n) **agreement** 33
disregard **admire** 27
disregard **consider** 92
disregard **watch** (v) 398
disrespectful **rude** 312
dissension **agreement** 33
dissent (v) **agree** 32
distaste **hate** (n) 194
distasteful **delicious** 114
distinct **dim** (adj) 118
•distinguish **know** 224
distinguished **famous** 152
distract **disturb** 122
distress (n) **misery** 245
•distress (n) **misfortune** 245
•district **zone** (n) 415
distrust (v) **doubt** (v) 125
distrust (n) **doubt** (n) 126
disturb 122
    See also **move** 250
disturb **amuse** 37
disturb **calm** (v) 70
disturbed **worried** 408
disturbed **calm** (adj) 69
diversion **amusement** 38
divert **amuse** 37
divide **decrease** (v) 110
divide **increase** (v) 213
divide **join** 222

E

F

- •fable **tale** 373
- fabricate **build** 68
- •fabrication **invention** 220
- fail **fall** (v) 151
- fail **succeed** 361
- **failure** 147
- failure **accomplishment** 21
- failure **conquest** 91
- **fair** (adj) 148
  - See also **right** 308
- fair (adj) **beautiful** 54
- •fairy tale **tale** 373
- faith **belief** 57
- faith **doubt** (n) 126
- faithful **loyal** 242
- faithless **loyal** 242
- **fake** (adj) 150
- fake (adj) **real** 301
- **fall** (v) 151
  - See also **go** 179
- fall (v) **rise** (v) 309
- fall back **advance** (v) 30
- false **fake** (adj) 150
- false **correct** (adj) 98
- false **loyal** 242
- false **real** 301
- famed **famous** 152
- familiar **ordinary** 263
- familiar **odd** 260
- familiar **special** 351
- **famous** 152
- fanciful **imaginary** 208
- fancy (v) **imagine** 209
- fantastic **imaginary** 208
- fashion (v) **create** 100
- **fast** (adj) 153
- **fast** (adv) 154

- **fasten** 155
- fasten **break** (v) 64
- fat **slender** 347
- fat **thin** 378
- fatigued **exhausted** 145
- favor (n) **present** (n) 287
- **fear** (n) 157
- fearlessness **fear** (n) 157
- feat **accomplishment** 21
- •federation **club** (n) 80
- feeble **weak** 399
- feign **pretend** 288
- fence (v) **limit** (v) 234
- fenced **enclosed** 134
- ferocious **fierce** 158
- ferocious **wild** 401
- fetch **carry** 71
- fickle **changeable** 77
- fickle **loyal** 242
- fictitious **imaginary** 208
- **fierce** 158
- fierce **tame** (adj) 375
- **fight** (v) 158
- fight (n) **battle** (n) 52
- figure (n) **shape** (n) 333
- filthy **unclean** 387
- •final **last** (adj) 228
- **find** (v) 160
- find (v) **hide** (v) 199
- •finding (n) **invention** 220
- fine **slender** 347
- finish (v) **end** (v) 134
- finish (v) **start** (v) 354
- finish (n) **end** (n) 136
- finish (n) **beginning** 56
- **firm** (adj) 161
- firm (adj) **tough** 382
- firm (adj) **thin** 378
- **firm** (n) 163
  - See also **gathering** 174

- first **basic** 50
- first **last** (adj) 227
- fit (adj) **appropriate** (adj) 44
- fit (v) **join** 222
- fit (v) **shape** (v) 334
- fitting (adj) **appropriate** (adj) 44
- fix (v) **repair** (v) 304
- fix (v) **break** (v) 64
- fix (v) **ruin** (v) 314
- fizzle (n) **failure** 147
- flabbergast **surprise** (v) 368
- flabby **firm** (adj) 161
- •flash (n) **gleam** (n) 178
- flaw (n) **spot** (n) 352
- flawless **perfect** (adj) 266
- flee **run** (v) 315
- fleet (adj) **fast** (adj) 153
- fleetly **fast** (adv) 154
- flexible **elastic** 132
- flexible **firm** (adj) 161
- •flicker (n) **gleam** (n) 178
- flighty **serious** 329
- flimsy **thin** 378
- flimsy **weak** 399
- flimsy **strong** 358
- fling (v) **throw** (v) 382
- float (v) **wander** 393
- flog **beat** (v) 53
- flourish **succeed** 361
- flow (v) **run** (v) 315
- fluctuating **changeable** 77
- fluster **disturb** 122
- •folk tale **tale** 373
- **follow** 163
  - See also **go** 179
- follow **imitate** 210
- fondness **hate** (n) 194
- fond of, be **enjoy** 138

G

fool (v) 165
foolish 166
foolish **wise** 404
foolishness **wisdom** 403
forbid **allow** 36
force (v) 167
   See also **move** 250
force (n) **strength** 357
forceful **powerful** 282
foreboding (n) **warning** 396
forecast (v) 168
   See also **tell** 377
forecast (n) 169
foreign 170
foresee **forecast** (v) 168
foretell **forecast** (v) 168
forewarn **forecast** (v) 168
forewarning (n) **warning** 396
forge (v) **shape** (v) 334
forged **real** 301
forget **find** (v) 160
forget **remember** 303
forgo **obtain** 259
form (n) **shape** (n) 333
form (v) **create** 100
form (v) **shape** (v) 334
forsake **leave** (v) 230
fortitude **endurance** 136
found **start** (v) 354
fracas **quarrel** (n) 298
fraction **portion** (n) 280
fracture (v) **break** (v) 64
fragile **breakable** 67
fragile **weak** 399
fragile **tough** 382
fragment **piece** 268
•fragrant **delicious** 114
frail **weak** 399
frame (n) **edge** (n) 131
frantic **worried** 408

free (v) 171
free (v) **catch** (v) 72
free (v) **fasten** 155
•freedom **liberty** 232
freight **load** (n) 238
frequent **rare** 300
friendly 172
fright **fear** (n) 157
frighten **scare** (v) 325
frightful **dreadful** 127
frisky **playful** 273
frivolous **serious** 329
frolicsome **playful** 273
frontier **limit** (n) 235
frustrated **happy** 190
fun **amusement** 38
function (v) **act** (v) 23
function (v) **work** (v) 407
fundamental **basic** 50
funny **foolish** 166
funny **humorous** 205
funny **odd** 260
furious **wild** 401
further (v) **advance** (v) 30
fury **anger** 39
fuse (v) **mix** (v) 247
fusion **mixture** 248
fuss (n) **quarrel** (n) 298

gallantry **bravery** 63
gallop (v) **run** (v) 315
•gang **party** 265
gather 173
gather **scatter** 326
gathering 174
gaunt **thin** 378
gawky **clumsy** 81
gay **sad** 317
gaze (v) **look** (v) 240
general **rare** 300
general **special** 351
genial **friendly** 172
genial **rude** 312
gentle 176
gentle **fierce** 158
gentle **harsh** 193
gentle **rude** 312
gentle **wild** 401
genuine **real** 301
genuine **fake** (adj) 150
•gesture (n) **sign** (n) 341
get **present** (v) 288
get **send** 328
gift **present** (n) 287
gigantic **large** 226
give 177
give **obtain** 259
give **win** (v) 402
give up **attempt** (v) 49
give up **obtain** 259
glad **sad** 317
gladness **sadness** 318
glance (v) **look** (v) 240
glare (v) **look** (v) 240
gleam (n) 178
glimmering **shining** 336
•glint (n) **gleam** (n) 178
gloat **brag** 61
gloom **sadness** 318
gloomy **dark** 106
gloomy **sad** 317
gloomy **happy** 190
gloomy **pleasant** 274

H

glorious **splendid** 352
•glow (n) **gleam** (n) 178
glue (v) **join** 222
go 179
go **come** 82
goad (v) **urge** 388
goal **object** (n) 256
go away **come** 82
good **fair** (adj) 148
gorgeous **beautiful** 54
gorgeous **splendid** 352
govern 179
grab **grasp** (v) 182
graceful **beautiful** 54
graceful **clumsy** 81
gradual **sudden** 362
gradually **suddenly** 363
grand 180
grant (v) **present** (v) 288
grant (n) **present** (n) 287
grapple **battle** (v) 51
grasp (v) 182
　　See also **take** (v) 373
gratify **satisfy** 320
grave (adj) **serious** 329
grave (adj) **humorous** 205
great 183
　　See also **big** 58
green **adult** (adj) 29
grip (v) **grasp** (v) 182
group 184
　　See also **gathering** 174
•group **party** 265
grow 186
grown-up (adj) **adult** (adj) 29
growth 186
gruff **harsh** 193
•guarantee (n) **pledge** (n) 276
guard (v) **protect** 290
guard (v) **watch** (v) 398
guard (v) **attack** (v) 48
guess (v) **imagine** 209
guide (v) **direct** (v) 119

habit 188
halt (v) **end** (v) 134
handsome **beautiful** 54
handy **convenient** 94
handy **skillful** 345
handy **useful** 389
handy **clumsy** 81
hankering **yearning** 412
•happen **come** 82
happening **event** 141
happiness 189
happiness **misfortune** 245
happiness **misery** 245
happiness **sadness** 318
happy 190
happy **sad** 317
harbor (v) **protect** 290
•harbor (n) **shelter** (n) 335
hard **difficult** 115
hard **firm** (adj) 161
hard **convenient** 94
hard **gentle** 176
hard **simple** 343
•hardship **difficulty** 116
•hardship **misfortune** 245
harm (v) 192
harm (n) 191
harm (n) **help** (n) 198
harmless **safe** (adj) 319
harmless **fierce** 158
harmless **harm** 191
harmless **wild** 401
harsh 193
harsh **gentle** 176
harvest (v) **gather** 173
hasten **hurry** (v) 206
hastily **suddenly** 363
hasty **sudden** 362

hatch (v) **plan** (v) 272
hate (v) 194
hate (v) **enjoy** 138
hate (n) 194
hatred **hate** (n) 194
haughty **proud** 292
haughty **humble** (adj) 204
haul (v) **pull** (v) 293
hazard **danger** 105
hazardous **safe** (adj) 319
healthy **powerless** 284
healthy **weak** 399
heart **center** (n) 74
heave **lift** (v) 233
heavy 196
heavy **slender** 347
heavy **thin** 378
heedless **thoughtless** 381
heedless **alert** (adj) 34
help (v) 197
help (v) **block** (v) 59
help (n) 198
help (n) **misfortune** 245
helpful **useful** 389
helpless **powerless** 284
helpless **powerful** 282
helpless **useful** 389
herald (v) **announce** 41
heroism **bravery** 63
hidden **visible** 390
hide (v) 199
hide (v) **announce** 41
hide (v) **find** (v) 160
hide (v) **show** (v) 337
hideous **beautiful** 54
hike (v) **walk** (v) 391
hinder **block** (v) 59
hinder **advance** (v) 30
hinder **help** (v) 197
hinder **hurry** (v) 206
hindrance **help** (n) 198

I

ineffectual **useful** 389
inexact **correct** (adj) 98
inexpensive **precious** 285
inferior **great** 183
inflate **enlarge** 138
inflate **shrink** 339
inflexible **firm** (adj) 161
inflexible **elastic** 132
influential **powerful** 282
inform 214
   See also **tell** 377
information 215
•infrequent **rare** 300
ingenious **skillful** 345
ingenuity **ability** 20
inhabit **live** (v) 237
inherit **obtain** 259
initiate (v) **start** (v) 354
injure **harm** (v) 192
injury **harm** (n) 191
inquire 216
inquire **answer** (v) 42
inquiry **inspection** 218
inquiry **answer** (n) 43
inquisitive **curious** 102
•insight **wisdom** 403
insignificant **important** 211
insinuate **suggest** 365
insinuation **suggestion** 366
insipid **dull** 128
insipid **tame** (adj) 375
insipid **delicious** 114
inspect **examine** 142
inspection 218
instant **fast** (adj) 153
instant **sudden** 362
instantaneous **fast** (adj) 153
instantaneously **fast** (adv) 154
instantly **fast** (adv) 154
instantly **suddenly** 363

instruct **command** (v) 85
instruct **inform** 214
instrument 219
integrity **honesty** 203
•intelligence **information** 215
intend **plan** (v) 272
intent **object** (n) 256
intercept **interfere** 220
interest (v) **amuse** 37
interest (n) **amusement** 38
interest (n) **concern** (n) 86
interesting **dull** 128
interfere 220
interfere **disturb** 122
intermission **break** (n) 66
interpret **explain** 146
interrupt **disturb** 122
interrupt **interfere** 220
interruption **break** (n) 66
intimidate **scare** (v) 325
intricate **simple** 343
introduce **start** (v) 354
invade **attack** (v) 48
invade **enter** 140
invent **create** 100
invention 220
investigate **examine** 142
investigate **inquire** 216
investigation **inspection** 218
iridescent **changeable** 77
irk **worry** (v) 409
irregular **normal** 254
irritation **anger** 39

J

jagged **rough** 310
jerk (v) **pull** (v) 293
job **task** 376
jog (v) **run** (v) 315
join 222
join **break** (v) 64
•journal **history** 200
joy **happiness** 189
joy **misery** 245
judgment **decision** 109
judgment **opinion** 262
•judgment **wisdom** 403
juicy **moist** 249
jumble (v) **disturb** 122
just **fair** (adj) 148
just **dishonest** 121
justification **defense** 112
justification **reason** (n) 302
justify **explain** 146
juvenile **adult** (adj) 29

K

keen **eager** 130
keep **protect** 290
keep **save** 321
keep **surrender** (v) 371
•kind (n) **group** 184
kind (adj) **friendly** 172
kind (adj) **thoughtful** 380
kind (adj) **harsh** 193
know 224
   See also **think** 379
•knowledge **information** 215
•knowledge **wisdom** 403

L

labor (v) **work** (v) 407
labor (n) **work** (n) 406
laborious **difficult** 115
large 226
   See also **big** 58
large **little** 236
last (adj) 227
last (adj) **basic** 50
late **new** 252
•latest **last** (adj) 227
launch (v) **start** (v) 354
law 229
lay **put** 296
lead (v) **direct** (v) 119
lead (v) **follow** 163
leading **important** 211
•league **club** (n) 80
lean (adj) **thin** 378
lean (v) **slant** (v) 346
learn **find** (v) 160
leave (v) 230
   See also **go** 179
leave (v) **come** 82
leave (n) **permission** 268
legacy **present** (n) 287
•legend **tale** 373
leisure **work** (n) 406
lengthen 231
   See also **make** 243
lengthen **decrease** (v) 110
lessen **decrease** (v) 110
let **allow** 36
let **block** (v) 59
let go **catch** (v) 72
let go **grasp** (v) 182
let go **obtain** 259
let go **save** 321
level (adj) **rough** 310

•levelheaded **wise** 404
liberate **free** (v) 171
•liberation **liberty** 232
liberty 232
•license **liberty** 232
license (n) **permission** 268
lift (v) 233
   See also **move** 250
light (adj) **dark** 106
light (adj) **heavy** 196
lighthearted **serious** 329
like (v) **enjoy** 138
like (v) **hate** (v) 194
•likeness **copy** (n) 97
liking (n) **yearning** 412
liking (n) **hate** (n) 194
•limb **branch** (n) 62
limit (v) 234
limit (n) 235
limited **enclosed** 134
limp (adj) **firm** (adj) 161
line (n) **limit** (n) 235
linger **hurry** (v) 206
linger **leave** (v) 230
link (v) **join** 222
list (v) **slant** (v) 346
little 236
little **large** 226
live (v) 237
lively **active** 26
lively **sad** 317
load (n) 238
loathe **hate** (v) 194
loathe **enjoy** 138
locality **location** 239
location 239
lofty **grand** 180
lofty **humble** (adj) 204
•log **history** 200
loiter **hurry** (v) 206
longing (n) **yearning** 412
look (v) 240
   See also **see** 327

loosen **fasten** 155
lope (v) **run** (v) 315
lose **defeat** (v) 112
lose **find** (v) 160
lose **obtain** 259
lose **win** (v) 402
loss **harm** (n) 191
loud **calm** (adj) 69
loud **gentle** 176
loud **silent** 343
loud **tame** (adj) 375
love (v) 241
love (v) **hate** (v) 194
love (n) **hate** (n) 194
lovely **beautiful** 54
lower (v) **lift** (v) 233
lowly **humble** (adj) 204
lowly **grand** 180
loyal 242
lull (n) **break** (n) 66
lump (n) **piece** 268
lurk **sneak** (v) 348
luscious **delicious** 114
lustrous **shining** 336

M

made-up **real** 301
magnificent **grand** 180
magnificent **splendid** 352
magnify **enlarge** 138
mail (v) **send** 328
main **important** 211
maintain **support** (v) 367
maintain **change** (v) 75
majestic **grand** 180
major **important** 211
make 243
make believe **pretend** 289
mammoth (adj) **large** 226
mannerly **rude** 312
manufacture (v) **build** 68
march (v) **walk** (v) 391
margin **edge** (n) 131
mark (n) **object** (n) 256
mark (n) **spot** (n) 352
mask (v) **hide** (v) 199
massive **large** 226
mastery **power** 281
mature (adj) **adult** (adj) 29
mature (adj) **new** 252
mature (v) **grow** 186
maturity **growth** 186
mean (adj) **friendly** 172
mean (adj) **gentle** 176
mean (adj) **thoughtful** 380
meander **wander** 393
meddle **interfere** 220
meek **humble** (adj) 204
meeting 244
　See also **gathering** 174
melancholy (adj) **sad** 317
melancholy (adj) **happy** 190
melancholy (adj) **pleasant** 274
melancholy (n) **sadness** 318
member **portion** (n) 280
menace (n) **danger** 105

mend **repair** (v) 304
mend **break** (v) 64
mention **say** 323
merge **mix** (v) 247
merger **mixture** 248
merry **sad** 317
messy **neat** 252
middle (n) **center** (n) 74
might (n) **strength** 357
mighty **powerful** 282
mild **gentle** 176
mild **humble** (adj) 204
mild **fierce** 158
mild **harsh** 193
mimic (v) **imitate** 210
mingle **mix** (v) 247
miniature **little** 236
minor **important** 211
minor **serious** 329
minute (adj) **little** 236
minute (adj) **large** 226
mischievous **playful** 273
miserable **sad** 317
miserable **comfortable** 84
miserable **happy** 190
misery 245
misery **happiness** 189
misfortune 245
•misfortune **difficulty** 116
misgiving **doubt** (n) 126
misinform **inform** 214
mislead **fool** (v) 165
miss (v) **catch** (v) 72
miss (v) **notice** (v) 255
mistrust (n) **belief** 57
mix (v) 247
mixture 248
mob (n) **crowd** (n) 101
mock (v) **imitate** 210
model (v) **shape** (v) 334
model (n) **example** 143
•moderate **gentle** 176
modern **new** 252

modest **humble** (adj) 204
modest **shy** 341
modest **proud** 292
modify **change** (v) 75
moist 249
mold (v) **shape** (v) 334
money **wealth** 400
monotonous **dull** 128
monumental **great** 183
motion **action** 24
motive **reason** (n) 302
mount (v) **rise** (v) 309
mournful **sad** 317
movable **firm** (adj) 161
move 250
movement **action** 24
multiply **increase** (v) 213
multiply **decrease** (v) 110
multitude **crowd** (n) 101
murky **dark** 106
•murmur (n) **sound** (n) 348
murmur (v) **say** 323
muscular **strong** 358
mute **silent** 343
mutter **say** 323
mysterious **odd** 260
mystery 251
•mystery **story** 356
•myth **tale** 373

N

- narrate **report** (v) 305
- narrow (v) **enlarge** 138
- natural **normal** 254
- natural **odd** 260
- **neat** 252
- neat **unclean** 387
- necessary **basic** 50
- need (v) **want** (v) 395
- needy (adj) **poor** 279
- neglect (v) **consider** 92
- neighborly **friendly** 172
- nervous **worried** 408
- nervous **calm** (adj) 69
- net (v) **catch** (v) 72
- **new** 252
- news **information** 215
- nice **correct** (adj) 98
- noble **grand** 180
- noise **sound** (n) 348
- noise **calm** (n) 71
- noiseless **silent** 343
- noisy **calm** (adj) 69
- noisy **silent** 343
- noisy **tame** (adj) 375
- nonessential **basic** 50
- nonplus (v) **surprise** (v) 368
- nonsensical **foolish** 166
- **normal** 254
- normal **odd** 260
- normal **rare** 300
- nosy **curious** 102
- notable **great** 183
- note (v) **notice** (v) 255
- noted **famous** 152
- **notice** (v) 255
  - See also **see** 327
- noticeable **visible** 390
- notify **inform** 214
- notion **idea** 207
- notorious **famous** 152
- novel **story** 356
- nucleus **center** (n) 74
- nudge (v) **push** (v) 295

O

- obey **command** (v) 85
- **object** (v) 257
- **object** (n) 256
- **objection** 258
- objective (n) **object** (n) 256
- obnoxious **disagreeable** 120
- obnoxious **pleasant** 274
- obscure (adj) **dim** (adj) 118
- obscure (adj) **clear** (adj) 79
- obscure (adj) **famous** 152
- obscure (v) **hide** (v) 199
- observe **notice** (v) 255
- observe **watch** (v) 398
- obsolete **new** 252
- obstacle **difficulty** 116
- obstruct **block** (v) 59
- obstruct **advance** (v) 30
- obstruct **help** (v) 197
- obstruction **difficulty** 116
- **obtain** 259
  - See also **take** (v) 373
- obvious **clear** (adj) 79
- occupy **live** (v) 237
- occurrence **event** 141
- **odd** 260
- offensive **disagreeable** 120
- offensive **beautiful** 54
- offering (n) **present** (n) 287
- old **new** 252
- old-fashioned **new** 252
- omen **sign** (n) 341
- omnipotent **powerful** 282
- open (adj) **clear** (adj) 79
- open (adj) **enclosed** 134
- open (v) **start** (v) 354
- open (v) **end** (v) 134
- open (v) **shut** (v) 340
- operate (v) **run** (v) 315
- operate (v) **work** (v) 407
- operation **action** 24

- **opinion** 262
- order (v) **command** (v) 85
- order (n) **arrangement** 46
- order (n) **confusion** 89
- orderly **neat** 252
- ordinance **law** 229
- **ordinary** 263
- ordinary **odd** 260
- ordinary **rare** 300
- ordinary **special** 351
- ordinary **splendid** 352
- organization **arrangement** 46
- origin **beginning** 56
- origin **end** (n) 136
- original (adj) **real** 301
- original (n) **example** 143
- original (n) **copy** (n) 97
- originate **create** 100
- originate **end** (v) 134
- ornate **clear** (adj) 79
- outcome **result** (n) 307
- outdo **defeat** (v) 112
- outlandish **foreign** 170
- outline (n) **edge** (n) 131
- outline (n) **plan** (n) 270
- outline (n) **shape** (n) 333
- outset **limit** (n) 235
- outstanding **rare** 300
- overcome **conquer** 90
- overlook (v) **notice** (v) 255
- overlook (v) **watch** (v) 398
- overpower **conquer** 90
- oversee **watch** (v) 398
- overthrow **conquer** 90
- overwhelm **conquer** 90

P

Q

R

race (v) **run** (v) 315
radiant **shining** 336
rage (n) **anger** 39
raging **fierce** 158
rainy **moist** 249
raise (v) **lift** (v) 233
ramble (v) **wander** 393
range (v) **wander** 393
ransom (v) **free** (v) 171
rapid **fast** (adj) 153
rapidly **fast** (adv) 154
rare 300
raspy **harsh** 193
rattle (v) **disturb** 122
ready **alert** (adj) 34
real 301
   See also **right** 308
real **fake** (adj) 150
real **imaginary** 208
realize **imagine** 209
•realize **know** 224
reason (v) **consider** 92
reason (n) 302
•reason (n) **wisdom** 403
•reasonable **wise** 404
reasonable **foolish** 166
recall **remember** 303
recede **advance** (v) 30
receive **obtain** 259
receive **present** (v) 288
receive **send** 328
recent **new** 252
recess (n) **break** (n) 66
•recite **report** (v) 305
reckless **thoughtless** 381
•recognize **know** 224
recognize **remember** 303
recollect **remember** 303
•record (n) **history** 200
recreation **amusement** 38
reduce **decrease** (v) 110
reduce **enlarge** 138
refined **rude** 312

•reflect **remember** 303
reform (v) **correct** (v) 99
refreshing **pleasant** 274
•refuge **shelter** (n) 335
refuse (v) **choose** 78
refuse (v) **request** (v) 306
regard (v) **admire** 27
•region **zone** (n) 415
regular **normal** 254
regular **odd** 260
regulate **govern** 179
•regulation **law** 229
reign (v) **govern** 179
reject (v) **choose** 78
•relate **report** (v) 305
relax **work** (v) 407
release (v) **free** (v) 171
release (v) **catch** (v) 72
release (v) **contain** 93
release (v) **grasp** (v) 182
reliable **changeable** 77
reliable **dishonest** 121
relief **help** (n) 198
relinquish **surrender** (v) 371
relinquish **obtain** 259
remain **leave** (v) 230
remain **wander** 393
remedy (v) **correct** (v) 99
remember 303
   See also **think** 379
remind **remember** 303
remove **put** 296
renounce **surrender** (v) 371
renowned **famous** 152
repair (v) 304
repair (v) **break** (v) 64
repair (v) **harm** (v) 192
repair (v) **ruin** (v) 314
•repeat **practice** (v) 284
repeat **say** 323

replace **substitute** (v) 360
reply (v) **answer** (v) 42
reply (v) **inquire** 216
reply (n) **answer** (n) 43
report (v) 305
   See also **tell** 377
•report (n) **account** (n) 22
repulsive **disagreeable** 120
repulsive **pleasant** 274
request (v) 306
request (v) **answer** (v) 42
require **force** (v) 167
rescue (v) **free** (v) 171
rescue (v) **save** 321
•resemblance **copy** (n) 97
reside **live** (v) 237
resign **surrender** (v) 371
resilient **elastic** 132
resolution **decision** 109
resolve **decide** 108
respect (v) **admire** 27
respectful **rude** 312
respond **answer** (v) 42
respond **inquire** 216
response **answer** (n) 43
rest (v) **work** (v) 407
rest (n) **action** 24
rest (n) **work** (n) 406
restless **calm** (adj) 69
restless **silent** 343
restore **repair** (v) 304
restrain **block** (v) 59
restrict **limit** (v) 234
restricted **enclosed** 134
restriction **limit** (n) 235
result (n) 307
result (n) **beginning** 56
retort (v) **answer** (v) 42
retort (n) **answer** (n) 43
•reveal **report** (v) 305
reveal **show** (v) 337
reveal **hide** (v) 199

S

reversible **changeable** 77
rich **poor** 279
riches **wealth** 400
riddle **mystery** 251
ridiculous **foolish** 166
right 308
rigid **firm** (adj) 161
rigid **elastic** 132
rim **edge** (n) 131
rip (v) **break** (v) 64
ripe **adult** (adj) 29
ripen **grow** 186
rise (v) 309
   See also **go** 179
rise (v) **fall** (v) 151
risky **safe** (adj) 319
roam **wander** 393
•roar (v) **yell** (v) 413
•roar (n) **sound** (n) 348
rock (v) **shake** (v) 331
•romance **story** 356
root **beginning** 56
rough 310
rough **rude** 312
rough **gentle** 176
rout (v) **conquer** 90
routine **normal** 254
rove **wander** 393
rude 312
rude **polite** 278
rude **thoughtful** 380
rugged **rough** 310
ruin (v) 314
•ruin (n) **misfortune** 245
rule (v) **decide** 108
rule (v) **govern** 179
rule (n) **habit** 188
•rule (n) **law** 229
ruling **decision** 109
•rumble **sound** (n) 348
run (v) 315
   See also **move** 250
rush (v) **hurry** (v) 206

sacrifice (v) **surrender** (v) 371
sad 317
sad **happy** 190
sad **pleasant** 274
sadness 318
sadness **amusement** 38
sadness **happiness** 189
safe (adj) 319
safety **danger** 105
•sale **deal** (n) 107
sample (n) **example** 143
•sanctuary **shelter** (n) 335
satisfaction **happiness** 189
satisfied **comfortable** 84
satisfied **happy** 190
satisfy 320
satisfying **pleasant** 274
saunter (v) **walk** (v) 391
savage **fierce** 158
savage **wild** 401
save 321
savory **delicious** 114
say 323
   See also **tell** 377
•scarce **rare** 300
scare (v) 325
scatter 326
scatter **gather** 173
scatter **mix** (v) 247
scatterbrained **thoughtless** 381
•scheme (v) **plan** (v) 272
•scheme (n) **plan** (n) 270
scorn (v) **hate** (v) 194
scrawny **thin** 378
•scream (v) **yell** (v) 413
•screech (v) **yell** (v) 413
screen (v) **protect** 290

scrutinize **examine** 142
scrutiny **inspection** 218
secret (n) **mystery** 251
section (n) **portion** (n) 280
secure (adj) **safe** (adj) 319
secure (v) **fasten** 155
•security **pledge** (n) 276
security **danger** 105
see 327
see **look** (v) 240
segment **portion** (n) 280
seize **catch** (v) 72
seize **grasp** (v) 182
select (v) **choose** 78
self-control **anger** 39
selfish **thoughtful** 380
self-reliant **confident** 88
send 328
   See also **move** 250
send **obtain** 259
•sense **wisdom** 403
•sensible **wise** 404
sensible **foolish** 166
separate (v) **fasten** 155
separate (v) **gather** 173
separate (v) **join** 222
separate (v) **mix** (v) 247
separation **mixture** 248
serene **calm** (adj) 69
serenity **calm** (n) 71
serious 329
serious **humorous** 205
serious **playful** 273
service (n) **help** (n) 198
serviceable **useful** 389
set (v) **put** 296
set (v) **rise** (v) 309
•set (n) **group** 184
settle **decide** 108
settlement **decision** 109

sever **fasten** 155
shadowy **dim** (adj) 118
shake (v) 331
shape (v) 334
   See also **make** 243
shape (v) **create** 100
shape (n) 333
share (n) **portion** (n) 280
sharp **dim** (adj) 118
sharp **dull** 128
sharp **gentle** 176
shatter **break** (v) 64
shelter (v) **protect** 290
shelter (n) 335
shield (v) **protect** 290
shield (n) **defense** 112
•shield (n) **shelter** (n) 335
shift (v) **change** (v) 75
shift (v) **substitute** (v) 360
shimmering **shining** 336
shining 336
ship (v) **send** 328
shipshape **neat** 252
shiver (v) **shake** (v) 331
•shoot (n) **branch** (n) 62
short **little** 236
shorten **decrease** (v) 110
shorten **lengthen** 231
•shout (v) **yell** (v) 413
shove (v) **push** (v) 295
shove (v) **pull** (v) 293
show (v) 337
show (v) **hide** (v) 199
show (n) 338
•shriek (v) **yell** (v) 413
shrink 339
   See also **make** 243
shrink **enlarge** 138
shrivel **shrink** 339
shudder (v) **shake** (v) 331
shuffle (v) **walk** (v) 391
shut (v) 340
   See also **stop** (v) 356

shy 341
sign (n) 341
sign (n) **warning** 396
•signal (n) **sign** (n) 341
signal (n) **warning** 396
significant **important** 211
signify **show** (v) 337
silence **sound** (n) 348
silent 343
silhouette **shape** (n) 333
silly **foolish** 166
simple 343
simple **difficult** 115
simulate **pretend** 289
sincerity **honesty** 203
sink (v) **fall** (v) 151
site **location** 239
situation **condition** 87
situation **location** 239
skepticism **doubt** (n) 126
•sketch (n) **plan** (n) 270
skill **ability** 20
skillful 345
skillful **clumsy** 81
skinny **thin** 378
skirmish **battle** (n) 52
skulk **sneak** (v) 348
slant (v) 346
slap (v) **hit** (v) 202
slash (v) **cut** (v) 103
slender 347
slice (v) **cut** (v) 103
slight (adj) **little** 236
slight (adj) **slender** 347
slight (adj) **heavy** 196
slight (adj) **large** 226
slim **slender** 347
sling (v) **throw** (v) 382
slink (v) **sneak** (v) 348

slip (v) **sneak** (v) 348
slit (v) **cut** (v) 103
slope (v) **slant** (v) 346
sloppy **neat** 252
slovenly **unclean** 387
slow (adj) **active** 26
slow (adj) **alert** (adj) 34
slow (adj) **fast** (adj) 153
slow (adv) **fast** (adv) 154
slow (v) **advance** (v) 30
slow down **hurry** (v) 206
slowly **fast** (adv) 154
slug (v) **hit** (v) 202
sluggish **alert** (adj) 34
sluggish **fast** (adj) 153
sluggishly **fast** (adv) 154
small **little** 236
small **grand** 180
small **great** 183
small **large** 226
•smart **wise** 404
smash (v) **break** (v) 64
smooth **harsh** 193
smooth **rough** 310
smudge (n) **spot** (n) 352
smug **proud** 292
snare (v) **catch** (v) 72
snatch **catch** (v) 72
snatch **grasp** (v) 182
sneak (v) 348
   See also **go** 179
snoopy **curious** 102
snug **comfortable** 84
snug **safe** (adj) 319
soar **rise** (v) 309
sober **serious** 329
sociable **friendly** 172
•society **club** (n) 80
soft **gentle** 176
soft **firm** (adj) 161
soft **rough** 310
soft **tough** 382

T

subdue **conquer** 90
subdued **tame** (adj) 375
submit **surrender** (v) 371
submit **conquer** 90
substitute (v) 360
subtract **decrease** (v) 110
subtract **increase** (v) 213
succeed 361
succeed **win** (v) 402
success **conquest** 91
success **failure** 147
success **misfortune** 246
succulent moist 249
sudden 362
suddenly 363
suffer 364
suffering **misery** 245
suggest 365
  See also **tell** 377
suggestion 366
suitable **appropriate** (adj) 44
suitable **convenient** 94
sunny **dark** 106
superb **splendid** 352
superior **great** 183
support (v) 367
support (n) **help** (n) 198
suppose **imagine** 209
suppress **announce** 41
supreme **great** 183
sure **confident** 88
sure, be **know** 224
surpass **defeat** (v) 112
surprise (v) 368
surprise (n) 370
surrender (v) 371
  See also **give** 177
surrender (v) **conquer** 90

surround 372
surrounded **enclosed** 134
suspect (v) **doubt** (v) 125
suspend **shut** (v) 340
suspicion **doubt** (n) 126
sustain **support** (v) 367
swagger (v) **walk** (v) 391
swap (v) **trade** (v) 384
swat (v) **hit** (v) 202
sway (v) **shake** (v) 331
swear **promise** (v) 290
swear **say** 323
swell (v) **enlarge** 138
swell (v) **shrink** 339
swift **fast** (adj) 153
swiftly **fast** (adv) 154
switch (v) **change** (v) 75
switch (v) **substitute** (v) 360
swoop **fall** (v) 151
•symbol **sign** (n) 341
sympathetic **thoughtful** 380
•symptom **sign** (n) 341
symptom **warning** 396
•system **arrangement** 46
•system **habit** 188

•tactful **polite** 278
tactless **polite** 278
take (v) 373
take **carry** 71
take away **put** 296
take back **present** (v) 288
tale 373
talent **ability** 20
talk (v) **speak** 350
talkative **silent** 343
tame (adj) 375
tame (adj) **fierce** 158
tame (adj) **wild** 401
tantalize **worry** (v) 409
target **object** (n) 256
task 376
taste (n) **yearning** 412
tasty **delicious** 114
teach **inform** 214
•team **party** 265
tear (v) **break** (v) 64
tear (v) **repair** (v) 304
tear down **build** 68
tease (v) **worry** (v) 409
tedious **dull** 128
tell 377
tend **watch** (v) 398
tender **gentle** 176
tender **tough** 382
tenuous **slender** 347
terminate **end** (v) 134
terminate **lengthen** 231
termination **end** (n) 136
terrible **dreadful** 127
terrify **scare** (v) 325
terror **fear** (n) 157
terrorize **scare** (v) 325
test (v) **examine** 142
tether (v) **fasten** 155
thick **heavy** 196
thick **slender** 347
thick **thin** 378

thin 378
thin **slender** 347
thin **heavy** 196
thing **object** (n) 256
think 379
thirst (n) **yearning** 412
thought (n) **idea** 207
thought (n) **opinion** 262
thoughtful 380
thoughtful **serious** 329
thoughtful **thoughtless** 381
thoughtless 381
thoughtless **thoughtful** 380
thrash **beat** (v) 53
threat **danger** 105
thrive **succeed** 361
throng (n) **crowd** (n) 101
throw (v) 382
   See also **move** 250
throw away **save** 321
thrust (v) **push** (v) 295
thump **beat** (v) 53
tidy **neat** 252
tidy **unclean** 387
tie (v) **fasten** 155
tilt (v) **slant** (v) 346
timid **wild** 401
timidity **bravery** 63
tiny **little** 236
tiny **large** 226
tip (v) **slant** (v) 346
tire (v) **amuse** 37
tired **exhausted** 145
tiresome **dull** 128
toil (v) **work** (v) 407
toil (n) **work** (n) 406

•token **sign** (n) 341
•tolerate **allow** 36
tolerate **suffer** 364
•tool **instrument** 219
torment (n) **misery** 245
toss (v) **throw** (v) 382
tough 382
tough **breakable** 67
tough **gentle** 176
tough **weak** 399
tow (v) **pull** (v) 293
trace (v) **imitate** 210
track (v) **follow** 163
•tract **zone** (n) 415
trade (v) 384
•trade (n) **deal** (n) 107
trail (v) **follow** 163
•train (v) **practice** (v) 284
training 386
traitorous **loyal** 242
tramp (v) **walk** (v) 391
tranquil **calm** (adj) 69
tranquilize **calm** (v) 70
tranquillity **calm** (n) 71
•transaction **deal** (n) 107
transfer (v) **change** (v) 75
transform **change** (v) 75
transmit **send** 328
transparent **clear** (adj) 79
transport (v) **carry** (v) 71
trap (v) **catch** (v) 72
treacherous **loyal** 242
tread (v) **walk** (v) 391
treasure **wealth** 400
•treaty **agreement** 33
tremble **shake** (v) 331
tremendous **large** 226
•tributary **branch** (n) 62
trick (v) **fool** (v) 165
trim (adj) **neat** 252
trip (v) **walk** (v) 391

triumph (v) **win** (v) 402
triumph (n) **conquest** 91
trivial **little** 236
trivial **basic** 50
trivial **grand** 180
trivial **great** 183
trivial **heavy** 196
trivial **important** 211
trivial **serious** 329
•troop (n) **party** 265
trot (v) **run** (v) 315
trouble (v) **disturb** 122
•trouble (n) **difficulty** 116
•trouble (n) **misfortune** 245
troubled **worried** 408
trounce **beat** (v) 53
•troupe **party** 265
truck (v) **send** 328
trudge (v) **walk** (v) 391
true **loyal** 242
true **real** 301
true **changeable** 77
true **fake** (adj) 150
true **imaginary** 208
trust (v) **doubt** (v) 125
trust (n) **belief** 57
trust (n) **doubt** (n) 126
trustworthy **loyal** 242
trustworthy **dishonest** 121
truthful **dishonest** 121
truthfulness **honesty** 203
try (v) **attempt** (v) 49
tug (v) **pull** (v) 293
turn (v) **change** (v) 75
twinkling **shining** 336
typical **normal** 254

U

ugly **beautiful** 54
•ultimate **last** (adj) 227
unable **skillful** 345
unappetizing **delicious** 114
unbiased **fair** (adj) 148
unbind **fasten** 155
unbreakable **breakable** 67
uncertain **confident** 88
unchangeable **changeable** 77
uncivilized **rude** 312
unclean 387
uncomfortable **comfortable** 84
uncomfortable **convenient** 94
•uncommon **rare** 300
uncommon **ordinary** 263
uncomplicated **simple** 343
uncomplicated **difficult** 115
unconcern **concern** (n) 86
unconcerned **worried** 408
undergo **suffer** 364
•understand **know** 224
•understanding (adj) **wise** 404
•understanding (n)
   agreement 33
•understanding (n) **wisdom** 403
undertake **attempt** (v) 49
undisturbed **worried** 408
uneasy **comfortable** 84
uneasy **confident** 88
uneven **rough** 310
unexpected **sudden** 362
unexpected **ordinary** 263
unexpectedly **suddenly** 363
unfair **fair** (adj) 148
unfit **appropriate** (adj) 44
unfold **enlarge** 138
unfriendly **friendly** 172
unfriendly **thoughtful** 380
ungainly **clumsy** 81
unhappiness **misery** 245
unhappiness **happiness** 189
unhappy **sad** 317
unhappy **happy** 190

unhurried **sudden** 362
unhurriedly **suddenly** 363
unimportant **important** 211
uninterested **curious** 102
uninterested **eager** 130
uninteresting **dull** 128
•union **club** (n) 80
union **mixture** 248
•unique **rare** 300
unique **special** 351
unit **portion** (n) 280
unite **join** 222
unite **break** (v) 64
unjust **fair** (adj) 148
unkind **friendly** 172
unkind **thoughtful** 380
unknown **famous** 152
unknown **great** 183
unlimited **enclosed** 134
unmannerly **rude** 312
unmask **hide** (v) 199
unnatural **normal** 254
unnecessary **basic** 50
unpalatable **delicious** 114
unpleasant **disagreeable** 120
unpleasant **pleasant** 274
unreal **fake** (adj) 150
unreal **imaginary** 208
unreal **real** 301
unreasonable **wise** 404
unreliable **changeable** 77
unrestricted **enclosed** 134
unripe **adult** (adj) 29
unruly **tame** (adj) 375
unsafe **safe** (adj) 319
unsatisfied **comfortable** 84
unsavory **delicious** 114
unshaken **firm** (adj) 161

unskillful **skillful** 345
unsoiled **unclean** 387
unstable **changeable** 77
unsteady **changeable** 77
unsteady **firm** (adj) 161
unsuitable **appropriate** (adj) 44
unsuitable **convenient** 94
unsure **confident** 88
untamed **wild** 401
unthinking **thoughtless** 381
untidy **unclean** 387
untidy **neat** 252
untie **fasten** 155
untroubled **worried** 408
untrue **fake** (adj) 150
untrustworthy **dishonest** 121
untruthful **dishonest** 121
untruthfulness **honesty** 203
unusual **odd** 260
•unusual **rare** 300
unusual **ordinary** 263
unveil **hide** (v) 199
unwise **wise** 404
uphold **support** (v) 367
uplift (v) **lift** (v) 233
upright **dishonest** 121
upset (v) **disturb** 122
up-to-date **new** 252
urge 388
   See also **move** 250
usage **habit** 188
useful 389
usefulness **worth** (n) 411
useless **useful** 389
usual **ordinary** 263
usual **odd** 260
usual **rare** 300
usual **special** 351
•utensil **instrument** 219
utility **worth** (n) 411
utter **speak** 350

V

vacate **leave** (v) 230
vacation **break** (n) 66
vague **dim** (adj) 118
vague **clear** (adj) 79
vain **proud** 292
vain **shy** 341
valor **bravery** 63
valuable **precious** 285
valuable **useful** 389
value **worth** (n) 411
vanish **come** 82
varied **dull** 128
vary **change** (v) 75
vast **large** 226
vast **little** 236
veil (v) **hide** (v) 199
verdict **decision** 109
•version **account** (n) 22
vex **worry** (v) 409
vexation **anger** 39
vibrate **shake** (v) 331
victory **conquest** 91
view (v) **notice** (v) 255
view (n) **opinion** 262
vigilant **alert** (adj) 34
vigor **strength** 357
vigorous **active** 26
vigorous **strong** 358
violent **fierce** 158
violent **wild** 401
visible 390
vital **basic** 50
voice (v) **speak** (v) 350
vow (v) **promise** (v) 290
•vow (n) **pledge** (n) 276

W

wade **walk** (v) 391
walk (v) 391
    See also **move** 250
wander 393
    See also **go** 179
want (v) 395
warn **advise** 31
warn **forecast** (v) 168
warning 396
watch (v) 398
    See also **see** 327
watchful **alert** (adj) 34
watery **moist** 249
weak 399
weak **powerless** 284
weak **thin** 378
weak **powerful** 282
weak **strong** 358
weak **tough** 382
weakness **endurance** 136
weakness **strength** 357
wealth 400
wealthy **poor** 279
weary **exhausted** 145
weigh **consider** 92
weight **load** (n) 238
weighty **heavy** 196
weighty **important** 211
well-mannered **polite** 278
well-to-do **poor** 279
•whimper (v) **yell** (v) 413
•whine (v) **yell** (v) 413
whisper (v) **yell** (v) 413
wide **slender** 347
widen **enlarge** 138
wild 401
wild **tame** (adj) 375
win (v) 402
win (v) **defeat** (v) 112
win (v) **obtain** 259
•wing (n) **branch** (n) 62
wiry **strong** 358
wisdom 403

wise 404
wise **foolish** 166
wish (v) **want** (v) 395
withdraw **come** 82
withdraw **present** (v) 288
withhold **announce** 41
withhold **present** (v) 288
witty **humorous** 205
woe **sadness** 318
wonder (n) **surprise** (n) 370
wonderful **splendid** 352
•word **pledge** (n) 276
work (v) 407
work (n) 406
work (n) **action** 24
work (n) **amusement** 38
worried 408
worry (v) 409
worry (n) **concern** (n) 86
worship (v) **adore** 28
worth (n) 411
wrath **anger** 39
wreck (v) **ruin** (v) 314
wrestle **battle** (v) 51
wrong (adj) **correct** (adj) 98

Y

Z

Answers to questions on pages 4-18.

Exercises
Reviewing the Parts
(page 8)
1. delicious
2. Something that is pleasant or appealing.
3. Any two of the following: luscious,
   delightful, delectable, delicate,
   appetizing, savory, tasty
4. palatable, fragrant
5. pleasant
6. any two of the following: insipid,
   unappetizing, unpalatable,
   distasteful, unsavory
7. no

Choosing Synonyms and Related Words
(page 9)
1. damp
2. juicy or succulent
3. rainy
4. watery or damp
5. humid

1. small
2. tiny
3. minute
4. brief
5. trivial

Choosing Antonyms
(page 10-11)
1. true - false
2. plentiful - scarce
3. bright - dull
4. unusual - ordinary
5. easy—hard

1. false
2. fake or forged
3. false or artificial or fake
4. false or artificial or made-up

Using a Thesaurus When You Write
Nouns
(page 11)
1. implements
2. appliances
3. instruments
4. tool

Verbs
(page 12)
1. jogged
2. running
3. running or racing or operating
4. sprinted or raced
5. running or flowing
6. run

Adjectives
(page 13)
1. notable
2. most illustrious
3. noble
4. most famous
5. imposing or an imposing
6. superior
7. distinguished
8. monumental

Adverbs
(page 14)
1. immediately
2. unexpectedly
3. instantly
4. abruptly
5. fast or quickly

1. awfully
2. appallingly
3. terribly

The Index
(page 15)
1. narrate
2. enlarge
3. 254, 252
4. synonym
5. 260
6. 5
7. 2
8. verb
9. the bullet or dot next to it
10. neat

Other Uses
Idioms
(page 16)
1. act on
2. act up
3. act for

Formal and Informal Words
(page 17-18)
The first letter is formal.
The second letter is informal.
1. started or began
2. said or mentioned
3. new
4. trying or attempting
5. want
6. trade
7. ask